SOCIAL WORK RESEARCH METHODS

To *the students and faculty of the Department of Social*
Work at California State University, San Bernardino

SOCIAL WORK RESEARCH METHODS

Four Alternative Paradigms

Teresa Morris

California State University, San Bernardino

SAGE Publications
Thousand Oaks ▪ London ▪ New Delhi

For information:

Sage Publications, Inc.
2455 Teller Road
Thousand Oaks, California 91320
E-mail: order@sagepub.com

Sage Publications Ltd.
1 Oliver's Yard
55 City Road
London EC1Y 1SP
United Kingdom

Sage Publications India Pvt. Ltd.
B-42, Panchsheel Enclave
Post Box 4109
New Delhi 110 017 India

Printed in the United States of America on acid-free paper

Library of Congress Cataloging-in-Publication Data

Morris, Teresa.
 Social work research methods : four alternative paradigms / Teresa Morris.
   p. cm.
 Includes bibliographical references and index.
 ISBN 1-4129-1673-9 (cloth) — ISBN 1-4129-1674-7 (pbk.)
   1. Sociology—Research—Methodology. 2. Social sciences—
 Research—Methodology. I. Title.
 HM571.M67 2006
 361.3'072—dc22   2005019924

05 06 07 08 09 10 9 8 7 6 5 4 3 2 1

Acquiring Editor:	Todd R. Armstrong
Editorial Assistant:	Veronica Novak
Production Editor:	Sanford Robinson
Copy Editor:	Diana Breti
Typesetter:	C&M Digitals (P) Ltd.
Indexer:	Sheila Bodell
Cover Designer:	Edgar Abarca

Contents

Preface

I wrote this book because I thought it was time to acknowledge that there is more than one way to do systematic social work research. Like social work practice, social work research requires knowledge and skills in a range of paradigms, theories, and methods. Thus, four paradigms and their associated theories and methods are explained here. One of the reviewers for this book forcefully stated that it should not be written. Rather, this reviewer argued, we should put our energies into writing about ways to address Type I and Type II error in positivist research. To me, this reflects an overreliance on one worldview. Positivism is great for some things but cannot do everything. Give it a break, applaud what it does well, and find other approaches for what it cannot do. Yes, indeed, positivism can test causal and correlational theories, but post-positivism can build theory and critical theory can promote action to address social injustice and, what is more, constructivism offers the tools to comprehend and act on subjective knowledge and understanding.

Think of it this way: you may have been brought up in one religion but then "grew out" of that original childhood belief system and developed your own worldview of spirituality; you may well start your research career as a positivist but then change to a post-positivist or find that critical theory or even constructivism resonates more with your stage of intellectual maturation. Of course, this leads us to two important questions. How can one person accept four contradictory paradigms? How can you believe there is objective knowledge and subjective knowledge at the same time? The best way I can explain it is to ask you, the reader, some questions. Do you like to sing? Do you like to dance? Do you like to play music? Do you like to listen to music? However you relate to music, there is something called music, and we all know what it is, don't we? But we all experience it differently and we experience different music in different ways. We don't do the same dance, no matter what the music. We don't sing the same song regardless of the accompaniment. Music is both an objective entity and a subjective experience, something to be explored and something to be engaged. In the same way, when we consider approaches to research we realize that, yes, there is a place for positivism, just as there is something out there called music, which is sometimes written down. Yes, there is a place for post-positivism just as there is a place out there for varieties of ways of doing a waltz or singing a song. Yes, there is a place for critical theory, just as there is a place for the modern composer who thinks that the structure of the symphony orchestra has oppressed us for too long and creates a classical piece for a differently structured orchestra without three or four movements, or for that matter for Beethoven writing in German rather than Latin and thus throwing off the hegemony of the Italian intellectuals and artists to use the language of the people rather than the language of court. And yes, there is a place for constructivism just as there is a place for the myriad sounds that people of the world perceive as music.

When I came to America to learn and then teach research, I came with a European philosophical outlook that entertains the possibility of any point of view being valid as long as its pros and cons can be argued out. I came to a land of multiple-choice exams where correct knowledge is certain and the right and wrong answers are clear. What joy, I thought, the doubt in my life has been wiped away; all is certainty. I soon found that I was kidding myself, especially when I failed every multiple-choice exam I ever took because I could see pros and cons for all alternative answers. As someone who wrote a high school paper proving that Shakespeare's *A Midsummer Night's Dream* was a tragedy, not a comedy, this was second nature to me. Thus I needed to make the compromise between my European and American selves if I was going to succeed in my studies, develop an academic career in the U.S., and sleep at night. I found a book by Egon Guba that talked about four paradigms. I decided to use this as a starting point. I gave all four paradigms equal credibility and taught research methods for them all. God bless the students who went along with my experiment. It is their work that you are about to read about. Yes, in this book, because alternative research designs are not generally funded through traditional sources, many small-scale student research projects are used as examples. These studies, because of the constraints of resources, time, and the students' level of expertise, are not always perfect examples of the approach they are using, but they do illustrate aspects of the approach if not the whole approach.

In this book, the positivist worldview is used as a starting point for exploring various approaches to gathering knowledge in a scientific manner. Positivism is discussed as one of many intellectual traditions, and its perspective on science is presented as only one piece of the total picture. The discussion of the history of thinking on how we know and understand the world, given in the first part of this book, gives a context for this position. Also, this book modifies a generalist model of social work practice to parallel the tasks of social work research. In this way, the notion of a social work researcher is integrated with the idea of a social work practitioner at both the micro and macro levels of social organization.

There are reasons for this desire to explore alternative paradigms, beyond my own personal preference. In most social work research texts, positivism is the accepted paradigm for doing "scientific research." Its assumptions and methods are a marriage of philosophy of science and mathematical theory. Even with this credible foundation, however, parts of this approach rest on untested assumptions or simply the rationale of accepted practice as the key justification for a particular way of doing things. The positivist approach to research is not as clear-cut as it first appears and, at times, it makes assumptions that cannot be proved. For example, Rubin and Babbie (2001), in their research methods text, state at the end of a long and detailed discussion of sampling and probability theory that,

> You should be cautioned that the survey uses of probability theory as discussed previously are not wholly justified technically. The theory of sampling distribution makes assumptions that almost never apply in survey conditions. The number of samples within specified increments of standard errors, for example, assumes an infinitely large population, an infinite number of samples, and sampling with replacement. Moreover, the inferential jump from the distribution of several samples to the probable characteristics of one sample has been grossly oversimplified in the preceding discussion.
>
> These cautions are offered as perspective. Researchers often appear to overestimate the precision of estimates produced by using probability theory in connection with social research. . . . Nevertheless, the calculations discussed in this section can be extremely valuable to you in understanding and evaluating your data. Although the calculations do not provide estimates that are as precise as some researchers might assume, they can be quite valid for practical purposes. They are unquestionably more valid than less rigorously derived estimates based on less rigorous sampling methods. (p. 269)

Well, are they? Reading the above one cannot be faulted for thinking that if practical utility is the criterion for validity, then other approaches to research hold up as valid and useful knowledge-generating strategies. If you have precise lines of reasoning intertwined with guesswork and acknowledged incorrect assumptions and call it science, this may be pleasing to think through but what makes it rigorous? It is as if a religion has been established which is a combination of faith, theories, and enough observed phenomena (tossing coins ad nauseam) to be convincing. Social work students are asked to believe in the religion because of tradition and a false hope that we can add theology to this religion until it becomes hard science and makes considerable contributions to social work practice.

When we consider the classical experimental design, it quickly becomes clear that studies addressing social work practice confront ethical problems regarding withholding service to control groups, practical problems associated with random assignment of human beings to experimental and control groups, and methodological problems concerning the application of findings derived from a controlled experiment to the hurly burly world of social work practice. One author suggests that we can only be really sure about causality through replicating studies (Cohen, 1994), and others suggest that we will never be able to accurately address causality with people in real-world settings (Lincoln & Guba, 1985). When we move on to consider correlational designs, the threats that low response rates make to applying probability theory and sampling theory to research on humans again reveal flaws in trying to generalize findings from such studies to real-world settings. Also, as is explained in the discussion of the history of the philosophy of science below, the practice of rejecting the null hypothesis instead of testing the relationship between the independent variable and the dependent variable is not the solution to induction that it is meant to be. When we do this, we are still generalizing from one study to all situations. These kinds of concerns have led this author, on the one hand, to acknowledge the contribution that positivism can make to establishing knowledge about social work practice but, on the other hand, to explore alternative paradigms and examine their capacity to contribute to scientific knowledge about social work practice.

The question is, do we "fix" the positivist paradigm by creating additional procedures such as weighting samples for oppressed groups; adding qualitative pieces to quantitative instruments; adding designs such as single subject and program evaluation, including qualitative data analyses procedures; and being more sensitive to the diversity of participants in research projects and call this the evolution of the paradigm? Or do we retrace our steps and realize that the need for all these "add-ons" or "plug-ins" to positivism comes from a more basic problem? The positivist approach to research can no longer hold the monopoly on how to answer the questions that need to be asked about social work practice. Positivism is like a little lifeboat that is now heading into complicated choppy waters. As it enters those waters, it is starting to break up. We try to fix the sinking little boat as it bravely sails further into the rough waters, but we really don't need to. There are other boats that are sturdy enough and designed to sail these other waters. We can leave the positivist boat in the waters that it was designed to sail and take our other lifeboats into the raging waters of complicated human experience, social problems, and social work practice.

Acknowledgments

I have been interested in philosophy for a long time, but I want to thank Fiona McDermott at the University of Melbourne for taking the time to have a number of conversations with me in the late 1980s about how we know what we know. Not many people would take that on. I also want to thank Nancy Mary for always being encouraging about our "off the wall" ideas. The enthusiasm and good humor of the students at California State University, San Bernardino, cannot be overvalued in its contribution to the development of the methodologies described here. Also, thanks to Jim Midgley for challenging me to write this book rather than waste a good sabbatical. Lastly I want to thank my brother Michael, my nephews Paul and Michael and Elaine their mother, big Michael, the McMurray family, and Joy and Sue for being proud of me. I'm proud of you, too.

Introduction

In a sense, we are all researchers every day of our lives. To survive we need to find things out, build and test theories, and take action based on that knowledge-generating activity. Each of us has our own worldview, built on a personal history, that guides our approach to our daily research. The aim of this book is to build on that personal approach to research by offering fresh alternatives for social work practice research that acknowledge different worldviews. This is a social work research methods textbook for upper level undergraduate and graduate social work students as well as social work researchers in general. It proposes that social workers can not only adopt a positivist approach to research, but also build authentic knowledge by adopting other paradigms and methodologies that resonate with the social work mission and its diverse information needs. In this way, social workers are given a range of approaches to creating evidence for practice. Guba (1990), in his book *The Paradigm Dialog,* proposed four paradigms: positivism, post-positivism, critical theory, and constructivism. Positivism combines traditional philosophies of science with probability theory and sampling theory. The other paradigms combine philosophies of postmodernism, critical realism, and phenomenology with the linguistic work of authors such as Edward Sapir (1884–1939), Leonard Bloomfield (1887–1949), and Noam Chomsky, who developed theories of "transformational grammar." Positivism takes a deductive, objective view of the world and is the paradigm that underlies almost all social work research method books. Post-positivism uses positivism as its starting point but notes that adherence to the strict methodological prescriptions of the natural sciences results in data gathering, analysis, and findings that cannot always capture the complexity and richness of the human experience. A post-positivist approach to research is generally inductive, favoring qualitative methods that capture the data contained in language. Critical theory, like positivism and post-positivism, takes an objective view of the world but rejects the requirement for a neutral researcher whose presence does not affect what is going on in that world. While a post-positivist commits to awareness and control of the influence of the researcher's values on the research study, critical theorists approach all research with an explicit ideological position on the power relationships operating in the proposed site of the study. Research projects with the critical theory starting point take a particular ideology, such as neo-Marxism or feminism, and not only gather data on the impact of that ideology on a particular social issue or population but also take action to empower those who are oppressed by that ideology. Finally, constructivists challenge the objective reality that is assumed by the other three paradigms. Constructivists propose that knowledge about the human condition is a set of shared understandings, or constructions, and the most valid way to understand and carry out research about people is to collect, analyze, and report data on subjective knowledge of social phenomena.

When describing these paradigms, Guba (1990) differentiates them using three dimensions: the nature of reality, epistemology, and methodology. Positivism assumes an objective reality governed by laws and mechanisms that can be identified; reality is separate from the observer and scientific observation requires objective methodologies that manipulate reality. Post-positivism assumes an objective reality governed by laws and mechanisms that can never be truly understood; although the observer can never be truly separate from reality, researchers should work to control the influence they might have on reality, and data gathered in naturalistic settings gives us an accurate understanding of reality. Critical theory assumes an objective reality governed by laws and mechanisms; the observer distorts this reality using the ideologies of his or her social group, and true research uncovers the impact of such ideologies and takes action to address oppression. Constructivism assumes a subjective reality; the observer discovers this reality in partnership with participants in that reality, and data is gathered by means of a hermeneutic dialectic from which a joint construction of a reality, unique to time and place, evolves.

Thus each paradigm has a different perspective on a given research question and each has a different goal for the research project. For example, imagine we are interested in studying social work interventions with homeless families in a particular region. As Table I.1 shows, each paradigm would use its own approach to gather a different kind of knowledge about that research focus.

What we see here is a gradual building of knowledge about social work practice with homeless families from different perspectives. Anthropologists have developed the notions of emic and etic understandings of humanity. These terms come from the words phonetic and phonemic. Put simply, an etic understanding of a human situation is that of the outside observer looking inwards, while an emic understanding of a human situation is that of the insider looking outwards. If we use these perspectives as our categorizing concepts, we can see that positivism and post-positivism give us etic

Table I.1   Alternative Approaches to Research on Social Work Interventions with the Homeless

Paradigm	Question	Data Collection	Analysis	Goal of Research
Positivism	Which intervention is most effective with homeless families in this region?	Experimental or correlational design using a representative sample and gathering quantitative data.	Quantitative analysis using statistics based on probability theory and sampling theory.	To test effectiveness of interventions with homeless families
Post-Positivism	How do we intervene with homeless families in this region?	Interviews and observations, gathering qualitative data.	Qualitative analysis techniques using "top down" or "bottom up" approaches to build theory.	To build theories of interventions with homeless families
Critical Theory	What action must be taken in this region to address poverty and thus empower homeless families?	Ideological position developed, teaching-learning process carried out with study participants.	Ideological analysis of literature and history, action analysis to develop and implement action plan based on political theory and power analysis.	To empower homeless families
Constructivism	How do the key stakeholders in the issues of homelessness in this region understand homeless families and the interventions they need?	Hermeneutic dialectic circle of key informants developed, interviewed individually and as a group.	Building individual and joint constructions throughout the data-gathering period. Participants review constructions for accuracy. A process of research-participant joint development of findings built on existential philosophy and linguistic theory.	To engage key homelessness stakeholders in building a joint understanding of homeless families and the interventions that must be implemented

understandings of a situation while critical theory and constructivism give us emic understandings of a human situation. In addition, the goal of positivist and post-positivist research is to gather knowledge for its own sake while the critical theorist and constructivist gathers knowledge to take action. To select the appropriate paradigm, then, the researcher needs to make a decision about whose perspective he or she is taking and the goal of the research.

This book does not favor one paradigm over any other. It simply suggests that an imaginative researcher can choose to approach a research topic from different perspectives and that the chosen perspective will dictate problem formulation, the appropriate data collection methodology, and the nature of the impact of the research. As noted above, current social work research method books tend to adopt the positivist paradigm when explaining the correct approach to social work research. This is a paradigm borrowed from the natural sciences. It was favored by these disciplines when they adopted a more Newtonian approach to gathering knowledge than they do today. Newtonian worldviews have given way to theories of relativity, quantum mechanics, and the proposition that chaos has a theoretical structure that can inform prediction. In the social sciences there have been similar changes in thinking, as illustrated by the literature on symbolic interactionism and phenomenology. In social work, when we discuss practice we say that we must "start where the client is" when planning and implementing interventions. We therefore support taking a flexible approach to micro or macro practice and develop the intervention that most appropriately meets client needs. However, social work research has been left behind when it comes to the exciting possibilities that are associated with a diversity of worldviews. It is time for us to have the courage to acknowledge that we can approach generation of new knowledge on our own terms. This is not the first time alternative approaches to research have been suggested. However, such discussions have either been at the philosophical and theoretical level or at the methodological level where qualitative and quantitative methods have been described as alternative methods without consideration of context and the paradigms they imply (Thyer, 2001; Neuman & Kreuger, 2003). The unique value of this book is that it offers the conceptual clarity to link different worldviews with different research questions requiring different methodologies, achieving different goals when researching social work practice at the micro and macro levels of human organization.

Research and Generalist Practice

In this book, research methods associated with the four paradigms are integrated with social work practice by using a generalist practice model to structure the discussion of how to do research. A generalist social worker has the knowledge, values, and skills to intervene at the micro (individuals, families, and groups) and macro (organizations and local, national, or international communities) levels while acknowledging the interlocking influences of all those levels of human organization on the target of the social work intervention. Kirst-Ashman and Hull (2002) have suggested that when a generalist social worker intervenes, he or she should follow the following stages of a planned change process.

1. Engagement: "the initial period where you orient yourself to the problem at hand and begin to establish communication and relationships with others who are also addressing the problem" (p. 31).

2. Assessment: "the investigation and determination of variables affecting an identified problem or issue" (p. 31).

3. Planning: "specifies what should be done: work with client, prioritize problems, translate problems to needs, evaluate levels of intervention for each need, establish goals, specify objectives, specify action steps, formalize contract" (p. 35).

4. Implementation: "the actual doing of the plan" (p. 38).

5. Evaluation: "proof that intervention has been effective" (p. 38).

6. Termination: "a process of disengagement and stabilization" (p. 40).

7. Follow Up: "reexamination of client's situation at some point after the intervention" (p. 41).

These stages have a certain logical order, but in real life the practitioner may well go back and forth between the stages as the intervention requires. The social work researcher, like any other social worker, is a practitioner involved in a planned change process. Such researchers intervene with clients at both micro and macro levels of social organization to gather knowledge scientifically and, in some cases, take action as a result of that knowledge. The steps of the above generalist model can be modified to parallel the necessary tasks that a researcher must complete. For the generalist social work researcher generating knowledge about interventions at micro or macro levels of practice, the tasks are

Engagement = Gaining entrée to the research setting

Assessment = Developing an understanding of the research focus

Planning = Rationales and plans for carrying out the research project

Implementation = Gathering the data

Evaluation = Developing an understanding and interpretation of the data

xxii   Social Work Research Methods: Four Alternative Paradigms

Termination = Reporting on findings and exiting the research setting

Follow Up = Communication and distribution of research findings

The order in which these steps or tasks are completed will depend on the paradigm being adopted by the social work researcher. For the positivist researcher, there is a sequential order:

1. Engagement

2. Assessment

3. Planning

4. Implementation

5. Evaluation

6. Termination and Follow Up

The positivist researcher makes a formal contract with the research site and gains permission for data gathering. The project is then developed without the biasing influence of the study sponsors and participants. The research plan is based on the philosophical principles of causality and correlation, previous literature on the research topic, and the guidelines of "science" dictated by probability and sampling theory. The research plan is finalized before data gathering begins, and good science dictates that it does not change during data gathering. In this book, only quantitative data is considered appropriate for the positivist researcher since this is the only data that can meet the requirements of the philosophical and theoretical foundations of the positivist paradigm regarding the nature of reality, epistemology, and methodology. This position is expanded below in the discussion of the history of the philosophy of science and in the introduction to Part I. Given this position, analysis of data using statistics based on mathematical theories of probability and sampling theory is carried out when data collection is completed and the research findings are usually reported in the academic literature.

For researchers using the post-positivist paradigm, many of the stages of the generalist change model are interwoven:.

1. Assessment and Engagement

2. Planning and Implementation and Evaluation

3. Termination and Follow Up

Post-positivist researchers, like the positivist researchers, develop a formal contract with the sponsors of the research, obtaining permission to gather data. However, the research question(s) and understanding of the research focus are developed both from previous literature on the topic and through initial engagement of the research setting using interviews and observations. This initial data gathering may well modify and expand the questions to be asked. Thus assessment and engagement are interwoven processes that influence each other. As the focus of the research is settled upon, data gathering plans are developed. Data is gathered and then immediately analyzed since the results of each analysis will influence future data gathering strategies, refining the focus of interviews, observations, and other data to be gathered. Since both researchers and study participants have experienced an intense personal engagement, termination involves similar preparation and explanations as those used to terminate with a client in the practice setting. Postpositivist researchers tend to report findings to study participants as well as to the academic community.

For researchers using the critical theory approach, again there is interweaving between the stages of the generalist model.

1. Assessment and Engagement (with initial Implementation) and Planning

2. Implementation

3. Evaluation

4. Termination and Follow Up

The critical theory researcher starts with a plan that is guided by ideology, whether it is feminism, neo-Marxism, class theory, or theories of ethnic and cultural discrimination. The ideology explicitly provides an assessment of the research focus. However, the critical theorist does not develop the ideological position in isolation from the research setting. One of the initial tasks for the critical theorist is to engage key informants in the research setting using a teaching-learning partnership to raise consciousness of oppression and promote empowerment. For both the researcher and study participants, ideological positions are modified as the result of discussion and agreement is reached on an action plan. Thus after initial engagement and initial implementation for development of the ideological position in the context of the research setting, an action plan is developed and a second stage of implementation is carried out where action is taken and later evaluated for its impact on empowerment. Termination of the critical theory research project involves reporting back and celebrating the impact of the research project in the research setting as well as reporting to the academic community.

For the constructivist, we have another interwoven structure of the generalist model.

1. Engagement and Assessment and Planning

2. Implementation and Evaluation

3. Termination and Follow Up

The constructivist researcher, gathering subjective data, develops the plan for the focus and implementation of the study with study participants. The key is gathering data that brings valid descriptions of study participants' understanding of the research focus. Thus engagement, assessment, and planning all happen together and influence each other. This continual development of the research focus continues during implementation and evaluation in which data is gathered and analyzed immediately so the results of the analysis can influence the selection of study participants and the building of study participants' joint construction of the research topic.

To clearly describe and explain the above approaches to research, the discussion of alternatives is divided into four parts addressing each of the four paradigms. Within each part, a brief overview of the paradigm is given followed by description of associated methodologies. Chapter headings within each of the four parts of the book reflect the steps of the generalist model (see Table I.2).

This book structure automatically leads to chapters of varying lengths, since each paradigm interprets stages of the generalist model in differing ways with varying emphases. However, within each chapter there is an explanation of the research assumptions, methods, and tasks illustrated with examples of research at the micro and macro practice levels. Some of these examples are drawn from completed M.S.W. student projects. At the end of each chapter there is a listing of the main points and a series of student learning assignments. Part V of the book addresses cross-cutting themes that can only be discussed in an informed manner after the four approaches to research have been explained. These are the ethics and politics of research, the researcher's responsibility to diversity, and the uses of technology at each stage of the research process. However, before we move on to discuss each paradigm in detail, a brief history of the philosophy of science is outlined below as both a rationale and a context for the book's approach.

Brief History of the Philosophy of Science

To explain the emergence of positivism and mathematics as the dominant paradigm for research and the more recent challenges to this dominance stressing humanity, politics, and language, a brief background on the philosophy of science is needed. Please try not to skip over this; it's important because it explains why we should accept the propositions contained in the

Table I.2   Structure of Discussion of Paradigms

Part I: Positivism	Part II: Post-Positivism	Part III: Critical Theory	Part IV: Constructivism
Chapter 1: Engagement	Chapter 7: Assessment and Engagement	Chapter 10: Assessment, Engagement, and Planning	Chapter 14: Engagement, Assessment, and Planning
Chapter 2: Assessment	Chapter 8: Planning, Implementation, Evaluation	Chapter 11: Implementation	Chapter 15: Implementation and Evaluation
Chapter 3: Planning	Chapter 9: Termination and Follow up	Chapter 12: Evaluation	Chapter 16: Termination and Follow Up
Chapter 4: Implementation		Chapter 13: Termination and Follow Up	
Chapter 5: Evaluation			
Chapter 6: Termination and Follow up			

rest of the book. Kuhn (1970), in *The Structure of Scientific Revolutions*, suggested that science is a social construct or invention and Feyerabend (1988), in *Against Method*, challenged the existence of a specific method of scientific enquiry. Such propositions have sparked debates in the scientific community that have caused a complete reevaluation of the scientific method and led to suggestions in Gleick's (1988) *Chaos* that new fresh approaches to science are emerging.

Three themes are the focus of this discussion. The first theme is how researchers' thoughts about the nature of reality are linked to identifying relevant data. The second and third themes adapt Turbayne's (1962) and Oldroyd's (1986) concept of a two-fold pathway for the establishment of knowledge. The pathway first travels from an examination of observable phenomena to general rational "first principles," which is termed "analysis," and second travels back from "first principles" to observable phenomena, which are therefore explained in terms of principles from which they are deducible, which is termed "synthesis."

Identification of Data

How do we know what we know and how do we know we're right? How can someone, starting from observations of the world, find the theoretical principles that govern the world? These are questions that have occupied philosophers of science rather than social work researchers. A brief history of highlights of the debate around these questions is outlined in Table I.3, where major thinkers' approaches to identification of the relationship between thought and reality, analysis and synthesis are noted along with whether each approach is generally included in standard social work research texts.

Representatives of Ancient and Medieval thinkers such as Plato (428/7–348/7 B.C.E,), Aristotle (384–322 B.C.E.), the Stoics (ca. 280 B.C.E.–ca. 480 C.E.), and the Paduan School (ca. 1126–1590 C.E.) saw philosophy, theology, and science as one body of unified knowledge. Data was knowledge gathered through the senses or "first principles." Later, Galileo (1564–1642 C.E.) suggested that data had "primary" and "secondary" qualities. Primary qualities were measurable objectively, for example, shape, position, motion, rest, and contingency to other objects. Secondary qualities were deemed in the mind of the observer, for example, taste and feel. Bacon (1561–1626 C.E.) challenged this thinking by taking a more interventionist approach to seeking knowledge. He separated science from other forms of enquiry such as religion, philosophy, astrology, and alchemy. According to Oldroyd (1986), Bacon believed that "man is to try to 'command' nature, and wrest her secrets from her" (p. 60). According to Bacon, therefore, the role of the scientific investigator was to search for causes. However, Bacon's approach has been criticized by authors such as Charlesworth (1982), who noted that Bacon's approach was limited in three ways: first, it did not address the theoretical context or framework within which we make empirical observations; second, general assumptions about the world, such as nature being knowable or that nature operates in a regular fashion, are not recognized; and third, cultural circumstances that facilitate the emergence of science, such as a belief in the value of scientific knowledge, are not addressed. Nevertheless, Bacon's approach became the legitimate approach to linking thought and reality and was further developed by Hume (1711–1776), who offered eight rules of cause and effect.

Table I.3   Progression of Thought on Approaches to Generation of Knowledge

Scientist(s)	Nature of Data	Analysis	Synthesis	Included in SW Research Texts
Ancient/Medieval	knowledge gained through senses	dialectical discussion	theoretical propositions	no
Galileo	objective/subjective	mathematical models	physical principles	no
Bacon	regularities in nature	laws of causality	high-level principles	yes, the idea of causality is included but not Bacon's laws of causality
Hume	regularities in nature	rules of cause and effect	high-level principles	yes
Comte	hierarchy of knowledge	search for laws	high-level principles	yes
Pragmatists	how to do a task	what works	it worked	?
Russell	regularities in nature	logic & mathematics	high-level principles	no
Einstein	regularities in nature	metaphors, mathematical experimental tests	high-level principles	no
Popper	regularities in nature	falsification	high-level principles	yes
Kuhn	regularities in nature	paradigms of thinking influenced by history and culture	high-level principles	sometimes mentioned
Lakatos	regularities in nature	objective methods & cultural paradigms	high-level principles	no
Feyerabend	regularities in nature	counter-intuitive thinking, there are no objective methods	high-level principles	no

xxviii Social Work Research Methods: Four Alternative Paradigms

To summarize Oldroyd's (1986) quotation of Hume:

1. The cause and effect must be contiguous in space and time.

2. The cause must be prior to the effect.

3. There must be a constant union betwixt the cause and the effect.

4. The same cause always produces the same effect.

5. If several objects produce the same effect it must be by means of some quality which we discover to be common amongst them.

6. The difference in the effect of two resembling objects must proceed from that particular in which they differ.

7. When any object encreases or diminishes with the encrease or diminution of its cause, 'tis to be regarded as a compounded effect, deriv'd from the union of the several different effects, which arise from the several different parts of the cause.

8. An object which exists for any time in its full perfection without any effect is not the sole cause of that effect, but requires to be assisted by some other principle, which may forward its influence and operation. (p. 117)

The nineteenth- and twentieth-century positivist tradition, which defined science as a search for laws, began with Comte (1788–1857), who extended Bacon's and Hume's approaches to the study of society. Comte believed that there was a hierarchy of science in the following order: mathematics, astronomy, physics, chemistry, physiology, and sociology. He suggested that there could be a unification of these sciences through which the laws of nature could be successfully determined by empirical enquiry. In the United States such laws were discovered via pragmatism. Chauncey Wright (1830–1914), William James (1842–1910), and John Dewey (1859–1952) tended to believe that if something worked it was true. For example, if a bridge stays up then the principles that guided that bridge's construction must be true. However, critics of this stand note that theories that work in certain situations cannot always be generalized as correct in all situations. For example, Ptolemy's model of the cosmos worked for navigational purposes, but it was an incorrect theory. The pragmatist, though, influenced an empirical tradition that stressed the link between truth and pragmatic success.

Challenges to positivists' identification of data as objective observation of cause and laws have come from "the new physics" and Einstein's (1879–1955) contention that scientific theory is made up of axioms or principles freely chosen by the creative mind of the scientist and then tested experimentally. Einstein suggested that such axioms do not necessarily derive logically from empirical experience but that observations are molded by theories held by the observer. For example, light behaves as if it has a wave structure but it doesn't look like a wave. This wave image helps scientists use their own creativity to construct theories. Since Popper (1902–1994) did not focus on identifying the link between thought and reality because he felt that this was the domain of psychologists rather than scientists, Thomas S. Kuhn (1922–1996) emerges as the next challenger of the positivists' approach to identification of data by linking science to its social and historical context. He suggested that each of the sciences goes through certain phases of thinking which affect identification of data. The first of these phases he termed the pre-paradigm periods, in which facts are gathered almost randomly without reference to any plan or theoretical structure. Gradually one theory takes precedence over others and becomes the discipline's first paradigm. A paradigm is a worldview that molds the education of new scientists and directs research agendas and methodologies. For example, Ptolemy's geometric representation of the motion of heavenly bodies meant that astronomers at that time learned geometric methods that would allow the collection of data to support that position. This is the period of "normal science" when information is forced into an inflexible framework. The business of science becomes "puzzle solving" because the overall framework dictates that there is a solution to the problem. Any findings that contradict the accepted paradigm are either dismissed as inaccurate or receive ad hoc hypotheses. When there are too many ad hoc hypotheses, the science enters a crisis period in which the current paradigm is questioned and a new paradigm reaches general acceptance so that the science can settle into a new period of normal science and puzzle solving. Thus science is not a linear progression using basically the same methodology to increase knowledge but a series of shifts in thinking, which take place when an old mode of thinking has too may anomalies. The scientific community then comes to some consensus on the most credible new mode of thinking.

This relativist orientation was developed still further by Feyerabend (1924–1994), who insisted that science is an irrational enterprise. Feyerabend believes that the progress of science depends on scientists who think counterintuitively. For example, when Galileo insisted the earth moved when all the senses suggested that the earth was stationary, he was acting in an irrational manner but he was correct. Feyerabend concluded that no particular science, no particular form of knowledge, no particular methodology, no particular way of thinking can claim any kind of privileged status. The above account shows that philosophers of science have moved from a holistic conceptualization of knowledge being interrelated to a narrower conceptualization of the search for causes being the most legitimate approach to knowledge building. Only in this century has the cultural relativity of the interpretation of reality been identified.

Social workers in direct practitioner, community organizer, and administration and policy maker roles have a need for both an objective search for causality and the more relativistic metaphorical knowledge about individuals, family functioning, community members' perception of community functioning, agency members' perception of good process, clients' perception of good outcome, and researchers' awareness of the value of subjective knowledge. In addition, an awareness of the cultural context of these perceptions is needed. Social work students can be encouraged to recognize current paradigms, consider problems in a counterintuitive manner, value subjective interpretation of knowledge, and develop metaphors to interpret what they observe in client groups and agency settings. In addition, cultural influences on the way different client groups or professional groups identify a problem or issue can be explored as a way of illustrating the value of subjective data.

Analyses

When analyzing their data, Ancient and Medieval thinkers believed that knowledge should be subjected to "dialectical discussion," which would reveal theoretical generalizations and principles regarding objective existence. Aristotle suggested some methodologies for gaining first principles using classification systems and the relationships between classes of things. In the syllogism he also offered some principles of deductive reasoning that would lead to theoretical generalizations. Later, with the "New Science" of the seventeenth century, Galileo substituted Aristotelian logic with mathematical models that could explain phenomena such as motion.

Bacon introduced his own methods of analysis. The steps of Bacon's methodology were first, to systematically collect and tabulate data; second, having considered the findings, to eliminate "non-causes" of findings; third, to note the cause that would be the explanation left when all the non-causes had been excluded. The final step was to test this explanation. This test would formulate "low level" principles, which would then be used to understand "higher level" principles with increasing generality. However, this method was inadequate even for Bacon's own research on the causes of heat since at step three he was left with several alternative explanations. He was forced to guess, or hypothesize, which explanation among those alternative explanations was correct. He guessed correctly with heat (motion), but when researching the cause of color, he guessed incorrectly (parts of different sizes mixed in different proportion). Again, Charlesworth (1982) criticizes Bacon's approach because it does not address the problem of induction, that is, how we move from our limited empirical observations to general laws. Bacon's methodology leads to generalizations about observations; it does not lead to statements about scientific theory. For example, the rule that energy can be transformed but never destroyed could not be discovered through Bacon's method. In addition, Bacon ignored the role of mathematics in science.

In the twentieth century, Bertrand Russell (1872–1970) moved away from empirical ideas of analysis and offered logical procedures to identify the truth or falsity of complex statements by analyzing these statements' atomic constituents. He suggested a link between the logical operations of the mind, the logic of mathematics, and the way things happen in the real world. Einstein's ideas about the creative use of metaphor in science also stressed the effects of different ways of thinking about analysis. However, Popper returned thinking on analysis to the position that there was a need for one specific scientific method. His methodology includes the following steps: (1) formulate or conjecture a hypothesis or theory that may account for a problem or difficulty of interest; (2) rigorously test the hypothesis by drawing logical consequences from the hypothesis and testing these consequences experimentally; and (3) show whether the hypothesis is false, since it is not possible to prove that the hypothesis is true from one observation. Results of this analysis will lead to new problems, which will lead to new tests of hypotheses

Popper also introduced the term "corroboration" to mean "failure to falsify." A theory with high corroborative ability must have the capacity to make risky predictions that can be readily falsified. Popper believed that the scientific method made science better than other forms of seeking knowledge. He differed from the positivists, however, in suggesting that science is driven by bold theoretical conjectures that are tested by observation rather than in the logical positivist mode of looking for the logic in observations and then developing theory. He, therefore, condones and emphasizes the creative and imaginative aspects of generating hypotheses for testing. Critics of Popper suggest that it is as difficult to refute a theory after one study as it is to confirm a theory after one test. In addition, it is not always clear what is being refuted. A hypothesis does not stand alone; it rests on other presumptions and it is not always clear which presumption is being refuted by the results of a study (Charlesworth, 1982).

Lakatos (1922–1974) tried to find common ground between Popper's "objective" approaches and Kuhn's ideas on cultural relativity. His solution was to suggest that there are certain "hard core" methodological rules that are useful in developing research programs, but when the research program is coming to an end, certain ad hoc hypotheses are developed that lead to new research agendas. He also suggested that there are three kinds of falsification: dogmatic, naïve, and sophisticated. Sophisticated falsification rejects a complex of hypotheses. However, Feyerabend responded to Lakatos by noting scientists are ready to use any and every method. He said that the successes of science, such as limiting disease and the moon shot, were not the result of the use of correct scientific methods but a combination of intuition, lucky guesses, and manipulation of data.

This account of the history of ideas on analysis reflects a "seesawing" debate between stressing logical thought processes as the appropriate form of analysis and stressing specific objective steps of analysis of empirical data as the appropriate form of analysis—until, in this century, it is suggested that the "scientific method" is a combination of logical thought, specific method- ology, and inspired guesswork.

When we review the social work analysis, we see that for the direct practitioner there is a need for objective measurable goals, but there is also a need for analysis of clients' subjective interpretation of how treatment is progressing. Interventions might change as a result of these analyses, and insights into the nature of the problems will emerge during these discussions. There is clearly a need for specific methodology, logical thought, and inspired guesswork when analyzing the results of such interventions. In the community organization role, a social worker is likely to be involved in action research in which a specific problem is addressed at the community level. Analysis of this research will involve objective outcomes but will also involve insight into community dynamics, power structures, and the explicit and implicit methods for" getting things done." In the administration and policy maker role, social workers will need the objective data for summative studies but will also need subjective data on processes and explicit and implicit agendas within the agency when doing formative studies.

Synthesis

When it comes to synthesis, there appears to be more agreement through- out the history of the scientific method debate than in any other part of the knowledge creation process. Most thinkers state that they are looking for "the truth" or "knowledge." The Ancient and Medieval thinkers saw this truth in terms of theoretical propositions, while thinkers since Galileo have been searching for principles that govern the regularities in nature. When science was separated from the rest of knowledge development, the search for truth or knowledge was equated with scientific investigation. The goal of science has been to develop "high-level principles" or theories that predict how nature works. This goal has been transferred to the social sciences where, for example, economists "model" the economy and predict consequences of budgetary policy and sociologists and psychologists use surveys and experimental designs to predict or find the causes of social phenomena such as child abuse, crime, and mental disorders.

Social science has found these goals, which have been transferred from a traditional "scientific method," unsatisfactory (Tudor, 1982; Bernstein, 1988; Mulkay, 1985; Hesse, 1980). As Hesse, when quoted by Bernstein, notes,

> In natural science a one way logic and method of interpretation is appropriate, since theory is dependent on self-subsistent facts, and testable by them. In human science, on the other hand, the "logic" of interpretation is irreducibly circular: part cannot be understood without whole, which itself depends on the relation of its parts; data and concepts cannot be understood without theory and context, which themselves depend on relations of data and concepts. (Bernstein, 1988, p. 32)

In social science, the effects of the relationship of thought and reality, analysis, and synthesis on each other are being recognized. Synthesis goals of generalizability or causality are not appropriate if the identification of the data or the problem definition cannot be separated from the theory that the research project is testing. For example, if a political orientation determines whether welfare recipients are deemed as a welfare dependency problem or victims of societal structural inequities, the identification of causality of increasing welfare roles will depend on that political orientation rather than any particular scientific method of synthesis.

In social work, synthesis needs are localized and pragmatic. Direct practice social workers need to know what interventions and services improve a client's functioning, a community worker needs to know how her or his community can work together to solve its problems and prevent other community problems, and the administrator/policy maker often just needs to know who her or his client community are and whether that group has changed over time as well as the effectiveness and impact of the program. In addition, in times of financial cutbacks social workers need to know about new practice methods to deal with large caseloads and multi-problem clients as well as effective use of resources. These needs are clearly not always searches for high-level principles and causality. Social work synthesis needs can be identified more clearly when the difference between natural science and social science realities are identified. Social work research can then have confidence in noting unique synthesis needs within both social science and the social work profession.

Implications for Social Work Research Education

Tudor (1982) suggests that sociological thinking on the scientific method falls into four camps:

1. Those who accept that there is one correct logical structure of scientific method but who do not believe in one ideal unified science;

2. Those who believe that scientific inquiry includes a logical structure but that this structure is not necessarily the correct form;

3. Those who believe that scientific theories have an "intellectual structure" but no mathematical or logical form; and

4. Those who believe that the natural sciences can no longer be understood in terms of "structure" or "system" or any correct systematization. (pp. 47–48)

This gives us a useful framework to review current thinking on social work research methods. In which of these camps does social work research intend to rest and why? Social work research texts suggest that we are in the first camp. However, the above discussion illustrates a need to review this position. In order to decide which of Tudor's camps to join, we can use his delineation of the common elements in any process of inquiry. He suggested that these elements are,

1. Experience of some aspect of the world that is significant or problematic to us;

2. Interpretation of this experience in the light of our preconceptions relating to this experience;

3. Derivation of these preconceptions from our earlier experience, peers, interests, social world, and what we have already accepted as knowledge;

4. Testing of these interpretations from our own and significant others' experiences;

5. Establishment of socially approved knowledge or truth; and

6. Explanation of further experiences or making sense of the world in light of the above elements. (p. 28)

These elements can be applied to social work research using the example of child abuse as a research problem. The political/economic climate surrounding child welfare policy can range from a positive support for a full range of primary, secondary, and tertiary prevention programs to a sentiment that only minimal services can be funded and that, therefore, only minimal tertiary prevention or treatment programs can be provided. This political/economic climate then dictates the approach to child abuse that social workers may adopt in their working environments. Orientations to child abuse treatment can range from a rehabilitative treatment model to a corrective punishment model. Such orientations imply value systems ranging from a belief that people are basically good and just need more education or self-awareness to improve their behaviors to a belief that people are basically bad and need to know that they will be caught and punished if they exhibit bad behavior. In addition, protection of children can be seen as a private family responsibility or a more public community responsibility. Social theories on the etiology of child abuse can range from critical theories, such as Marxist and feminist ideas of class or gender conflict that create societal structural inequities that affect the family and lead to child abuse, to functionalist theories suggesting that equilibrium in the family has been threatened in some manner and needs to be regained. Interventions in child abuse could be with the child victim or perpetrator as individuals, with family, with community (e.g., child abuse prevention programs or parent education), or at state and federal community levels in terms of legislating programs to address child abuse. Social workers finding themselves in a "supportive" political/economic environment might, at the farthest end of each continuum, be free to adopt a rehabilitative approach to child abuse, implying a belief in peoples' basic goodness, and incorporating a full range of community responsibility and treatment programs, implying a Marxist or feminist orientation. However, a social worker finding herself or himself in the minimalist political/economic environment might be forced to the other end of each continuum, regardless of professional or personal ethics or values. This social worker might adopt a coercive approach, implying that people are basically bad and that only a minimal treatment program can be offered for the most severe offenders who must change at the individual level to restore the functionalist status quo. While acknowledging that social workers can vary independently on each continuum, for ease of discussion we will use the "ideal types" at the anchoring point of each continuum as illustrations. The former orientation will be referred to as the comprehensive social worker while the latter orientation will be referred to as the minimalist social worker. This idea is illustrated in Figure I.1.

If we apply the comprehensive or minimalist orientations to Tudor's (1982) elements of the process of enquiry and the direct practice social worker role, we have the following ranges of possible research methodologies for the direct practice social worker. A comprehensive direct practice social worker with a rehabilitative perspective who sees people as basically good might *experience* the data on child abuse cases by focusing on positive aspects of families' functioning and looking for potential for change. A belief that child protection from abuse is a public rather than a private responsibility would lead to a belief in proactive intervention assessing "at risk" families and offering family support services, which would lead to the *experience* of

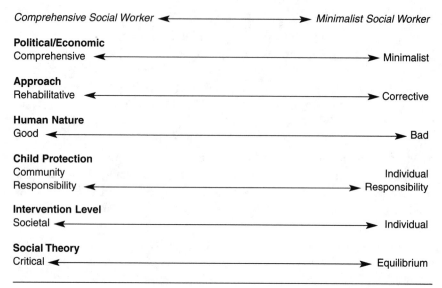

Comprehensive Social Worker ←——————————————→ *Minimalist Social Worker*

Political/Economic
Comprehensive ←——————————————————————→ Minimalist

Approach
Rehabilitative ←——————————————————————→ Corrective

Human Nature
Good ←——————————————————————————→ Bad

Child Protection
Community
Responsibility ←—————————————————————→ Individual
Responsibility

Intervention Level
Societal ←——————————————————————————→ Individual

Social Theory
Critical ←—————————————————————————→ Equilibrium

Figure I.1   Example of Continua of Possible Orientations to Child Protection

data on risk assessment. A Marxist or feminist conflict orientation to child abuse would stress data at a community or societal level that illustrates structural inequalities that lead to child abuse. This comprehensive social worker might *interpret* data on child abuse as information for making community changes and instigating a full range of services. This social worker is likely to *interpret* data in terms of its contribution to changing the class or gender inequities in the community and adopt an action approach to research. Preferred *testing* techniques might be subjective explorations of the impact of oppression and a comprehensive, detailed understanding of all aspects of child abuse, techniques that tend to be favored by action researchers. This social worker might *establish* findings by gaining the approval of other comprehensive social workers by reporting back to professionals with a conflict orientation to society for assessment. The findings might then *explain* further incidents of child abuse via a comprehensive framework that suggests a broad range of impact and services and possible social action strategies to change structural inequalities.

A minimalist social worker in the direct practice role who has a corrective approach implying people are basically bad might *experience* child abuse cases by focusing on the severity of incidents and families' dysfunction. The resultant treatment orientation would support intervention only when the abuse has become so severe that private responsibility for child protection has clearly broken down. This orientation contradicts the belief that people are basically bad and, therefore, need surveillance, but it is a cheaper service.

This orientation would emphasize study of severe child abuse cases as a research need. The functionalist orientation of this social worker would focus on individual child abuse cases rather than community, societal, class, or gender relations. The minimalist social worker might *interpret* data in terms of individual or family dysfunction and *derive* from this data that certain therapeutic interventions should be developed at the individual or family level. This social worker might *test* his or her interpretation by studying individual cases and looking for generalizations about variables at the individual or family level that appear to cause child abuse. Such generalizations would be *established* by presentation to other professionals with a minimalist orientation and suggest *explanations* of further cases of child abuse in terms of needs for better direct practice techniques. The above discussion of ideal types with regard to the direct practice role illustrates the limitations of suggesting that the traditional scientific method is the only method for carrying out research. The interrelations of all the continua that influence identification of the problem, analysis, and synthesis put social work research in Tudor's (1982) third or fourth camps.

Frequently instructors in social work research method courses comment that students do not know how to define a problem. Students, it is said, use all the technology available for library searches or statistical analysis without really thinking through what it is they want to know. When we review standard social work research method texts, we see that this problem is not all the student's fault. Usually, in these texts, there are comprehensive chapters on measurement, sampling, data collection, and analysis but only one brief introductory chapter on developing an orientation to the research focus and problem definition. In terms of Tudor's model, little is said about experience, interpretation, and derivation but everything is said about testing, establishment, and explanation. This "lopsided" approach leads students to believe that "good" testing is the essence of research while understanding the problem is an easy task that should be quickly passed over. In social work practice courses, students learn that a range of clients can be addressed with a range of interventions and a major part of their professional skill is to decide which of these interventions is appropriate for particular clients. It is time to use this approach to social work research.

Main Points

- There are four alterative paradigms that can guide social work research: positivism, post-positivism, critical theory, and constructivism
- These paradigms can be integrated with a generalist model of social work practice to offer approaches to generalist social work research

- Each of the four paradigms will interpret the stages of a generalist model of practice in different ways and in different sequential patterns
- The history of thought on the philosophy of science shows us that the accepted approach to knowledge generation has always been debatable
- There are four possible camps in relation to natural science. This book suggests that these camps can also be applied to current thinking on social work research. Most social work research thinkers are currently in camp (1) and we need to entertain the idea of moving to at least camp (2) and maybe even camps (3) and (4)

  1. Those who believe that there is one correct logical structure of scientific method but who do not believe in one ideal unified science;

  2. Those who believe that scientific inquiry includes a logical structure but that this structure is not necessarily the correct form;

  3. Those who believe that scientific theories have an "intellectual structure" but no mathematical or logical form; and

  4. Those who believe that science can no longer be understood in terms of "structure" or "system" or any correct systematization.

Learning Assignment

1. Think of a social work practice question that is interesting to you. Make a chart like Table I.1 and identify the questions you would ask about each of those topics, how you would gather data, how you would analyze that data, and what the goal of the research project would be. In pairs, share your charts and discuss the social work practice knowledge that would be generated by these projects.

2. Using the same social work question, pick one of the paradigms and questions and discuss with your partner how you might implement each stage of the generalist model when carrying out that research project.

3. Form four groups in the classroom: positivists, post-positivists, critical theorists, and constructivists. Consider the questions "How should social workers intervene at the micro and macro levels of practice with adolescents who are suicidal?" Discuss the question in small groups for 10 minutes and then present to the class how your group would study the question.

4. Form pairs and, using Figure I.1, one of you assume the role of a comprehensive social worker while the other assumes the role of a minimalist social worker. Discuss how each of you would address the research question "How should we intervene with child neglect?" Use the stages of the generalist change model to describe your approaches.

PART I

The Positivist Paradigm

Introduction to Part I

The positivist worldview assumes that an objective reality exists outside of personal experience that has demonstrable and immutable laws and mechanisms. Some authors refer to this worldview as the traditions of rationalism and empiricism (McCarl-Neilson, 1990). Positivist researchers suppose that one can identify the laws and mechanisms of human behavior and therefore reveal cause and effect relationships. Finding these causes and correlations is the goal of positivist research. This worldview assumes that "it is both possible and essential for the inquirer to adopt a distant, non-interactive posture. Values and other biasing and confounding factors are thereby automatically excluded from influencing the outcomes" (Guba, 1990, p. 20). As outlined in the brief history of the philosophy of science and knowledge in the introduction to this book, positivism emerged during the nineteenth century when Comte narrowed Bacon's notion of a separate objective "scientific" approach to gathering knowledge to a search for the laws of nature. Later, Hume's laws of cause and effect developed this proposition into a foundation for a scientific method. The laws of cause and effect are that

1. The cause and effect are contiguous

2. The cause is prior to the effect

3. There is a constant union between the cause and the effect

4. If there are several causes of the effect, they have a common feature

5. If causes have different effects, then they are different

6. If a correlation is observed between cause and effect, this correlation is derived from the relationship between cause and effect

7. If a cause appears to have no effect at certain times it is because that cause only creates the effect in combination with other causes.

Thus we have a set of principles aimed at determining causes and correlations so that scientific knowledge can be advanced. In the nineteenth century in the United States this thinking was combined with the pragmatism school of thought that led to empirical testing being the proof of the truth of knowledge. Later, in the twentieth century, Karl Popper offered the methodology for this "logical empiricism" when he noted that science has the following stages:

1. Formulate a hypothesis

2. Test the consequences of the hypothesis experimentally

3. Show whether the hypothesis is false

4. Formulate predictive principles

To operationalize this scientific method in the social sciences, psychologists have developed the experimental design while sociologists have developed the survey design. The experimental design addresses causality while the survey design addresses correlation. The experimental design has it roots in psychology's early history as a discipline that needed to prove that it was not just a philosophy or branch of metaphysics. Herbert Spencer (1902), in his book *Principles of Psychology,* noted that psychologists study the reasons for the connections between stimuli from the external world and the responses of humans to those stimuli. Ernest Mach (1883/1959), in his book *The Analysis of the Sensations,* linked this definition to the physical sciences and their related experimental research methodologies. This linking later fitted neatly with the evolution of behaviorism in the United States with its focus on the study of stimulus and response (Skinner, 1953; Watson, 1963).

The survey design aims to generate findings that can be generalized to a wider population than the sample included in the research project. It is a response to Emile Durkheim (1895/1938), who, in his book *The Rules of Sociological Method,* stated that a scientific treatment is a treatment that demands such generalization. He further stated that for sociologists, causality is addressed through the comparative method and that "the method of concomitant variations, or *correlation*" is *the* method of sociology (pp. 143–144). Although other thinkers, such as J.S. Mill, challenged these positions (Manicas, 1988), they are still apparent in the rationales offered today for the legitimacy of the survey design.

These deterministic designs have been combined with sampling and statistical procedures based on probability theory, again, not without controversy (Cohen, 1994), to make the case for a "scientific" approach to research aimed at gathering knowledge and making predictions about people. The above philosophers and thinkers did not entertain likelihood or significance levels when developing their principles of causality. They were assuming an absolute statement of fact, not a percentage probability of causality or correlation. This modification was made during the debates at the beginning of the twentieth century that extended the logic of Bertrand Russell's (1903) book *Principles of Mathematics*. Bertrand Russell linked mathematics to philosophy, suggesting that the logic of philosophical propositions could be proved mathematically. This entry of mathematics into proofs meant that confirmation of causality, which was originally framed as needing absolute proof, could be reframed to mean verification of probability of causality.

So, who made this jump from the need to prove absolute causality to the need to prove probability or likelihood of causality? Probability theory was developed in the 1620s by a French civil servant named Pierre Fermat, for whom mathematics was a hobby. Thomas Bayes, who lived from 1702–1761 in England, set out his theorem of probability in his paper "Essay towards solving a problem in the doctrine of chances," published in the *Philosophical Transactions* of the Royal Society of London in 1764. According to Charles Hull (1914), at this time in the eighteenth century, Achenwall invented the word "statistics" from the Italian word for a statesman. The term referred to information needed by statesmen and those in public life. Such information was gathered in numerical form but with no commonly accepted methodologies. These emerged in the nineteenth century when a Belgian astronomer named Felt Quetelet developed "social physics" when he developed the idea of the "statistical man" to make predictions about society as a whole and promote the idea that we can identify "laws deduced from inference" (Hull, 1914, p. 36). Thus a natural scientist transferred the methods of the "hard" sciences to the study of society. This gave the newly developing social sciences of "folk-psychology and sociology" an improved prestige as they emerged from their natural science benefactors. At the same time, according to Stephan (1948), in the United States there was an extensive use of sampling, where inferences were made about a larger phenomenon from a selection assumed to represent that phenomenon in agricultural crop and livestock estimates; economic statistics of prices, wages, and employment; social surveys and health studies; and public opinion polling. According to Stephan, the application of probability theory to the selection of samples was not made until the twentieth century with Bowley's sampling of bonds and their interest rates in 1906 and Student's testing of the t-distribution in 1907. Then Tippett's table of random numbers was published in 1927. It was Bowley and his colleagues who estimated errors associated with various approaches to stratified random sampling. The students of Bowley, working for the Russell Sage Foundation and influenced by the Social Science Research Council, gave serious attention to sampling methodology, especially with the demands of the social programs developed under the New Deal in the 1930s. From then until now, sampling and statistics based on probability theory have been the accepted methodologies for studying society.

In the middle of these developments, though, critics noted that probabilistic statements could not be made on the basis of the finding of one study, since this would be making the assumption that one can generalize from the specific case to all cases. In 1934 Karl Popper stepped into the breach and suggested that since a hypothesis cannot be confirmed because of this problem of induction, then let us simply reverse the logic, and rather than confirm the hypotheses, let us reject the null hypothesis. To clarify, since we cannot generalize a finding about one relationship (e.g., effective parenting skills in one particular sample of parents reduced child abuse) from one study to the general population (effective parenting skills causes a reduction of child abuse in the general population), we can assess the absence of the finding in our study (is there an absence of a relationship between effective parenting skills and child abuse in this particular sample of parents?). If we can reject this null hypothesis then the relationship must hold (if we can answer "no" to the above question). If we can repeat this study and reach the same conclusion then we have a logical empirical proof of the relationship. Again, this position is controversial but has gained acceptance.

The last step in this line of thought is the linking of probability statements and testing the null hypothesis to quantitative methods. If positivist, logical empiricism aims to make probabilistic statements about the absence of a relationship between cause and effect, the only way to do this is to gather data in terms of numbers that can then be manipulated via statistical procedures based on probability theory. This book, therefore, concludes that the only way to faithfully carry out this methodology and meet the requirements of positivist logical empiricism is to gather quantitative data to test hypotheses about the absence of a relationship or correlation between cause and effect. Data collected in the form of numbers facilitates probabilistic statements; data collected in the form of words does not facilitate statements about the precise relationships between cause and effect as specified by Hume. Thus in the following discussion of positivism, causal and correlational research using quantitative methods will be discussed. All other approaches to research are discussed under the appropriate alternative paradigm in other parts of this book.

1

Engagement—Entrée
to the Research Setting

The positivist researcher engages the research setting on two occasions: the first is during the initial stages of developing the project when formal contracting with the research sponsors must be completed and the second is when data gathering begins and study participants are contacted. For the positivist researcher, engagement of the research setting tends to be a formal agreement to gather data and use the site as a source of data. Although negotiation of the terms of the research project with the site's gatekeepers is crucial, further involvement of study sponsors and participants in design and data collection planning is not considered appropriate. A sponsor may identify the focus of the study, but it would not be considered an independent scientific study if the process of engagement with the research setting included study participants influencing the research design. For the positivist, it is important that these assessment and planning stages are completed using literature on previous knowledge about the topic and the principles of research design. Also, all data collection instruments should be developed before data collection begins. Study participants are not engaged as partners in developing the focus of the study but as "subjects" from whom data will be collected.

Often the hardest part of research, especially for students, is finding a setting that is willing to be the research site. Usually field placement settings or places of employment are approached. Otherwise professional contacts are used to find gatekeepers to sites where the desired data can be gathered. It is important to remember that hosting a research project may bring extra work to an agency setting or other research site. When initial telephone, e-mail, or letter contact is made, a willingness to explore the research site's information needs as well as the researcher's interests should be communicated. These communications should include

- A brief explanation of who you are and why you would like to do research at this particular site
- An invitation to discuss a range of possible research topics within both the researcher's and the research site's arena of interest
- An indication of time lines and the potential intrusion into the daily life of the research site
- An indication of the benefits of the research project to the research site
- An indication of the commitments the researcher and the research site would need to make to each other
- An indication of how the findings of the research project will be used, including the potential usefulness of these findings to the research site

It is important to find out about the site's procedures for approving research projects. A verbal commitment from a gatekeeper is a good start, but a formal agreement signed by the appropriate decision maker should follow. Certain settings, such as hospitals and prisons, have time-consuming procedures requiring approval by several levels of the hierarchy. Allow time for this possibility.

When engaging study participants for data collection, the informed consent provisions that were included in the human subjects review come in to play.[1] A review of the project is offered to the study participant and an informed consent agreement is signed. Then the interview or observation can be carried out. Of course, a positivist researcher carrying out quantitative research should be able to personally engage study participants. However, the requirements of positivist science downplay any further engagement between researcher and researched. The need for uniformity of interview conditions and the need to limit the influence of the researcher on the study call for a more neutral relationship between the researcher and the study participant. Study participants are considered to be the source of data, not the source of input on the direction of the research. This limited engagement of study participants by positivist researchers has led to some dissatisfaction among study participants who are from oppressed groups or from various minority ethnic groups; it is one of the reasons for the exploration of alternative approaches to carrying out research. The idea of being sensitive to study participants and acknowledging their worldviews while engaging them for data collection has been developed particularly by feminist researchers (McCarl-Nielson, 1990; Reinharz, 1992). They tend to suggest collecting qualitative rather than quantitative data as a way of respecting study participants and engaging them more fully. This call for sensitivity to study participants creates a dilemma for social work positivist researchers whose epistemology states that the researcher must take a distant, non-interactive posture but whose ethics require sensitivity to diversity. This dilemma has been at the root of much of the blurring of positivism and post-positivism in recent developments of research methodologies. In many ways, the alternative paradigm approach in this book resolves this dilemma.

Main Points

- For positivists, engagement of study participants tends to be limited to formal contracting and creating a relaxed atmosphere for data collection
- Further engagement between researcher and researched will threaten the objectivity required by the science of positivism

Learning Assignment

- Think of a research topic that you are interested in. In a class discussion, explore how as a positivist social work researcher you might resolve the dilemma of needing to adopt a distant stance to gather quantitative data and, at the same time, engage study participants at the start of the research project.

Note

1. The Human Subjects Review process is reviewed in Chapter 17.

2

Assessment—Development of Understanding of the Research Focus

The positivist approach to research dictates that questions and hypotheses about causes and correlations be stated in advance of data collection and that they be subject to testing in controlled conditions. The researcher taking a positivist worldview asks questions addressing explanation or description. Explanations are causal questions, such as "How did the intervention program affect clients' depression?" or "How did refugee adaptation improve after the introduction of focused resettlement programs?" A specific hypothesis is stated and a controlled experimental design is used to measure the predictive link between an independent variable (the cause) and a dependent variable (the effect). Units of analysis are identified, such as individuals, families, groups, organizations, or communities, and they are precisely defined and measured. Descriptions are correlational questions, such as "What is the link between poverty and child abuse?" or "What is the link between an individual's self-esteem and coping mechanisms?" A hypothesis about the direction of relationship between the variables that were identified in the question is developed and the correlations are generally tested through surveys of randomly selected samples.

Most research texts identify exploration as a third arena for positivist research. Exploratory questions are asked when there is very little literature or data on an issue and generally start with a broad question, such as "What are the causes of homelessness in Native American communities?" or "Why are certain children in the Latino culture unaffected by abuse?" They are exploratory questions with no hypothesis regarding the answer to the question. This book takes the position that such research is not positivist research, since it does not meet the criteria, offered by Guba (1990), of the positivist paradigm. It does not adopt an ontology that addresses immutable laws and natural mechanisms and aims to generalize findings; it does not adopt an epistemology that gives the researcher a distant, non-interactive posture; and it does not adopt a methodology that is experimental or manipulative. Rather, this approach is better described as a post-positivist approach to research and is described in Part 2 of this book.

The Literature Review

Whether the proposed study is causal or correlational, a positivist researcher will begin the development of the research project by carrying out a literature review. Developing hypotheses about causal or correlational relationships relies on drawing assumptions based on established knowledge of regularities and mechanisms in human interaction. The scholarly literature (scholarly journals, books, dissertations, reports, and presented papers) is the primary source of established knowledge for the positivist, and it frames the researcher's understanding of the research focus. Neuman and Kreuger (2003) offer useful advice on the function of, and techniques for, carrying out a literature review. They suggest that the first step is to narrow down the research topic. For example, a topic such as "refugee resettlement" is too broad. However, a topic such as "South East Asian refugees' experience of welfare" sharpens the focus of the search. The next step is to make a plan for searching the literature, given the time you have and the types of materials you need to access. Generally, students have access to a university library Web site. Universities are increasingly subscribing to electronic sources of scholarly journals such as EBSCOhost or Wilson OmniFile. In recent years, these sources have increased remarkably their subscription to social work journals, and they also allow you to download a full text version of an article that you are interested in to your computer at home. Other services are abstracting services (Social Work Abstracts, Psychology Abstracts, Social Science Citation Index) which are also available online; they provide citation information, but you will need to retrieve the full text of the article from another source. Dissertations are a good source for more recent research, and they can be searched by accessing Dissertation Abstracts International. Government documents can be accessed through sources such as the Monthly Catalog of Government Documents and The Federal Register. Using the Internet you can also track down authors of presentations and conference papers you would like to review. When carrying out these searches, make sure you try several key words since not all databases understand words in the same way. Your library Web site will also be a source for your library's and other libraries' book catalogs.

Having found the sources of your literature there is a decision to be made. How will you read and synthesize all of this literature? You check out all the books, print the full text articles and reports, and photocopy hard copy sources. Now you have a big pile of books and paper that makes you feel like you have achieved something. You take it home and there it is, this overwhelming stack of information. You circle it, leave the room, come back and sit down, but where to begin? The best idea, as with any project, is to take it one step at a time. Have a system of recording in mind. Decide beforehand the information you need to glean from each source. Citations should include at least

1. Author, year, title, and journal source or publisher; all the citation information you will need for your reference list.

2. The abstract of the article, or a summary of the book's preface (or perhaps the table of contents for the book), or the executive summary of the report.

3. Specific quotes that illustrate points you want to make about the topic, including page numbers.

4. If it is a publication describing a research study, the research question, hypotheses, measurement of concepts, design (sample and data collection strategies), and major findings.

5. It is a good idea to look at the references or bibliography of your sources to see if there is something there you might want to look up.

The most efficient way to record your citations is in a word processing program. Think about how you want to organize them, though. Is it by author, topic, or source? I strongly recommend that you organize the citations by topic. When writing the literature review, remember that you are synthesizing your understanding of the literature, not writing an annotated bibliography. The biggest mistake students make when writing their literature reviews is to give a succession of brief abstracts of each source without discussing the common threads or how they relate to the research topic. This mistake happens, I think, because students start with the author as the organizing principle of their literature review, rather than the topics to be reviewed. If you have your citations grouped according to topic, it is easier to synthesize. For example, in a review of literature on South East Asian refugees' experience of the welfare system in the United States, concepts being explored could include

- Characteristics of South East Asian refugees
- Historical context of their refugee status
- The refugee experience of transition to the host country
- Typical welfare services available to refugees
- Resettlement experiences of refugees (divided into women, men, old and young, or other relevant subgroups)

These concepts can then be the organizing headings for the literature review, and, by the way, they might be the source of the variables you develop later to operationalize your hypotheses when you move on to developing your problem statement.

Problem Statement

A positivist researcher develops a problem statement in the early phases of the assessment stage. Such a researcher may begin with a vague interest in a topic, for example, poverty. As a social work positivist researcher interested in practice knowledge, this researcher may narrow the focus of the study to "interventions with poverty." As a generalist, this researcher will then consider interventions at the micro and macro levels of human organization and social work practice. The micro level could be employment and work training programs, benefit programs, and ancillary substance abuse or mental health services, if needed. The macro level could be organizations such as the Temporary Assistance for Needy Families (TANF) administrative divisions and communities of recipients of TANF. Then the researcher decides whether to investigate current interventions with poverty or initiate and evaluate innovative programs. This leads to the identification of questions and hypotheses and the operationalization of variables described in the questions and hypotheses.

Thus we see that social work research's primary function is to inform social work practice. A social work research question should address an aspect of practice with individuals, families, groups, organizations, or communities (local, national, or international). The positivist must decide whether

Table 2.1   Causal and Correlational Micro and Macro Practice Research Questions

	Causal (Explanatory)	*Correlational (Descriptive)*
Micro Practice (target is individuals, families, or groups)	What is the differential effectiveness on TANF clients of two approaches to employment training where one group receives training and the other receives no training and is simply placed immediately into a job?	How does the family assessment device (FAD)[1] assess families from three different ethnic groups?
Macro Practice (target is organizations or communities)	What is the impact uptake of county mental health services where one county has neighborhood mental health clinics and the other has a central mental health clinic?	How do the contrasting supervisory styles in two departments of children's services affect staff retention rates for social workers?

1. The Family Assessment Device (FAD) was developed by Epstein and Bishop (1981). For a study of its sensitivity to diversity see Morris (1990).

the research question is causal or correlational and ask him or herself, "Is the research question addressing explanations of events or describing patterns of events?" As stated above, in most research texts, these two purposes are termed "explanatory" and "descriptive." Questions associated with these two purposes are illustrated by the examples in Table 2.1.

In the examples in Table 2.1, we see the distinction illustrated for micro and macro practice. The causal micro practice question targets individuals and the correlational micro practice question targets families; the causal macro practice question targets communities and the correlational macro practice question targets organizations. Just to be clear, the target of the question is not only the level of practice to be addressed but also the unit of analysis. The unit of analysis is the category of people about whom assertions rising from the findings of the study will be made.

Having developed questions, the positivist researcher's next step is to develop proposed answers to these questions, that is, hypotheses. Hypotheses, in positivist research, are based on current knowledge found in the scholarly literature. Thus, for our example questions, the proposed answers might be

- The TANF recipients who receive *work training* are more likely to gain *permanent employment* than those who do not
- The FAD is more likely to assess Anglo *families* as functional than Japanese American and Hawaiian American *families.*
- The county with neighborhood *mental health clinics* will experience a higher *uptake of services* than the county with a central *mental health clinic.*
- The organization in which *supervision* offers encouragement and support is more likely to have a high *staff retention rate* than the organization in which *supervision* offers assessment and direction only.

By operationalizing the concepts within the proposed questions as *variables* with identified dimensions, the hypotheses facilitate a clear statement of the relationship between the variables that we intend to test. They narrow down the focus of the study and clarify exactly who and what the study is about. To be clear, this is illustrated in Table 2.2.

We are now ready to state our hypotheses in terms of relationships between variables.

- For TANF recipients, the higher the score on approaches to work training, the lower the score on permanent employment.
- For families, the higher the score on ethnicity of families, the higher the score on the FAD.
- For counties, the higher the score on mental health clinics, the higher the score on uptake of mental health services.
- For the organization, the higher the score on supervision, the lower the score on staff retention rate.

So now we have stated the direction of the relationship of the variables in the hypotheses that we anticipate. The first relationship is negative; that is, as one variable increases the other decreases. The second relationship is positive; that is, both scores increase or decrease together. The third relationship is also positive and the fourth relationship is negative. In addition, we have identified two different types of variables, dependent and independent variables. The dependent variable is the variable that you think will change because of the effect of the cause—it is usually the focus of your study—and the independent variable is the variable that you think will cause, or correlate with, that change. Put more precisely, the dependent variable shows the effect and the independent variable is the cause. In our examples, the dependent variables are permanent employment, scores on the FAD, uptake of mental health services, and staff retention rates. The independent variables are approaches to training, families, mental health clinics, and supervision. Having identified our hypotheses, we have reached the final stage of the assessment and can now move on to planning or rationales for gathering data.

Table 2.2   Operationalization of Concepts and Variables

Concept/Variable	Operationalization	Dimension
Approaches to work training (i.v.)	Provision of a training program or placement directly into employment with no training.	Range has two values: training = 1 no training = 2
Permanent Employment (d.v.)	Presence or absence of paid employment that lasts for six months or more	Range with 2 values: unemployment = 1 employment = 2
FAD (d.v.)	Specific Family Assessment Device created by Epstein and Bishop (1981).	Scores from 1 to 4 on each item of assessment device: 1 = strongly agree, 2 = agree, 3 = disagree, and 4 = strongly disagree
Families (i.v.)	Families from three ethnic groups: Anglo, Japanese American, Hawaiian American.	Range with 3 values: Japanese American = 1 Anglo = 2 Hawaiian American = 3
Mental Health Clinics (i.v.)	A county system of providing mental health services to the community either by providing one large central clinic or a number of smaller neighborhood clinics.	Range with 2 values: centralized = 1 neighborhood = 2
Uptake of Mental Health Services (d.v.)	Rates of usage of mental health services as a proportion of rates of mental health problems such as depression, suicide, and schizophrenia	Percentage of eligible population in county using mental health services.
Supervision (i.v.)	A style of staff management that ranges from authoritarian and directive to supportive and facilitative.	Range with values from 1 to 10 with 1 and 10 being the anchors at each end of the scale 10 = authoritarian and directive 1 = supportive and facilitative.
Staff Retention Rate (d.v.)	The rate at which social workers leave the organization per year.	The percentage of staff that leave each year.

Main Points

- Positivist research is causal or correlational (explanatory or descriptive)
- The assessment phase starts with a literature review
- Social work research addresses questions of micro and macro practice
- A question and hypothesis is developed that includes concepts/variables, operationalization, dimensions, and the direction of relationships between variables

Learning Assignment

- Think of a social work practice topic that you are interested in. Using Tables 2.1 and 2.2 as examples, write down causal and correlational questions about that topic at the micro and macro level of practice. Give hypotheses for each question. Identify the concepts and variables. Identify the independent and dependent variables. State how your questions address social work practice. Get into pairs and then explain your questions and hypotheses to your partner.

3

Planning–Rationales for Carrying out the Research Project

I n positivist research, the question, hypothesis, research design, data collection strategy, and data analysis procedures are rooted in previous literature and identified before the project begins. Any changes in the proposed design while carrying out the research would be seen as weakening the validity of the research finding and, well, just bad research practice. An explanatory, also called classical experimental, design is seen as the most robust, since it follows procedures that meet the criteria for proving causality. It identifies independent and dependent variables, requires random assignment of research subjects to experimental and control groups so that both groups are the same, describes procedures for manipulation of the dependent variable(s), and requires development of pretest and posttest instruments and time frames. If this design is implemented then threats to internal validity (proving causality) are removed.

Descriptive designs address correlational relationships between independent and dependent variables, usually through large-scale surveys. Samples are preferably random (representative of the population being studied); however, these samples are not manipulated into control and experimental groups but are surveyed in their own settings using valid and reliable data collection instruments developed in advance of data collection. Such designs do not address threats to internal validity, but they are considered to have stronger external validity (generalizability of findings from the sample to the population of interest) than the explanatory design.

Explanatory Designs

An explanatory or causal design aims to prove that the independent variable(s) caused changes to the dependent variable(s) and that there are no explanations for changes noted in the dependent variable other than the influence of the independent variable. In our examples of causal studies, we want to prove that the two different employment training programs were the *cause* of differing employment experiences for TANF recipients in those programs, and we want to prove that the type of mental health clinic *caused* changes in the uptake of mental health services. To do this, we set up a research design that allows us to exclude all alternative explanations for the relationship we observe between our independent variables and dependent variables. We measure the dependent variable at the beginning of the study (pretest) and then again at the end of the study (posttest) and note the changes. We prove that the independent variable caused the changes to the dependent variable because we have controlled for alternative explanations for these changes. Alternative explanations for the changes measured in a dependent variable are called "threats to internal validity." Threats to internal validity are generally grouped under the following headings:

1. *History.* Something happened during the course of the study that was the real explanation for any changes noted in the dependent variable. In our sample micro practice causal study, this might be the opening of a new industrial plant in the neighborhood where TANF recipients were living that hired all TANF recipients regardless of training. In our example macro practice study, this might be a media campaign informing people about the range of services that local mental health departments offer that caused people to use more mental health services.

2. *Maturation.* Participants in the study simply changed because of the passage of time. In our micro practice study, this might be that TANF recipients, over time, simply had a better understanding of how to get and keep a job because time had passed and they literally had a more mature approach to the workplace. In our macro practice study, potential clients of mental health services might seek services because they had lived with their mental illness for longer.

3. *Testing.* Participants in the study simply changed because they were tested on the items that measure the dependent variable and thus became more conscious of potential change. In our micro practice study, being assessed for employability by employment specialists might have caused TANF recipients to pursue job search strategies that they were not aware of before being asked about them in the pretest interview. In our macro practice study, testing might be a problem if the focus on collecting aggregate statistics for use

of services in two counties led administrators to target their services more effectively.

4. *Instrumentation*. The instrument used to test respondents may cause changes in the dependent variable. TANF participants may receive a thorough employability assessment at the beginning of the study but may just receive a telephone call checking on their employment status at the end of the study. The two different ways of testing may cause changes in results. In our macro practice example, there might have been changes in the efficiency with which statistics on uptake of mental health services were collected that caused changes in the measurement of such services used between the time of the pretest and the time of the posttest.

5. *Statistical Regression*. This is a statistical concept regarding the obvious statement that group scores cluster around the average score. That is why it is the average score. If participants in a study have extreme scores on a dependent variable, then simple random error is likely to move their scores closer to the average score for that variable in that group of people. In our micro practice study, we probably have participants with extremely low scores on poverty and employability. Probability theory suggests that they are likely to improve their scores simply because their scores are so extreme. In our macro practice study, likewise, as a whole, the group of people with extremely low use of mental health services are likely to increase their use of services because they are at the extreme low end of usage.

6. *Selection Bias*. It is possible that there is something about the participants in the study that has caused changes noted in the dependent variable. In our micro practice example, it is possible that people who are more motivated to get a job chose the program where participants are immediately placed in employment, while those who were not chose to go to employment training. In our macro practice study, it is possible that potential mental health clients in one of the counties had cultural or religious beliefs promoting a cultural norm that frowns upon the use of mental health services. In the other counties there might have been a stronger acceptance of the positive function of mental health services.

7. *Experimental Mortality*. Participants in the study may simply drop out of the study before it is completed. In our micro practice study, TANF recipients who tend to be transitory populations living in marginal housing may be forced to move to another area. One of the counties in our macro practice study may experience a reduction in service use because people are leaving the county to live in a neighboring county with improved and more convenient services.

8. *The Effect of the Study*. This is the possibility that simply being in a study affects participants. TANF participants in each of the training programs may get to know each other and learn employment tips from each other so

that the training being received by the two groups of participants starts to merge. Also, the groups of TANF recipients might start to get into a rivalry with each other once they discover they are being compared. The researcher might start to affect TANF recipients by simply subtly communicating the expectation that one group is going to be more employable than another. In the macro practice study, these kinds of effects would be less likely because of the use of aggregate statistics and less personal contact between study participants and researchers.

We can best understand how the experimental design allows us to control for these threats to internal validity by reviewing a number of example designs and understanding their intrinsic threats to internal validity, as noted in Table 3.1.

Table 3.1 shows how we can develop a design that controls for all threats to internal validity. There are some practical problems with this design for our macro practice study that we will address in a moment, but for the purposes of understanding the implications of each of these designs, let us walk our way through each of them. In design One we simply measure employment in our micro practice study and uptake of services in our macro practice study after the independent variables have been implemented. We know the amount of the dependent variable at that time, but we do not know what caused that amount of employment or uptake of services. In design Two, we measure employment and uptake of services both before and after the dependent variable was implemented. At the end of the study we know the difference in employment and uptake of services, but, again, we do not know what caused that difference. In design Three we introduce comparison groups, but we have done nothing to check whether the two groups are similar. Thus we have, in the micro practice study, one group of TANF recipients receiving employment training and another receiving employment services only. We measure employment both before and after each group participates in its different programs. At the end of the program we can compare the employment rates of the two groups, but we do not know what caused those differences. Similarly, in our macro practice study we can compare the two counties' uptake of mental health services, but we do not know what caused those differences.

In design Four we randomly assign study participants to each of the two comparison groups, so we need to take a brief detour into a discussion of random assignment and what it means. To ensure that the researcher does not influence the composition of the two comparison groups to favor one of the employment programs or service delivery systems and make it appear to be more effective than it is, we need a systematic process for assigning study participants to the two comparison groups. Also, to be able to use statistical

Table 3.1   Research Designs

Design	Sample Question That Would Be Answered	Threats to Internal Validity
One One Group Posttest Only X O	1. Are recipients of TANF employment training employed after the end of the training? 2. Are recipients of no training only TANF employment placement services employed at the end of the program? **(Two separate micro practice studies)** 1. What is the rate of mental health service use in the county with neighborhood clinics? 2. What is the rate of mental health service use in the county with a centralized clinic? **(Two separate macro practice studies)**	History Maturation Testing Instrumentation Statistical Regression Selection Bias Experimental Mortality The effects of the study
Two One Group Pretest Posttest O X O	The above questions, as well as 1. What is the difference in employment for recipients of TANF employment training between the start of the program and the end of the program? 2. What is the difference in employment for recipients of no training only TANF employment placement services between the start of the program and the end of the program? **(Two separate micro practice studies)** 1. What is the rate of mental health service use in counties with neighborhood clinics?	History Maturation Testing Instrumentation Statistical Regression Selection Bias Experimental Mortality The effects of the study

(Continued)

Table 3.1 (Continued)

Design	Sample Question That Would Be Answered	Threats to Internal Validity
	2. What is the rate of mental health service use in the counties with a centralized clinic? **(Two separate macro practice studies)**	
Three Two Nonequivalent Groups Pretest Posttest O X O O X O	The above questions, as well as 1. What is the difference in employment between TANF recipients who receive TANF employment training and TANF recipients who received TANF employment placement services only? 2. What is the difference in uptake of mental health services between counties with neighborhood mental health clinics and those with a centralized mental health clinic?	History Maturation Testing Instrumentation Statistical Regression Selection Bias Experimental Mortality The effects of the study
Four Two Equivalent Groups Pretest Posttest (classic experimental design) R O X O R O X O	The above questions, as well as 1. What is the differential effectiveness on TANF clients of two approaches to employment training where one group receives training and the other receives no training and is simply placed immediately into a job? 2. What is the difference in uptake of mental health services between counties with neighborhood mental health clinics and those with a central mental health clinic?	Testing Instrumentation

Design	Sample Question That Would Be Answered	Threats to Internal Validity
Five Two Equivalent Groups Posttest Only R X O R X O	1. Did the difference in employment programs *cause*[1] the differences observed in employment for TANF recipients who received these services? 2. Did the difference in the structure of mental health service delivery *cause* the difference in service uptake observed?	

R = Random Assignment

X = Measurement of Independent Variable

O = Measurement of Dependent Variable

1. Causality is being assigned here because of the ruling out of threats to internal validity; the problem with assuming causality as a result of one study that rejects the null hypothesis is discussed below under data analysis.

procedures to analyze our data, which are based on probability theory, we need to know the probability of each study participant being assigned to each of the two groups. Random assignment is a process whereby all study participants have an equal chance of being assigned to either group. The researcher can, for example, give all TANF recipients a number before the employment services begin and then place all those with an even number in the employment training program and all those with an odd number into the employment services group. Or the researcher can use a table of random numbers, which is a table of random numbers that has been generated where every number had an equal chance of being included at any point in the table. You can generate a table of random numbers and see exactly what one looks like by going to a Web site such as http://www.randomizer.org/form.htm. The use of random assignment increases the likelihood that the two comparison groups in the study are similar. If the groups are similar, then we can rule out most of the threats to internal validity because if they had been the cause of the change in the dependent variable they would have had the same effect on each of our comparison groups. Thus the only explanation for differences between our two groups on the posttest is the impact of the independent variable. To be really sure, though, we need to consider design Four. In this design we have our two equivalent groups but we do not pretest them so that we can rule out the two remaining threats to internal validity, testing and instrumentation. If we need to know the difference between the pretest and the posttest, we can combine designs Three and Four and randomly assign participants to four comparison groups, two of which are pretested and two of which are not. This is known as a "Solomon four-group design."

These randomized designs work for our micro practice example, but what about our macro practice example? You have probably been muttering this to the page as you have read these explanations. We can't exactly randomly assign mental health clients to two different counties and uproot them for the duration of our study. Well, remember, this is a macro practice study— *we are not targeting individuals; we are targeting service structure.* Ideally, the way to carry out this study would be to identify all counties within a given area, say a state. They then would be randomly assigned to implement either a centralized or local system of mental health clinics. We would then measure service uptake in each of the groups of county service delivery systems. This is as impractical as moving people out of their homes for the purposes of a research project. Each county has its own history, culture, and resources for mental health services. Thus, in this case we will need to do something called "matching." It is not as statistically robust as random assignment, but it is the next best thing. As macro practitioners, we would need to identify characteristics of counties that we think are particularly relevant to delivery of mental health services. These might include counties' rates of chronic schizophrenia, dual-diagnosed clients with both a mental illness and a substance abuse problem, or distribution of ethnic groups within a county. We would then need to make sure that counties with similar rates on these characteristics were matched, one with a centralized system of mental health services and the other with a neighborhood system of mental health services. This is how we would develop our two groups.

So far, we have talked about comparison groups that are either equivalent or nonequivalent. As you can probably see, getting an equivalent group is not an easy matter. However, rather than give up on trying to find the cause, we can approximate proof of causality with a time series design. With this design, we can have either one or two groups, and rather than do one pretest and one posttest, we can (1) repeat the pretest several times to get a baseline, (2) introduce the independent variable, and (3) repeat several posttests. In our example micro practice study, we could have one group of TANF recipients for each of the employment strategies being used. We could assess their employment every week for six months before the programs begin, then introduce the employment strategies, and then assesses their employment for six months afterwards. We could then compare the trends in employment for the two groups and make the assumption that if there was a change in the employment trend after the employment strategy was implemented, the employment strategy had something to do with causing that trend. We cannot absolutely state the probability because we do not have random assignment, but we can rule out those employment strategies as effective programs if nothing changes in the employment data in the six months after the intervention.

This has been an overview of explanatory designs. Rationales for causal designs have been discussed and some practical guidance has been offered. It is clear that there are practical issues to be addressed when implementing a causal study, and some remedies have been suggested. We now move on to a discussion of the second kind of positivist design: descriptive or correlational designs.

Descriptive Designs

Just as a reminder, as discussed at the beginning of this section of the book, the causal designs addressed above are rooted in the history of psychology, while the proposition that a correlational study is the appropriate approach to understanding the causes of human behavior comes from the traditions of sociology. You might have noticed that many of the designs outlined in the discussion above could address correlation even though they could not address causality. A social work researcher could go ahead and set up the above designs and prove a correlation between the independent variable and the dependent variable. However, with the strategies for selecting study participants associated with those designs, such a correlation would only be true for the actual study that showed the correlation. This correlation could not be generalized beyond the unique setting of the study. Indeed, this is a problem with explanatory designs; their internal validity is strong but their external validity, that is, the ability to generalize study findings to the total population of interest, is weak. There are two ways we can generalize findings from a sample to a total population of interest. The first is to keep replicating a study until a finding has been found to be true in all relevant situations. The second is to find a short cut around such time-intensive repetition and find a rationale for generalizing the findings of one study to a larger group of people: enter probability theory combined with sampling distributions. Both Frankel (1983) and Rubin and Babbie (2001) show clearly

Table 3.2   Hypothetical Retention Rate of Social Workers in Children's
Services Departments

County Departments of Children's Services	Staff Retention Rate
1. A County in California	20%
2. A County in New York	40%
3. A County in Florida	70%
4. A County in Washington State	30%
5. A County in Wisconsin	60%
6. A County in Texas	50%
Mean = 45% and SD = 17	

how we can select various samples of people from a larger population of people and justify the assumption that what is true for the sample is true for the total population from which the sample was selected, using the classical theory of inference drawn from probability theory. This theory suggests that one sample is a sample of 1 from the many possible samples. The larger this one sample, the more likely it is that its characteristics approximate the characteristics of the population from which it was selected, since it is more likely to be drawn from the samples clustered around the mean of samples. This is the central limit theorem (CLT) that states that the distribution of sample means tend towards a normal distribution. Perhaps an example would help here. Here is one adapted from Frankel (1983). Let us return to the example macro practice correlational study in Table 2.1. The research question is "How do the contrasting supervisory styles in two departments of children's services affect staff retention rates for social workers?" Imagine that we are interested in six departments of children's services. Their hypothetical average staff retention rates for the last year are shown in Table 3.2.

The mean retention rate for this population of six county departments of children's services is 45%. Now suppose we consider all the possible random samples of 2 that we can draw from this population of children's services. There are 15 possibilities and they are tabulated in Table 3.3.

In the fourth column of Table 3.3, the distribution of means of hypothetical social work staff retention rates has some interesting properties. The mean of these means is 45%, which is the same as the mean for the total population of six children's services agencies listed in Table 3.2. Also, if you look at the distribution of the means, 45% occurs three times. This is the most frequently occurring mean. In addition, the values of the other means

Table 3.3   Fifteen Possible Samples of 2 Drawn From a Population of 6

Sample Number	The two counties selected into the sample	Staff retention rates for the two counties	The mean staff retention rates for the two counties	Standard Deviation (square root of total of differences between scores and mean squared, divided by sample size)
1.	1 and 2	20% and 40%	30%	15 squared = 225
2.	1 and 3	20% and 70%	45%	0 squared = 0
3.	1 and 4	20% and 30%	25%	20 squared = 400
4.	1 and 5	20% and 60%	40%	5 squared = 25
5.	1 and 6	20% and 50%	35%	10 squared = 100
6.	2 and 3	40% and 70%	55%	10 squared = 100
7.	2 and 4	40% and 30%	35%	10 squared = 100
8.	2 and 5	40% and 60%	50%	5 squared = 25
9.	2 and 6	40% and 50%	45%	0 squared = 0
10.	3 and 4	70% and 30%	50%	5 squared = 25
11.	3 and 5	70% and 60%	65%	20 squared = 400
12.	3 and 6	70% and 50%	60%	15 squared = 225
13.	4 and 5	30% and 60%	45%	0 squared = 0
14.	4 and 6	30% and 50%	40%	5 squared = 25
15.	5 and 6	60% and 50%	55%	10 squared = 100

$$SD = \sqrt{(1750/15)} = 11$$

range from 25% to 65%, while the values of the actual staff retention rates for the six agencies range from 20% to 70%. Thus the means tend to cluster around the actual mean more closely than in the original population of interest. These means also form a bell-shaped curve if they are plotted out in a graph. Such a curve is known as a "normal" distribution. It shows how far each mean deviates from the overall mean. Usually the deviations of scores from their mean are transformed into a standardized statistic known as a standard deviation, which is the average deviation of all scores from their mean. In this case, because we are talking about a distribution of means rather than a distribution of scores, we call this the standard error. When a standard error is calculated, it takes into account the sample size in relation to the population size. Whether it be a standard deviation or a standard error, in any normal distribution 95% of the area falling under the curve of that distribution falls between plus and minus two standard deviations (or two standard errors) from the mean. The fact that such means drawn from samples will have these properties is the central limit theorem noted above.

Using this theorem, we can estimate how closely the characteristics of one sample approximate the characteristics of the population from which it was drawn. We do this by calculating the standard error and using confidence intervals. The standard error, according to Frankel (1983), is calculated by the formula

$$\text{S.E. of Mean} = \sqrt{[(1 - n/N)\, S^2/n]}$$

Where n = the sample size and N = the size of the population of interest, S squared is the variance (i.e., the sum of the square of all the difference between scores and means divided by the sample size).

So imagine we are studying staff retention rates for a population of the six counties listed above. We only have the resources to select one sample of two counties. The sample we choose happens to be sample 12 where the mean staff retention rate is 60%. We want to know how close this retention rate is to the average retention rate for all six counties. We do this by calculating the standard error for our sample. That is, we use the characteristics of our sample to calculate where that sample falls in the normal distribution of means for all samples. We use the characteristics of our sample to make this estimate.

$$\sqrt{[(1 - 2/6)*200/2} = 8$$

Thus we use the sample to estimate an unknown characteristic of the population of interest. This can only hold true for simple random samples (or measurable samples), and even then, according to Frankel (1983),

> The satisfaction of the probability sampling conditions are necessary but not sufficient conditions for measurability. That is, measurable samples must be probability samples, but not all probability samples are measurable. (p. 32)

With this warning we continue with the discussion and assume that our selection of a random sample allows us to assume that we have a 95% chance that the mean for our sample falls within 2 standard errors of the population mean. Our standard error allows us to state that the average staff retention rate for all six counties falls between 44% and 76% (60% + or − 16). A Bayesian interpretation would simply say that there is a 95% likelihood that the mean staff retention rate for the six counties is between 44% and 76%. The Bayesian method of statistical inference does not rest on the notion of repeated sampling. It uses credible intervals rather than confidence levels and simply states the likelihood of a result. This is possible because the likelihood function of a given statistic is assumed to be a random variable with a normal distribution of its own. Just one more point before we move away from this discussion of rationales for external validity. The standard error in our example was quite large because our sample size was so small. According to Frankel (1983), the CLT holds if the sample is of a "reasonable size" (p. 30). He suggests 30 or more. Both the classical CLT and the Bayesian approaches to generalizing findings from a sample to a total population of interest make the assumption that randomization exists in the total population. This assumption facilitates the use of probability theory and sampling theory. The combination of probability theory and sampling theory gives us a rationale for generalizing findings from one probability sample to a population of interest.

We now need to introduce the vocabulary of sampling.

- *Element.* This is the unit about which the information is collected (individuals, families, groups, organizations, or communities).
- *Population.* This is the total of all elements, for example, all social workers in the United States.
- *Study Population.* This is the total of elements from which the sample is selected. Sometimes we do not know how many people are in the total population; for example, we don't know exactly how many social workers there are in the United States. To approximate the number we find a listing. For example, we might get a list of all social workers who are members of NASW. This would be our study population. However, note that moving from a hypothetical total population of social workers where randomization is assumed to exist to a membership list where randomization cannot be automatically assumed to exist threatens the assumptions of probability and sampling theory that allow us to generalize from one sample to a population of interest.
- *Sampling Unit.* This is the same as an element in simple designs. However, in a complex design the element could vary. It could be a selection of chapters of NASW at one stage and then a selection of individuals from those chapters at another stage.
- *Sampling Frame.* This is the actual list of sampling elements or units from which a sample is selected.
- *Observation Unit.* This is the source from whom data is collected. It may be the same as an element, but it may not. For example, the element might be the overall social work supervision style for a department of children's services, but the observation unit may be various individuals within that department.
- *Variable.* This is the set of attributes of an element. For example, a social worker's supervision style can range from authoritarian to supportive.
- *Parameter.* This is a summary description (e.g., mean) of a variable in the population of interest, for example, the mean staff retention rate for all agencies in our population of interest. In the example above it was 45%.

- *Statistic.* This is a summary description (e.g., mean) of a variable in the sample. For example, in our sample of 2 our mean staff retention rate was 60%, while in the population of interest it was 45%.
- *Sampling Error.* This is the degree of error between a statistic and a parameter.
- *Confidence Level and Confidence Interval.* These are the limits within which we can assume our estimates of sampling error, and therefore of the parameter, are correct.
- *Credible Intervals.* These are simply the percentage likelihoods that something is true.

Strategies for selecting probability samples include

- *Simple Random Sampling.* Each element in the sampling frame is given a number. A table of random numbers is then used to select the sample size required.
- *Systematic Random Sampling.* Each element in the sampling frame is given a number and then a structured selection takes place where elements are selected that are equally apart, for example every tenth or fifth element in the list. If you need a sample of 100 from a sampling frame of 1,000, then you would select every tenth element.
- *Stratified Sampling.* In this case, the sampling frame is divided into groups and then each group is either simply randomly sampled or systematically randomly sampled. We might divide our sampling frame into three ethnic groups and then randomly sample elements within each group.
- *Multistage Cluster Sampling.* We might get a list of all departments of children's services in the United States. We would then stratify the list according to regions in the United States. Then, within each region, we would randomly select a sample of agencies, and from each of these agencies we would randomly select supervisors to find about their supervisory style.

To return to our sample correlational studies, we have two study questions:

- How does a family assessment tool assess families from three different ethnic groups? (micro practice)
- How do contrasting supervisory styles in two different departments of children's services affect staff retention rates? (macro practice)

We are searching for answers to these questions that can be generalized from the sample in the proposed study to the populations of interest. In correlational, or survey research, the sample design is the key to being able to do this.[1] For each of our example studies, we will need to select a random sample.

Table 3.4   Sampling Terms for Each Correlational Question

Question	How does a family assessment tool assess families from three different ethnic groups (Hawaiian American, Japanese American, Anglo)?	How do the contrasting supervisory styles in two departments of children's services affect staff retention rates?
Concepts	Element = families Population = all members of three identified ethnic groups Study Population = all members of Catholic, Zen Buddhist, and Anglican churches in Honolulu who have identified their ethnicity as one of the three in this study Sampling Unit = individuals Sampling Frame = lists from churches where ethnicity is identified Observation Unit = individuals who will report on families Variable = family functioning Parameter = scores on FAD in population of church members Statistic = scores on FAD in selected sample Sampling Error = difference between FAD scores in sample and in total list of church members Confidence Level and Confidence Interval = statement of sampling error in FAD scores Credible Level = likelihood of FAD score in sample being correct	Element = children's services departments Population = all children's services departments in one region Study Population = all children's services departments in one region Sampling Unit = all children's services departments in one region Sampling Frame = listing of all children's services departments from county Web sites Variable = staff retention rates in each department of children's services in one region Parameter = percentage staff retention rate in each department of children's services in one region Statistic = percentage staff retention rate in sample of departments of children's services Sampling Error = difference between percentage staff retention rates in all departments of children's services in one regions and the percentage staff retention rates in the sample of departments of children's services Confidence Level and Confidence Interval = statement of sampling error in percentage staff retention rates Credible Level = likelihood of sample retention rate being correct

(Continued)

Table 3.4 (Continued)

Simple Random Sample	Selection of 300 church members with identified ethnicities from list of church members using a table of random numbers. (See discussion and Table 3.5)	Selection of 20 departments from list using a table of random numbers. (See discussion and Table 3.6.)
Systematic Random Sample	Select individuals at regular intervals from the list until a sample of 300 is selected.	Select departments at regular intervals from the list until a sample of 20 is selected.
Stratified Sample	Divide list of church members into three ethnic groups. Randomly or systematically select a sample of 100 from each of the three divisions of the list.	Divided departments of children's services into two groups, those with above average retention rates and those with below average retention rates. Randomly or systematically select a sample of 10 agencies from each division.
Multistage Cluster Sampling	Develop a list of all churches in Hawaii. Divide into regions where the densest populations of Hawaiian Americans, Japanese Americans and Anglos are found. Give all the churches in each region a number and randomly select five churches. Select a sample of 100 church members from each of these churches for a total sample of 1,500 [(5*100)*3]	Develop a list of all departments of children's services in the United States. Stratify the list according to regions in the United States. Then within each region divide departments into those with above average staff retention rates and those with below average staff retention rates. Select a sample of 10 departments in each division for each region. Randomly select a sample of 10 supervisors within each department for a sample total of 200 [20*10] for each region.

Sample Size?

There is no quick and easy way to know before the study begins exactly what your sample size should be. Rubin and Babbie (2001) give us a formula and table for selecting a sample size that reduces the standard error. However, the calculation depends on knowing the distribution of scores on the variables of interest before the study begins. We cannot know this until we have selected our sample and found out the distribution of the variable within the sample. Sudman (1983) gives us pragmatic guidelines for deciding on the sample size. First, he suggests "the sample should be large enough so that there are 100 or more units in each category of the major breakdown and a minimum of 20–50 in the minor breakdown" (p. 157). The "breakdown" is subgroups of the sample that are needed for analysis, such as divisions according to gender, ethnicity, or age. This depends on the research question. Sudman also gives us data that was gathered from a survey of average sample sizes. It turns out that national studies of people and households tend to have samples of 1000 to 1500 for a few subgroups and 2500 for many subgroups; regional studies have 200 to 500 and 1000 respectively. For samples of institutions, the numbers for national studies are 200 to 500 and 1000 plus; and for regional studies 50 to 200 and 500 plus. Weinberg (1983), in the same book, tells us that sample size must be adjusted to the task, time, cost of data collection, and budget. Cochran (1954) reviewed the theoretical implications of using one particular statistical test, the Chi square, with small samples and developed the following rule: "If no more than 20% of the cells have expectations (values) less than 5 then a single expectation (value) near 1 is allowable in computing chi square" (Taylor, 1983, p. 560). Given the above advice, with our examples the samples needed would be as follows.

1. How does a family assessment tool assess families from three different ethnic groups (Hawaiian American, Japanese American, Anglo)? Using the guidelines above, Table 3.5 suggests we need a sample of 300.

Table 3.5   Sample Size for Micro Practice Correlational Question

	Hawaiian American		Japanese American		Anglo	
FAD Score	Below Norm	Above Norm	Below Norm	Above Norm	Below Norm	Above Norm
	50	50	50	50	50	50

2. How do the contrasting supervisory styles in two departments of children's services affect staff retention rates? The advice above suggests a sample of 20 agencies (see Table 3.6).

With the minimal sample size requirements laid out, we can now consider the pros and cons of the various sampling strategies in Table 3.4. For question one, simple random sampling would *not* guarantee that we had the sufficient sample size for each ethnic group, nor would systematic random

Table 3.6   Sample Size for Macro Practice Correlational Question

	Departments with high staff retention rates	Departments with low staff retention rates
Autocratic Supervision Style	5	5
Facilitative Supervision Style	5	5

sampling. The stratified sample would give us the division into three ethnic groups that we need, but we would not be addressing the issue of the random selection of the churches that are the source of our list. The multistage cluster sample does address all our needs but may well not be practical. Thus we see the balance that must be achieved between theoretical requirements of the question and the practical feasibility of achieving the desired sample. The multistage cluster sample meets our theoretical needs. To implement it we would have to make some pragmatic decisions. We could divide the island of Oahu into three regions, find one church in each region that clearly serves the designated ethnic group, and then select our stratified sample from the three churches.

For question two, the simple and systematic random samples will not guarantee that we have a range of agencies with a range of staff retention rates. The stratified random sample will give us the range of agencies that we need but does not address the regional differences in the United States. The multistage cluster sample will give us the theoretically correct sample and may require excessive resources. If resources are limited then the same sample design could be used in just one region. Just as a reminder, though, once we move away from using the simple random sample the assumptions of normal distributions associated with probability theory and sampling theory may no longer hold true.

To sum up this section, we have reviewed the design issues for correlational studies. Since the aim of correlational studies is to generalize findings from one sample to a larger population of interest patterns, sample design incorporating probability theory and sampling theory is the key to developing a rigorous study. This facilitates calculation of the standard error between the sample and the population of interest. There are a number of strategies for selecting random sampling, and the most appropriate sample will depend upon the research question. We will now move on to discuss two specific forms of explanatory and correlational designs that tend to be most useful for social work practice researchers: program evaluation and single subject designs.

Program Evaluation

A program evaluation is simply a research project that addresses a particular kind of macro practice research question. It can be descriptive or explanatory. Positivist program evaluations are divided into summative (outcome) and formative (process) evaluations. Summative evaluations ask and answer the question "Does the program work?" Process evaluations ask and answer the question "How does this program work?" In essence, both of these types of evaluations use the designs identified in the discussions above. In their book *Evaluating Family Programs,* Heather Weiss and Francine Jacobs (1988) suggest that the kind of program evaluation to be carried out depends on the stage of development of the program to be evaluated. They identify five levels of evaluation that can be carried out as the program matures. Some are summative and others are formative.

Level 1: This is simply a needs assessment before the program is implemented documenting characteristics of proposed program, cost of program, community support for program, and statistics describing the population to be served. This is essentially a "one group posttest only" design. The group is the community and the posttest is the data on the community need for the program and the identification of services that will meet those needs.

Level 2: This is a formative study documenting the program's use and its penetration into the target population. This kind of evaluation gathers data that justifies current expenditures and makes the case for any requests for increases in funding. This is essentially a version of a "one group pretest posttest" design. The independent variable is the program and the community being served is the dependent variable. The pretest was the needs assessment carried out in the level one evaluation. The posttest is the documentation of the community use of services.

Level 3: This is a formative study of the program reviewing the mission and goals of the program, the characteristics of clients who receive services, and the services they are using. This is to check whether the original mission and program should be revised now that the staff has experience with the implementation of the program. This is essentially a version of a "one group posttest" design where the group is the program and the posttest is service use.

Level 4: With this level we move to summative outcomes. This is an outcome evaluation of success with individual clients. Data is collected on client need at the intake phase and then again at the end of the delivery of services. This is a "one group pretest posttest" where the pretest is the client assessment at intake and the posttest is client assessment at termination of services.

Level 5: This is the final level and the one where the ultimate question is addressed: what is the program's impact? Generally it is a two group comparison study of the effectiveness of the program. One group receives services and the other does not. Members of each group are pretested and posttested on progress with the problem being addressed. This is essentially the "two group nonequivalent groups pretest posttest" or, if possible, the classic experimental design. These authors suggest that this kind of evaluation should only be carried out when the program is up and running and the other tiers of evaluation have been completed.

Single Case Evaluations

The single case evaluation is a form of a micro practice research project. It can be descriptive or explanatory. Rubin and Babbie (2001) describe a range of designs that basically suggest that the practitioner should collect baseline information on the target problem (say depression), which is the dependent variable, and then intervene while continuing to track scores on the dependent variable. The designs where only one client is being tracked are descriptive while the designs where two or more clients are being tracked who receive the intervention at different times address causality, since they offer evidence for ruling out alternative explanations for the changes in the dependent variable.

Note

1. Some authors suggest that causality is addressed in survey research by means of multivariate statistical analysis or through a time series design. However, the threats to internal validity with their roots in Hume's statement of causality cannot be ruled out using a survey design.

Main Points

- There are two kinds of positivist designs: explanatory (causal) and descriptive (correlational)

- The classical experimental design is the favored explanatory design because it controls for all threats to internal validity
- When implementing the classical experimental design, practical issues may lead us to make modifications such as matching and time series designs
- Descriptive (correlational) studies require the selection of random samples for strong external validity
- The rationale for being able to generalize from one sample to the population of interest is developed from both the classical central limit theorem (CLT) and Bayesian theories of inference
- The key to being able to make such assumptions is the selection of a random sample because this allows the assumptions of the central limit theorem to be made regarding the prediction of a population mean from a sample mean using the standard error
- There are a range of strategies for collecting random sampling that include simple random sampling, systematic random sampling, stratified random sampling, and multistage cluster sampling
- Two commonly used adaptations of causal and correlational studies are program evaluations addressing macro practice questions and single-subject designs addressing micro practice questions

Learning Assignments

1. Think of a research topic that interests you. Briefly describe a causal and a correlational design that would address an aspect of that topic.
   a. Which level of social work practice are you researching, micro or macro?
   b. Identify any threats to internal validity in your causal design.
   c. Are there any practical problems with implementing this design?
   d. How will you guarantee external validity in your correlational design? Is this feasible?
   e. How will you select your sample and why will you use that particular sampling strategy?

2. Working in small groups, take a group member's topic and discuss whether the design does indeed answer causal and correlational questions about social work practice and discuss how easy or hard it would be to set up this design. Also, answer the "so what" question. How important are the answers to these questions to social work practice knowledge? Give reasons for your conclusions. Would your practice be improved if you knew the answers to these questions?

4

Implementation– Gathering the Data

To carry out precise measurement, make probabilistic statements about causality and correlation, and generalize findings from a sample to a broader population, information about human behavior is translated into numbers that can be manipulated by statistical procedures. To make this translation reliable and valid, measurement instruments are developed and tested before data gathering begins. Such instruments will be the pretest or posttest for causal studies or the standardized questionnaire that will measure the variables to be correlated in correlational studies. Sheatsley (1983) notes that a well-designed questionnaire should meet the objectives of the research, obtain the most complete and accurate information possible, and do this within the limits of available time and resources (p. 201). This author also suggests five simple steps for constructing a questionnaire (p. 202).

1. Decide what information is required

2. Draft some questions to elicit that information

3. Put them in a meaningful order and format

4. Pretest the result

5. Go back to step 1.

When considering the questions for a measurement instrument, the first issue to be addressed is whether they should be open or closed ended. Open-ended questions let the respondent verbalize the answer. Closed-ended, or multiple choice, questions ask the respondent to choose an answer from a list of alternatives. While open-ended questions encourage respondents to answer in their own terms, they can lead to repetition, the gathering of irrelevant information, and misunderstandings about the intent of the question. They also lead to considerable additional coding work in the analysis phase of the study. Closed-ended questions limit respondents' input into the wording of answers but ensure that the interviewer or anyone else is not influencing the answer by randomly encouraging elaboration or making suggestions for answers. Sometimes the researcher can combine closed- and open-ended questions by giving a list of possible responses to a question and then adding a section where other comments can be made if desired. Generally, though, as positivist researchers of causal and correlational questions, we will favor closed-ended questions wherever possible so that our quantitative data is easily gathered.

It is a common practice to use scaling techniques when developing closed-ended questions. The most common types of scales are Guttman scales and Likert scales. Guttman scales measure cumulatively while Likert scales measure dimensionally. A Guttman scale of items measuring supervision might include a list of statements that is ordered so that each one gradually describes a more authoritarian style of supervision. The respondent would be asked to select the item that reflects his or her supervision style. A Likert scale of supervision might list the same items, but instead would ask a respondent to strongly agree, agree, disagree, or strongly disagree with each statement. These scales would be measuring the same concept, but the conceptualization of measurement of the concept of supervision would be slightly different. For example, one item in a Guttman scale for supervision might be

When providing supervision I *(circle one choice only)*

- Encourage the supervisee to suggest the discussion topics in an open-ended free flowing discussion
- Suggest that the supervisee come prepared with some talking points that he or she would think we need to discuss
- Have some key talking points that I think we need to discuss
- Have a clear agenda with detailed descriptions of the learning that should take place during the session

However, a Likert scale using the same items would ask a slightly different question:

(Circle one response to each item)

1. In supervision the supervisee should suggest the discussion topics in an open-ended free flowing discussion

   Strongly Agree   Agree   Disagree   Strongly Disagree

2. In supervision the supervisor should suggest that the supervisee come prepared with some talking points that he or she would think we need to discuss

   Strongly Agree   Agree   Disagree   Strongly Disagree

3. In supervision the supervisor should provide some key talking points that need to be discussed

   Strongly Agree   Agree   Disagree   Strongly Disagree

4. In supervision the supervisor should have a clear agenda with detailed descriptions of the learning that should take place during the session

   Strongly Agree   Agree   Disagree   Strongly Disagree

Another form of Likert scale is a semantic differential where respondents are asked to choose between opposite poles on an issue. For example, if supervisees were being surveyed, they might be given an instrument with the following instructions and format.

On the items below circle the number on the continuum that best reflects the supervisory style that you experience in this organization.

positive feedback							negative feedback		
1	2	3	4	5	6	7	8	9	10

Makes you feel like you make a positive contribution							Never comments on your contribution		
1	2	3	4	5	6	7	8	9	10

Responds to your stress level							Never comments on stress level		
1	2	3	4	5	6	7	8	9	10

Helps you learn about best practice							Never addresses practice learning		
1	2	3	4	5	6	7	8	9	10

Helps you reflect on your practice							Never encourages reflection		
1	2	3	4	5	6	7	8	9	10

Certain principles should guide the writing of questions and scales.

- Keep it simple.
- Avoid lengthy questions. Sheatsley (1983) recommends 25 words or less.
- Specify alternatives, don't just give one side of the issue such as, "My supervisor is dictatorial: strongly agree, agree, disagree, strongly disagree."
- Avoid loaded questions such as, "Most experts think that a facilitative style of supervision is most effective. What do you think?"

Sheatsley (1983) notes that common mistakes when wording questions include:

- Writing a double-barreled question, where a respondent is asked about two different things in the same question. For example, "How satisfied are you with your supervisor both as a colleague and as a manager?" The respondent may have different feelings about the two roles.
- Assuming a false premise, where the respondent is thought to have an opinion that he or she might not have. For example, "What should be done to solve the problems with supervision?" This may leave the respondent wondering "What problems?"
- Writing a question that is vague and ambiguous, where the meaning of the question is not clear or can have several interpretations. For example, "Do you get supervision?" This leaves the respondent to define supervision and to define what "getting" it means.
- Writing a question that includes overlapping alternatives, where the alternatives in the question are not mutually exclusive and the respondent could truthfully answer "yes" or "no" to them all. For example, "Are you generally satisfied with supervision in this department or are there some things you do not like about it?" The respondent may be both satisfied and have some concerns.
- Writing questions that include double negatives, where the meaning of answering "yes" or "no" is not completely clear. For example, "Would you be in favor of not training supervisors?"
- Asking about intentions to act, where the respondent is asked what he or she would do in a hypothetical situation. For example, "If group supervision were offered, would you go to it?" Such statements are poor predictors of actual behavior.

Having decided on the questions, the next step is to decide on the structure of the data collection instrument. It should start with a brief introduction explaining the study, the questionnaire, who the study is for, and who you are. The opening questions should be easy and nonthreatening, and any difficult or controversial questions should come later. Make sure the instrument is not too long; justify every item. Also, it is important to ask the right person the question, that is, someone who is knowledgeable and interested in the topic.

Before we decide how we are actually going to measure our variables in our example studies, we need to review some issues in relation to measurement. Variables can be measured at four levels: nominal, ordinal, interval, and ratio. It is important to understand levels of measurement because later this will influence decisions about the appropriate statistics to be used when analyzing your data. *Nominal* measurement is simply categorization of data with no real numerical value for the number given to each category. The number is simply used as a way of identifying each different category of the variable. Thus the values cannot accumulate. In our example, approaches to training, permanent employment, families, and mental health clinics are nominal variables. Adding the values for dimensions of these variables makes no sense. The total would tell us nothing. *Ordinal* variables have levels of measurement that identify different values of the variable and can be added, but these values have been assigned for non-mathematical reasons. In our example, both items on the FAD and supervision are ordinal variables. The levels of the dimensions of these variables have value relative to each other; a score of 1 on the FAD items denotes more agreement with an item on that instrument than a score of 3. A score of 3 on the supervision variable denotes a more authoritarian supervision style than a score of 7. But the size of the difference between these scores is unknown. Two is not necessarily twice as high as one and three is not necessarily three times as high as one. Moving to the next level of measurement, scores on *ratio* and *interval* variables *do* have equal mathematical relationships, and for all practical purposes ratio and interval level of measurement are the same. Just to be clear, though, age and money are variables measured at the ratio level because they have a true zero; you can have no money (right?) and you can be aged zero. However, I.Q. is measured at the interval level since it has no true zero; you cannot have zero intelligence (yes, it's true!). In our examples, both uptake of mental health services and staff retention rates are variables measured at the ratio level.

So now we are ready to decide how we will measure our variables. For our nominal variables, measurement is quite straightforward; we simply count the numbers for each category. For our ordinal variables, we have one preexisting instrument (FAD) and one instrument that needs to be created for this study (measurement of supervision style). As we create our new instrument we must remember that it should be both reliable and valid. Reliability is the consistency with which the instrument measures the variables. That is, if the same situation recurs, will the instrument give that situation the same score each time it is measured? The best way to explain this idea is to think of a decision you might make to lose weight. You step on your weighing scales one day and you are shocked at the number you see on the scale. Your are sure it could not be correct, so you go to a friend's house and use the weighing scales in her bathroom. You see the same number staring back at you. Both of these scales are giving you the same message, and it turns out that your scale is *reliably* measuring your weight. So, you go on your diet and you lose 10 1bs. in the first week. Lo and behold, when you stand on your weighing scale, it shows a number that is 10 lbs. less than a week ago. You know this is true because you know that your weighing scale is reliable. Whatever you weigh, your scale reliably reflects that number of pounds, no matter how many times you step on and step off the scale. To return to our social work practice example then, given a series of supervisors with similar characteristics, we need to know if our instrument will reliably assess this supervision style. So, if there is a group of supervisors with authoritarian approaches to supervision, does our instrument label each one as having that style? Or, does it assess them as having different styles when this is not true? That is, does it measure the same thing the same way every time?

The concept of reliability becomes clearer when we contrast it with validity. Validity refers to the accuracy with which a measurement instrument reflects the variable or concept that it is measuring. If we return to our dieting plans, imagine that your weighing scale is actually calibrated incorrectly. Imagine that when you stepped on the scale it measured you as 10 lbs. heavier than you actually are. Every time you stepped on the scale it gave you that extra weight. Now, your scale is reliable, because it measures you with the same weight every time you step on the scale, but it is not a valid measure of your weight because the weight that the scale registers is wrong (thank goodness). To use our preexisting instrument measuring family functioning as an example, the FAD assesses families on problem solving, communication, roles, affective involvement, affective responsiveness, behavior control, and general functioning. Does this instrument appear to address all dimensions of family functioning (face and content validity)? Does this instrument measure the same way as other measures of family functioning or predict accurately how "problem free" a family might be (criterion related validity)? Does this measure of family functioning measure the same way as other aspects of family functioning, for example, family violence (construct validity)? For this preexisting instrument, the reliability and validity are known since it has been used in other studies. For the instrument we intend to create, we will need to assess validity and reliability before and during the study.

To create the instrument assessing supervision styles, we need to look at definitions of supervision. Since we are studying the difference between two contrasting styles, a semantic differential Likert-type scale would be a good choice. Gibbs (2001) suggests that elements of effective supervision include acknowledgement of the emotional intrusiveness of the work, building resilience in workers, and adopting the principles of adult learning theory that include reflective supervision. She suggests that an effective supervisor will move beyond a focus on the tasks to be completed and become a messenger who sends and receives messages to and from workers, affirming both the merit and necessity of exploring the impact of feelings and thoughts on action and perception. She suggests that supervisors must affirm the value of individual workers to the organization, building self-esteem and self-efficacy. These findings suggest dimensions that we might build into our supervision scale as follows.

In supervision we *(circle one number)*

Concentrate on the task	1	2	3	4	5	Reflect on the task to be done
Never address emotions	1	2	3	4	5	Acknowledge emotional impact of the work
Concentrate on	1	2	3	4	5	Acknowledge issues accountability of professional judgment
Feel blamed for failure	1	2	3	4	5	Learn about assessing and learning from each situation

These items can be pretested with respondents that are similar to but not included in the study sample and modified accordingly. A final issue with developing quantitative instruments is sensitivity to diversity. Rubin and Babbie (2001) offer some guidelines for addressing diversity when pretesting the instrument:[1]

- Immerse yourself in the culture to be studied before constructing instruments.
- Use preexisting instruments that have been tested for reliability and validity with the culture you are studying.
- Use key informants to get advice on the cultural sensitivity of an instrument you plan to use.
- Use bilingual interviewers or interpreters.
- Use the processes of back translation, where an instrument is translated from English into a desired language and then translated back to English by a second translator to check for accuracy of meaning.
- Pretest the instrument with members of the culture being studied who will not be participants in the proposed study.

Managing and Implementing Data Collection

The next step is to actually collect the data. The first decision is whether to administer the surveys in a face-to-face situation or adopt one of many self-administered questionnaire strategies. This decision will depend upon sample size, time, and resources. The larger the sample size and the less time and resources you have, the more likely you are to choose a self-administered strategy. However, if you have the time and resources, the face-to-face strategy ensures that you have control of the interview setting and any misunderstandings about the intent of questions can be immediately clarified.

Face-to-Face Interviews

Personal Interviews

Weinberg (1983) notes that the personal interview has traditionally been considered the most reliable method of collecting data. As you work your way through your data collection instrument, you can see the person, you can make a nonverbal assessment of how things are going and whether the respondent is offering reliable and valid information, and it is a more sensitive way to make contact with culturally diverse populations, poorer groups, older people, and those who live in more isolated communities. However, this approach to data gathering is expensive and time consuming. The interviewer must set up the interview, travel to the interview site, and generally engage someone in a personal exchange. A one-hour interview can take three or four hours when all of this is taken into account.

Group Discussion

Group discussion is an effective, quick way to pretest an interview instrument. A group of people who are not in the sample but who have similar characteristics to those who will be in the sample can be brought together to review and respond to the instrument.

Group Interview

A way to solve the problem of the time consuming nature of personal interviews is to organize group interviews. A preexisting group, such as a group of workers in the same agency, can be brought together at a regular meeting time, such as a staff meeting, to complete questionnaires. In this way, the researcher controls the data gathering setting, and any clarification questions can be answered but several questionnaires are completed.

Telephone Interview

Yet another compromise between individual interviews and self-administered questionnaires is the telephone interview. If participants are informed about the study, knowledgeable and interested in the topic, and are willing to put some time into an interview, this can be an effective strategy. It is important to have a script and check verbally that the respondent understands questions and the progress of the interview, but of course any visual cues such as flash cards cannot be used. Recently, electronic surveys in which computer voices ask the questions have been developed. These might be successful if study participants are committed to the study but may not gain a high response rate if used without preparation of study participants.

Self-Administered Questionnaires

These days there are various ways of administering self-administered questionnaires. The traditional mode is the paper questionnaire delivered to the study participant through the mail, but we can now add the use of e-mail attachments and Web sites. Dillman (1983), when discussing mail-out questionnaires, offers the following principles of the Total Design Method (TDM):

- The questionnaire is designed as a booklet but does not look like an advertising brochure. It is accompanied by a cover letter explaining the project.
- The cover page has no questions but does have an eye catching title, illustration, or graphic and instructions.
- The back cover has no questions but is used to thank the respondent and invite further questions.
- The order of questions is interesting questions followed by controversial questions with demographic questions coming at the end. Special attention is given to the first question so that it applies to everyone, is easy, and is interesting.
- Regarding the formatting of each page:
  a. Lower case letters should be used for questions and upper case for answers.
  b. Respondents should be able to answer in a straight vertical line rather than skipping back and forth horizontally. This way they are not tempted to skip questions.
  c. Questions should not overlap onto the next page.
  d. Explanatory transitions should be written in so that the respondent is guided through each part of the questionnaire.
  e. Visual cues can be used to provide direction and clarification.

These rules are equally useful when a survey is sent as an attached document to an e-mail or is set up on a Web site. Many data management packages found on today's computers have features that make it easy for the average computer user to set up an electronic questionnaire with point and click response mechanisms.

The other organizational tasks of data collection include monitoring the return of questionnaires and any follow up mailings and e-mails that might improve the response rate. This brings us back to a consideration of sampling and probability theory. From the discussion above you can see how crucial it is that a random sample is surveyed so that probability theory and sampling theory can be used as rationales for generalizing the results of a study to a wider population of interest. However, most surveys get a response rate of approximately 25%, and a 50% response rate is considered very good. However, even if you manage to gather data from 50% of your original sample, you no longer have a probability sample. In fact, you are now two steps removed from the original rules of causality. Your sample is not random and you are only estimating the likelihood that your statistics, which are estimates based on probability theory, are accurate estimates of the characteristics of the population of interest. One solution to this problem is to use replacement sampling, where you continue down your sampling frame list and add people to the sample as respondents fall out of your sample. However, these replacement members of the sample have equal likelihood of not responding. There comes a point where you have to end data collection and use the sample you have.

Note

1. The social work researcher's responsibility to diversity in general is discussed in more detail in Part 5.

Main Points

- Since quantitative data is needed for positivist research, standardized instruments are developed
- The favored form of instrument is one containing closed-ended questions using Guttman or Likert scaling
- When writing items for a questionnaire, be careful to follow suggested guidelines and principles with relation to item construction and diversity
- When organizing data collection, decide on a mode of communication with the respondent that is either face-to-face or at a distance
- Be sure to track your response rate

Learning Assignments

- For the questions you developed at the end of Chapter 3, for either the causal or correlational question, think of 10 questions you could ask a study participant. Remember the answers to these questions will provide data that answers your overall research question and tests your hypothesis.
- Get into pairs and ask your partner the 10 questions. Did you get data that answered your research question? Was the data nominal, ordinal, interval, or ratio? Did your data allow you to test your hypothesis? If so, did your data confirm or reject the null hypothesis?
- Ask your partner to give you feedback on the actual questions you used. Were they easy to understand? Could there have been a better way to ask these questions?

5

Evaluation—Developing an Understanding of the Data and Its Meaning

S ince this book has taken the position that true positivist research can only use quantitative data, to remain true to the paradigm's worldview, quantitative analysis is the focus of this chapter. Positivist researchers develop an understanding of the data and its meaning using statistical procedures. Recently, with the renewed interest in qualitative research, many authors have simply added field research, historical-comparative research, narrative case studies, ethnographic research, and so on to the possible approaches to positivist research without satisfactorily making the case that these approaches can provide data on immutable laws and natural mechanisms, allow the researcher to adopt a non-interactive posture in relation to the study, and test hypotheses. Hypothesis testing, whether through an explanatory or descriptive study, is the key to finding causality as defined by positivist thinkers. Remember, hypothesis testing is rooted in Karl Popper's philosophy regarding falsification and rejecting the null. Qualitative data cannot be analyzed in a way that permits rejection of the null hypothesis. Qualitative approaches tend to build knowledge rather than test hypotheses.

Taking the above position gives us the conceptual clarity we need to understand the contribution that positivism makes to knowledge development. Positivist analysis uses statistical procedures appropriate to the level of measurement (nominal, ordinal, interval, ratio) to manipulate the data. Descriptive statistics such as means, medians, modes, and cross tabulations are used to summarize the data and show relationships between variables. Inferential statistics give estimates of whether a finding in your study sample (e.g., that the TANF training program led to permanent employment) is indeed true. There are two kinds of inferential statistical tests: parametric and nonparametric. Parametric tests are considered to be more powerful tests than nonparametric tests because they rest on more stringent assumptions related to probability theory and sampling theory discussed in Chapter 3. They are used to test relationships between variables measured at the interval or ratio levels and give estimates of whether a statistic is accurately estimating a population parameter. Nonparametric tests do not assume normal distributions of variables and, therefore, do not use estimates of parameters to test relationships identified in a hypothesis. Thus nonparametric statistical tests are generally used to test relationships between variables measured at the ordinal and nominal levels.

The steps of analysis, after entering the numerical data in an analysis software program, are to first run descriptive univariate statistics and then tests of bivariate relationships between independent and dependent variables. The researcher will next develop and test models of multivariate relationships between independent and dependent variables. These analysis procedures are aimed at rejecting the null hypothesis and explaining as much of the relationship between variables as possible.

Data Entry

Generally a statistical package such as the Statistical Package for the Social Sciences (SPSS) is used to analyze data. Although there are other packages, this is the most commonly used package for social workers, and it will be the illustrative package used here to explain analysis. The first step in using a software package such as this is to enter the data. This takes us back to our unit of analysis and observation units described in Chapter 3. Our observation unit is the source of our numerical data and thus our data will be entered for each of these "cases." In our four example studies the observation unit cases are

- *Individuals,* for our study of TANF;
- *Counties,* for our study of mental health service uptake;
- *Individuals,* for our study of the FAD; and
- *Individuals,* for our study of supervision.

Table 5.1   Data Entry Screen

Variable	Variable	Variable	Variable	Variable	Variable	Variable
1.						
2.						
3.						
4.						
5.						

Table 5.2   Entered Data

	Problem Solving	Communication	Roles	Affective Responsiveness	Behavior Control	General Functioning	Ethnicity
1.	2	3	4	2	1	3	1
2.	4	2	1	4	2	3	2
3.	4	2	3	2	4	1	3

However, our unit of analysis for each of these studies is different. For the study of TANF it is the *programs,* for the study of mental health services it is *counties,* for the study of the FAD it is *families,* and for the study of supervision it is *departments or agencies.* Thus our data will be entered according to our observation unit, but our analysis will be organized in terms of our units of analysis. To clarify, the data entry screen for SPSS looks like Table 5.1, where "variable" needs to be replaced by the names of the variables in our study and the numbers down the side identify each person who has participated in the study.

If we use our study of the FAD as an example, in which individuals are asked to report on their families' functioning on a scale of 1 to 4, then the table would be as shown in Table 5.2. These are hypothetical scores for three participants in the study, one person from each of the designated ethnic groups. Remember, the scores are derived from the coding that was explained in Chapter 2 accompanied by the operationalizations and dimensions of concepts and variables that were also described there.

Once the data has been entered, we need to check for any errors. Errors are most often made when transcribing the data from the questionnaire to the computer screen. They are detected when frequencies show values that you did not assign, or you have some cases in your sample with a pattern of responses that is very different from those of other members of your sample. Rossi, Wright, and Anderson (1983) suggest five options for "cleaning the data" and correcting errors in data entry: (1) go back and check the original questionnaire; (2) if you can, contact the respondent and try to correct the error; (3) estimate a corrected response by, for example, substituting scores from a case with similar characteristics; (4) discard the error and label it as missing data; and (5) discard the entire case. Once errors in data entry have been addressed, you can proceed with data analysis.

Descriptive Statistics

Univariate Analysis

The first analysis to be run is usually a univariate (one variable at a time) analysis so that you can look at the distribution of the values of each variable. Running this analysis is simply a "point and click" procedure in SPSS, where you click on "analysis," then "descriptive," and then "frequencies" while selecting all variables to be included in the analysis. This will give you percentage and numeric frequencies of each value of each variable. As you look at the output for frequencies you will notice that it gives you a lot of detail. Reporting your data in this detail would be cumbersome and confusing to consumers of your research. The usual way to summarize frequencies is to report variables' central tendencies or averages. This is where the level of measurement of the variable, which was discussed above, comes back into play. There are three measures of central tendency: mode, median, and mean. The mode is the value of the variable that is most frequent. It can be used with all four levels of measurement (nominal, ordinal, interval, and ratio) but is usually used with nominal variables since more accurate summaries of data at the other levels of measurement can be given by the median or the mode. The median is the halfway point in a distribution of values. Half the values fall below the median and half the values fall above the median. Thus extremely high or extremely low scores have little effect on its value. It is always in the middle. The mean is calculated by adding up all the values of the variable for each person in the study and dividing that number by the number of people in the study. This measure of central tendency can misrepresent data if there are a number of extreme scores. For example, if 20 students took an exam and 5 students scored 100 while the other 15 students scored between 20 and 70, the mean student score would be "skewed" towards the 5 high-scoring students. In this case, the median would offer a more representative summary of what happened. You can get the mode, median, and mean for any variable by simply pointing, clicking, and selecting these options in the analysis window of "frequencies" in SPSS.

The measure of central tendency is a nice brief summary of the values for a variable, but you may also want to report the distribution of values around the measure of central tendency. For modes and medians, the usual way of doing this is to report the interquartile range of values of a variable. This is the range of values for the lowest 25% of cases, the range of values for the next 25% of cases, the range for the next 25% of cases, and the range for the highest 25% of cases. For example, if we carried out our study using the FAD and 50 families had a score of 1 and 50 families had a score of 4, we would have multiple modes of both 1 and 4 and multiple medians of both 2 and 3. To explain these results, we would also explain that the lowest 25% of cases had a value of 1 as well as the next 25% of cases, while the top two quartiles had a value of 4.

For an interval or ratio variable, there is a more sophisticated way of explaining the distribution of the values of the variable around the mean: the standard deviation. This was introduced when we discussed random samples and standard error in Chapter 3. This statistic not only reports the distribution of scores on a variable but also opens the door to parametric bivariate analysis (testing the relationship between two variables) and multivariate analysis (testing the relationships between more than two variables). Probability theory assumes that values for all variables in the population of interest are equally distributed around the mean; that is, they have a normal distribution. The standard deviation, because of the properties of a randomly selected sample based on probability theory, is based on the assumption that the values for each variable in the sample are equally distributed around the mean; that is, the values of the variables in our studies also have a normal distribution. In a normal distribution, 68.6% of the values for a variable are one standard deviation above and below the mean, and 95.4% of the distribution of the values for the variable are two standard deviations above and below the mean. Thus if the standard deviation is small, then the values are closely clustered around the mean and the mean is an accurate representation of the average value for the variable. If the standard deviation is large, then the distribution of the values for the variable is spread out and the mean is not a good representation of the value for the variable. The standard deviation is calculated by subtracting all values of the variable from the mean, squaring those values, and then adding them up (this is the sum of squares) and dividing the sum of squares by the number of respondents in the sample and calculating the square root of that amount. For example, if we were counting the number of children per family in our hypothetical study of 100 families and 50 families had 1 child and the other 50 families had 4 children

(I know it's unlikely but it is easy to understand), the mean number of children per family would be 2.5. The calculation of the standard deviation would be $\sqrt{((2.5-1)*50^2 + (2.5-4)*50^2/100} = 1.5$. So this suggests that 68.6% of the distribution is between 1 and 4 and 95.4% of the distribution is between 0.5 and 5.5. Since the range is between 1 and 4, the distribution is too spread out for the mean to be a good representation of the score for that variable.

So in our example studies, to carry out the univariate analysis we would run frequencies for our variables: approaches to training, permanent employment, all items of the FAD, families, mental health clinics, uptake of mental health services, supervision, and staff retention. We would also run frequencies on any variables that described the participants in the study such as demographics and characteristics of agencies and counties.

Inferential Statistics

Bivariate Analysis

The next step is to start testing our hypotheses. We do this *not* by actually testing the relationship between our independent and dependent variables but by carrying out statistical procedures that indicate the likelihood that we can reject the null hypothesis. That is, that we can reject the idea that there is no relationship between the independent variable and the dependent variable. Again, as a reminder, this principle comes from the writings of Karl Popper who, when discussing the problem of induction where we generalize the findings from one study to all situations, suggested that we could take the opposite train of thought and simply test rejection of the null. The reasoning is that rather than try to prove a theory, scientist should try to refute a theory. If it can't be refuted, that is, if the null hypothesis is rejected, then the theory must be true. According to Oldroyd (1986), this still leaves us with the problem of generalizing findings from one study to all situations. However, the idea has taken hold and it is the basis of the statistical procedures used in positivist quantitative research.

Bivariate analysis is the first stage of hypothesis testing. As its name suggests, it simply addresses the relationship between two variables without consideration of the possible influence of other variables. In making these tests we are assessing the likelihood of making Type I or Type II errors. A Type I error is made when the null hypothesis is rejected and it should not have been. For example, it may be true that in the real world TANF training has no effect on employment, but in our study we conclude that this training does affect employment. Then we have made a Type I error. A Type II error is made when the null hypothesis is not rejected and it should have been. Again, to illustrate, if indeed in the real world TANF training does affect employment but in our study we conclude that it does not, then we have made a Type II error. According to Weinbach and Grinnell (2004), the statistical test to be used for bivariate analysis will depend on

1. Whether the sample is randomly selected

2. Whether the variables have a normal distribution in the population of interest

3. The level of measurement of the variable (nominal, ordinal, interval, or ratio)

4. The power that the statistical test has to avoid making a Type II error

5. The degree to which a statistical test produces accurate findings when one or more of its assumptions are violated: the robustness of the test

Since only random samples can adequately meet the requirements of probability theory, we will assume the selection of random samples for all our example studies. As discussed above, this theory assumes that all samples of a particular size drawn from a population of interest have a normal distribution with a mean that is equal to the mean in the population of interest. Thus any sample drawn from the population of interest measures variables whose mean scores' distance from the population mean can be estimated. Thus in our example studies all our ratio level variables are assumed to have a mean whose proximity to the true mean in the population of interest can be estimated. Like Bayes, we will assume that such estimates, or likelihoods, are normally distributed in the population of interest. The only variables in the sample that have the potential to have normal distributions in the population of interest are our ratio variables. Variables measured at the nominal and ordinal level do not have means because they do not have regular distributions; they are categorical or order variables. To illustrate this point, our variable "approaches to training" has two values and therefore can only range between 1 and 2, and the same is true for our variable "permanent employment." There is some discussion among mathematicians that this is untrue because we could look at the proportion of one that responses to each category represent (e.g., 40% employed and 60% unemployed). However, it is unclear if this argument is strong enough to warrant the use of statistical tests that assume normal distributions with nominal variables. We will, therefore, use the currently accepted perspective on nominal variables. Regarding ordinal variables, according to Weinbach and

Grinnell (2004) there is some debate that variables measured at the ordinal level can be treated like ratio variables with a minimum of error, and such means are often used for ease of understanding. However, to do this the researcher needs to find a way to show that there is an equal distance between the levels of the scale being used. Also, the means of such variables cannot meet the assumptions of probability theory regarding their likelihood of estimating a population parameter.

Returning to our choice of bivariate statistical tests, we have variables at nominal, ordinal, and ratio levels of measurement. Having discussed criteria 1, 2, and 3 above, we now turn to criteria 4 and 5. The choices for our example studies are tabulated in Table 5.3.

These tests compare the distributions of our dependent variables in the pretest and posttest, or in the two conditions that are being correlated, and tell us whether we can reject the null hypothesis. They also tell us the likelihood of making a Type I error—that is, rejecting the null hypothesis when we should not have done so. Generally the accepted likelihood that we have committed a Type I error is set at less than 5 times in 100. This means that if we repeated this study 100 times we would make a Type I error 5 times. This is usually stated as $p<.05$. We could go as high as $p<.09$, which means that if we repeated this study 100 times we would make a Type I error 9 times, since the higher this number the lower the chance is that we will make a Type II error, which is the likelihood of failing to reject the null hypothesis when we should have done so. We can also avoid Type II errors by analyzing variables with small standard deviations and using larger samples. Power analysis to test the likelihood of a Type II error has been carried out by Cohen (1988), and charts in that book tell you the best size of sample to use to avoid a Type II error.

To be more specific, Table 5.3 tells us which bivariate tests to use to decide whether

- TANF training caused employment
- The organization of mental health clinics caused uptake of services
- The assessment of family functioning by the FAD correlated with ethnicity
- The supervisory style correlated with staff retention rates

However, this is only the beginning. Bivariate analysis does not take into account the possible effects of other variables on the bivariate relationship we are analyzing. If we have a concern that another variable may be affecting scores on our dependent variable at the same time as our identified independent variable, or that there are many influences on our dependent variable, then we need to carry out multivariate analysis.

Table 5.3   Bivariate Statistical Tests

	Causal (Explanatory)	Correlational (Descriptive)
Micro Practice (target is individuals, families, or groups)	What is the differential effectiveness on TANF clients of two approaches to employment training where one group receives training and the other receives no training and is simply placed immediately into a job? IV = Approaches to Training (Nominal) DV = Permanent Employment (Nominal) Appropriate Statistical Tests: Chi-Square Fisher's Exact NcNemar's	How does a family assessment tool assess families from three different ethnic groups? IV = Families (Nominal) DV = Scores on FAD (Ordinal) Appropriate Statistical Tests: One-way ANOVA or (if the idea that ordinal variables can be treated like ratio variables is rejected) Mann Whitney U Wilcoxon Sign Kruskal-Wallis
Macro Practice (target is organizations or communities)	What is the impact on uptake of county mental health services where one county has neighborhood mental health clinics and the other has a central mental health clinic? IV = Mental Health Clinics (Nominal) DV = Uptake of Mental Health Services (Ratio) Appropriate Statistical Test: T Test One-way ANOVA	How do the contrasting supervisory styles in two departments of children's services affect staff retention rates? IV = Supervision (Ordinal) DV = Staff Retention Rate (Ratio) Appropriate Statistical Test: Simple linear regression (or ordinal variable is treated like ratio variable, otherwise) T test One-way ANOVA Pearson r

Multivariate Analysis

Multivariate analysis tests the relationship between our dependent variable and several independent variables simultaneously. Thus it controls for the interaction between several independent variables. Rubin and Babbie

(2001) explain this process by means of an elaboration model that shows how we can identify whether the relationship between the independent and dependent variable is indeed true or whether it is spurious or affected by other variables that specify or suppress the relationship we are testing. For example, in our study of TANF training, using multivariate analysis we may find that age rather than training determines employment, or that training is most effective with older clients but getting a job immediately is more effective with younger clients, or that employment history suppresses the relationship between training and employment. These findings would be the result of tests such as MANOVA (Multiple Analysis of Variance) or various forms of multiple regression. The choice of multivariate analysis test will, again, depend on whether the sample is randomly selected, the distribution of the variables in the population of interest, the level of measurement of the variables to be included in the analysis, and the power and robustness of the test.

A Comment on Nonparametric Statistical Tests

Before ending this overview of positivist data evaluation procedures, there is one last issue to acknowledge: the implication of using nonparametric statistical tests. In this discussion of the evaluation of data that has been collected using methods based on sampling theory and probability theory, it has been assumed that the positivist researcher will always gather data using these theories to guide methodology because these are the theories that have emerged from the rationales the paradigm is based upon. If the positivist researcher has gathered data using methods that are not based on these theories, then he or she has violated the rationale for the worldview that was used to conceptualize the study. Positivist social work researchers have found, however, that there are numerous practical problems with carrying out research that remains true to the paradigm. Often samples cannot be randomly sampled or are small. Many of the variables we are interested in can only be measured at nominal or ordinal levels and, therefore, will not necessarily have normal distributions.

Our solution has been to go ahead and gather non-random samples, or gather data from small samples, or measure variables at the nominal and ordinal levels and use nonparametric statistical tests that do not rest on the assumptions of randomness and normal distributions. As stated above, these statistics do no rely on an estimation of the parameters in a population. Rather, they simply test the differences between groups regardless of assumptions about distributions and parameters. It is as if the history and philosophy described here as the foundation for "the scientific method," having been proposed as the touchstone for gathering knowledge, in the next breath is disregarded with a shrug of the shoulders and a muttered apology of "never mind." The most commonly used nonparametric bivariate statistical test is the Chi square, which is used to test the relationship between two variables measured at the nominal level by comparing expected scores for each variable, if the null hypothesis were true, with the scores that were actually observed in the study. This test does not assume normal distributions of variables in the population of interest or that independent samples have been selected.

Main Points

- Quantitative analysis is the approach that positivists take to understand the meaning of their data
- It is important to distinguish the units of observation and the units of analysis
- Data can be entered in a statistical software package and frequencies can easily be run to check for any errors in data entry
- Descriptive statistics such as means, medians, and modes summarize the data
- Bivariate analysis tests the relationship between an independent and dependent variable. Choice of a bivariate test depends on the characteristics of the measurement and distribution of the two variables
- Multivariate analysis is used to understand the relationship between more than two variables and measures such relationships simultaneously
- Nonparametric statistical tests are used when the assumptions of parametric tests have not been met

Learning Assignments

- Run the tutorial in the SPSS package.
- Having gained this overview, go back to the first screen of the SPSS software package. You will see a data spreadsheet layout. Click on the "Variable View" tab at the bottom of the screen. Type in some imaginary demographic variables and variables that could be used as your independent and dependent variables in the left-hand column (gender, ethnicity, age, years of education, whether TANF training was given, employment status). Now click on the "Data View" tab at the bottom of the screen and enter some imaginary scores for these variables. Now you have a data set.
  a. Click on the "Analyze" tab at the top, then click on "Descriptive Statistics." Run frequencies. What did you get? What does it mean?
  b. Click on the "Analyze" tab again and experiment with the various univariate and bivariate tests it offers you. Run them. What do they mean? Which tests were appropriate for your variables?

6

Termination and Follow Up—
Reporting on Findings and
Exiting the Research Setting

As you can see, this is a short chapter; for the positivist researcher, termination and follow up is not a protracted process. Generally a commitment is made to report findings to the sponsor of the project, to present at a conference, and to write a scholarly publication. The prime audience for the study findings is other social work researchers and practitioners rather than the participants in the study. Study participants are informed where to obtain a copy of the study report, and the researcher may well give a presentation of findings to key informants at the research setting. However, the aim is to present data rather than engage in a termination process. Generally, once the study is finished, researchers do not have further plans to engage study participants. The presentation of research findings can be in the form of a poster at a meeting or conference, a presentation at a meeting or conference, a report, or a scholarly journal article. All of these can be posted on the Internet for easy access.

Posters

A poster is usually an informal mode of presentation in which researchers display the key elements of their project and the interested audience can browse the display and discuss the project with the researcher on a one-to-one informal basis. The poster simply and clearly describes the background to the study, the methodology used in the study, the study findings, and the meaning of those findings. Don't forget the title and the names and affiliations of the researchers. One-page handouts are distributed that include a summary of the project and a source for the full report of the project. According to Pellecchia (1999), a poster can be a time-consuming project but is worth the effort if you can produce an attractive visual display using charts and graphs, as well as keep things orderly and concise. The display needs to be interesting and eye catching, with minimal text and illustrative color pictures and charts. The text that is used should be in bullet list form and large and clear enough for a browsing person to read.

Presentations

The style of the presentation will depend on the size and nature of the audience. For a small group meeting, handouts summarizing the study by giving the background, methods, findings, and interpretation of the findings are fine. There can be an informal discussion and question and answer atmosphere. For larger audiences in a formal setting, presentation software such as Power Point offers a clear visual focus for the audience. The presentation slides should just give key headings. More detail can be offered in handouts or by referring the audience to a Web site where the full report or article can be found. As a minor piece of advice, some of the sound and visual effects that come with presentation software programs need to be used sparingly. At first they seem amusing, but if overused they can be distracting and annoying for your audience.

Reports and Articles

The layout of the report follows the requirements of a style guide such as the *Publication Manual of the American Psychological Association* (APA) or *The Chicago Manual of Style*. It includes

Title: This is the first thing the reader will look at. It needs to be a simple, clear description of what the report or article is about. It is usually the last thing that you finalize for the report since it tends to change as you write the report.

Abstract or summary: This summarizes the purpose, methods, findings, and interpretation of findings of the study. It is the next thing the reader looks at.

It needs to be simply and clearly written if it is to convince the reader to read on. These days, abstracts are indexed online and thus they need to be doubly carefully written. Everyone in the world is able to read them. This is usually the second to last thing that you finalize. You really need to have finished the report to have enough of an overview to write this kind of summary.

Discussion of problem focus: This is a discussion of the information that was gathered as a result of the tasks described in Chapters 1 and 2. It gives a background to the problem, its significance, and the specific research question(s) and hypothesis(es).

Discussion of literature: This is a discussion of the information that was gathered as a result of the tasks described in the "literature review" discussion in Chapter 2. It should be organized under key topics that are the source of concepts and variables that were operationalized in the study.

Description of research methods: This is an account of how data was gathered using tasks described in Chapters 3 and 4. It should include a description of the design (causal or correlational), the study participants, the data collection instruments that were developed, the procedures for data gathering, and the analysis procedures.

Description of findings: This describes the information that was gathered as a result of the tasks described in Chapter 5. The results of each analysis procedure that was described in the research methods should be given with the tables of data, the significant test values, the degrees of freedom, and the probability levels.

Discussion and interpretation of findings: This interprets the information that was gathered as a result of the tasks described in Chapter 5. The APA suggests that this section should address the contribution that the study has made to new knowledge, the contribution this study has made to the resolution of the original research problem, and the overall conclusions and theoretical implications of the study findings.

References: This is a listing of all books, articles, and reports cited in the main body of the research report or article. It is not a bibliography, just a listing of citations. The function of a reference list is to give the reader the information needed to find a citation. Most social work publications use the APA guidelines for creating reference lists.

Main Points

- For positivists, termination and follow up is a reporting of the findings
- Findings can be reported by means of posters, presentations, or written reports

Learning Assignments

1. Find a research article in a scholarly journal on a topic that you are interested in. Review the article and evaluate whether it includes all the sections described above under reports and articles. Is anything missing?

2. With your partner, have a brief discussion of reporting as the method of terminating with study participants. What are the advantages of this approach to terminating with study participants and what are the disadvantages?

Conclusion

In this part of the book, positivist research has been described as explanatory (causal) and descriptive (correlational) research. A rationale and context have been offered for this definition and associated methodologies have been discussed as well as analysis and reporting procedures using the stages of the generalist intervention model. This understanding of positivism is now used as a launching point for an exploration of our first alternative to positivism: post-positivism.

PART II

Post-Positivism

Introduction to Part II

Post-positivism takes the positivist paradigm as its starting point and, on the whole, accepts that worldview. It concurs that, indeed, an objective reality exists but suggests that the "immutable laws and mechanisms" driving that reality can never be fully comprehended. Quantitative measurement and hypothesis testing only offers a part of the picture; the rest must be discovered through open exploration. Post-positivism's associated epistemology suggests that one can never step completely outside human experience to study it. However, since objectivity is the ideal, a good researcher must strive for objectivity by being aware of his or her biases, paying attention to the intellectual traditions of the field, and attending to the observations and judgments of key players through peer feedback. The post-positivist takes an inductive exploratory approach to understanding an objective reality. To research a topic, he or she interviews people or observes naturalistic settings. The data to be collected are words rather than numbers, qualitative rather than quantitative.

Post-positivists collect qualitative data through interviews, observations, and reviews of documents using an inductive exploratory approach. The aim is to develop holistic and comprehensive descriptions and analyses of research topics. In this way, theories are developed, formulated, and tested by logical, self-aware reasoning. For example, a post-positivist researcher might pose the question, "How can social workers intervene with gangs?" Interviews, observations, and relevant reports and newspaper articles would all be sources for the collection of initial exploratory data. There would be no specific hypotheses about intervention strategies at the beginning of the study, but there would be a search for emerging concepts and themes as the study progresses and the data is collected, such as "criminality," "family experience," "role of substance abuse," "economic deprivation," "organizational structures," and "roles." There would then be a search for the connections between those concepts and themes that facilitates formulation of a theory of social work practice with gangs.

Brewer and Hunter (1989) and Andrew Tudor (1982), as they reflected on and analyzed the limits of the positivist approach to scientific research, concluded that positivism cannot adequately investigate many of the links between the empirical world and scientific knowledge. The essence of their concern with positivism is its restricted perspective of, to use Tudor's terminology, (1) how we *experience* the world; (2) how we should *interpret* that experience; (3) the *derivation* of our preconceptions about experience and its interpretation; (4) how we should *test* our interpretations; (5) how we should *establish* knowledge; and (6) how we should use this knowledge to *explain* and predict truth. The post-positivist worldview broadens perspectives on these dimensions by suggesting that we do not empirically experience everything that happens in the world. Much happens that we are not conscious of; we need to expand consciousness, since this leads us to understanding and innovation. For example, in the nineteenth century child abuse was not empirically experienced; generally children were seen as "little adults" and a notion of developmental stages for human growth was left to twentieth-century theorists such as Piaget to propose. Indeed, before Freud, we had no conscious or unconscious mind.

This worldview also proposes that the relationship between the observer and what is observed changes as the observer becomes aware of and more familiar with the observed. In addition, what is observed will depend on the expectations (interpretations and derivations) of the observer. Hanson (1958) describes an experiment in which subjects were shown slides of playing cards for short periods of time. One card, however, was a trick card where the color was altered; for example, a black six of diamonds or a red two of spades. Participants seeing this trick card would either see a blur or see the expected color of the card. Phillips (1990) describes Hanson's additional thought on interpreting and deriving our experiences.

> He imagined Tycho Brahe, and Kepler (astronomers) watching the dawn together; because they had different assumptions about astronomy, one would see the sun moving above the horizon, while the other would see the earth rotating away to reveal the sun! (pp. 34–35)

However, both would see the same thing: the sun increasing its distance from the earth. This is the point the post-positivist is making. Something objective is observed, but what it means will need to be discovered. Explaining and establishing truth is an exploration of experience rather than numerical measurement of objective data camouflaged as neutrality.

Post-positivism, though, is more than an enhancement of positivism, rounding off its sharp numerical edges. It has a function and stance in its own right. Juliet Corbin (Strauss & Corbin, 1998), who has written much about this approach to research in terms of "grounded theory" methodologies, refers to it as "a way of life" (p. ix). She and her co-author have not been concerned generally about the philosophical implications of taking the grounded theory approach but have stated its mission in terms of how the approach molds the researcher and the qualities of researchers who tend to be attracted to this approach. These authors note that the personal involvement with data brings research to life, and the people who do this research tend to be flexible, enjoy working collaboratively, acknowledge the complexity of research, are continually open to new interpretations of theory and data, have both nonacademic and academic audiences in mind, and tend to be completely absorbed in their work. They are excited by their ground-breaking role in building new theory.

> A researcher does not begin a project with a preconceived theory in mind (unless his or her purpose is to elaborate and extend existing theory). Rather, the researcher begins with an area of study and allows the theory to emerge from the data. Theory derived from data is more likely to resemble the "reality" than is theory derived by putting together a series of concepts based on experience or solely through speculation (how one thinks things should work). (p. ix)

According to Crabtree and Miller (1992), such approaches have been found in various disciplines. In psychology we have ethology and ecological psychology researching behavior and events over time and in context. In sociology we have ethnomethodology, symbolic interactions, and grounded theory addressing how individuals achieve shared agreement, how they interact in symbolic environments, and how we understand relations among social categories. In anthropology, ethnography and ethnoscience are methods for researching culture as a whole and as a cognitive map of social organizations, shared meanings, and semantic rules. All these traditions are categorized here as examples of the post-positivist approach to research.

For these disciplines, using words as the source of data and meaning is rooted in the science of linguistics. While positivists have turned to mathematics to develop approaches to scientific discovery, post-positivists have turned to the science of linguistics. In the United States, at the beginning of the twentieth century, there was a need to describe the numerous indigenous American Indian languages. Thus American linguists quickly developed field methods for recording and analyzing language, and the "structuralist" approach to understanding language, which codified the unique grammatical structure of each language, became the accepted method. Linguists, at this time, used a combination of anthropology and language analysis. It was Edward Bloomfield (1887–1949) who was credited with making linguistics scientific by restricting its scope to the study of language that was observable and measurable, a perspective similar to the one taken by J.B. Watson, the behaviorist psychologist, at that time. Bloomfield did not believe that the meaning of language could be studied in a scientific manner, only its structure. It was Avram Noam Chomsky's work on phrase structure grammar and transformational grammar that offered sets of rules for not only analyzing sentences but also identifying underlying "strings" or phrases within the sentence. In his book *Syntactic Structures,* he gives rules for formalizing transformational phrase structure analysis. For example, if we take the sentence "The woman hugged the child," using phrase analysis we can give the following analysis.

(i)   Sentence -> Noun Phrase (The woman) + Verb Phrase (hugged the child)
(ii) Noun Phrase -> Definite Article (The) + Noun (woman)
(iii) Verb Phrase -> Verb (hugged) + Noun Phrase (The child)
(iv) Definite Article -> the
(v)   Noun -> (woman, child)
(vi) Verb -> (hugged)

Lyons (1970) notes that these rules progress as follows. The sentence is broken down into a noun phrase and a verb phrase. Both these phrases can be broken down into their constituent elements. The noun phrase includes a definite article and a noun (The woman). The verb phrase includes a verb and another noun phrase (hugged the child). These can be broken down still further into the definite article, nouns, and verbs. Such an analysis reveals the sentence string. Chomsky, through the rules of transformational grammar, suggested a more complicated analysis where we can reveal the underlying strings in any sentence. Using Chomsky's rules, the analysis of the sentence would look like this:

(i)   Sentence -> Noun Phrase (The woman) + Verb Phrase (hugged the child)
(ii) Verb Phrase -> Verb (hugged) + NP (the child)
(iii) Noun Phrase -> (can be singular or plural: woman, women; child, children). Singular would be definite article plus noun. Plural would be definite article plus noun plus "s"
(iv) Definite Article -> the
(v)   noun -> (woman, child)

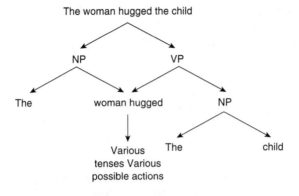

Figure II.1   Analysis of a Sentence

(vi) Verb -> (hugged, touched, watched, etc.)
(vii) Tense of verb (past or present)
(viii) Augmentation of verb (will, can, may, shall, must).

He then adds "transformational" rules for analyzing language, one of which breaks down the sentence into the dominant parts and the constituent parts. This is best illustrated by a diagram. (see Figure II.1)

These transformational rules will not be described in detail here (see Chomsky, 1968), but their function is acknowledged as one that reveals phrase markers as well as the grammatical structures of sentences so that we can understand both the sound and the structure of a sentence when analyzing the structure of language. In later works, Chomsky tied these analyses to cognitive psychology and the understanding of the human mind (Chomsky, 1968).

Up to this point, though, linguists analyzed language sentence by sentence to understand the structure of language as illustrated above. However, such an analysis ignored a vital piece of the data: the context of the sentence, namely the tone of voice, the social situation, and the identities of those who are creating the sentences. A more recent development in linguistics, "discourse analysis" according to Brown and Yule (1991), offers a compromise between a need for, on the one hand, form and regularity when analyzing narrative and, on the other hand, a need to include general principles of interpretation by which we all understand each other. When discussing discourse analysis these authors consider

- The form of language (spoken, written)
- The context of language (references, inferences, shared understandings)

- The sequencing of topics within the language
- The emergence of themes in language
- The structuring of information contained in language through tone and pauses
- The structuring of information contained in language through syntax
- Interpretation:
  - computing the communication function
  - using sociocultural knowledge to interpret meaning
  - determining inferences to be made

The explication of discourse analysis rules as rules that can be used for analysis of qualitative data will be discussed in more detail in Chapter 8. For the moment, it is enough to show a scientific foundation of linguistic thought and theory for the methodologies of post-positivist research and qualitative research in general. The qualitative researcher is analyzing language for meaning rather than structure. However, the use of guidelines from discourse analysis can focus this search for meaning. If the above issues are considered when interpreting data, then a uniformity of approach to understanding qualitative data can be developed. The rules for understanding qualitative data are based on the researcher's definition of concepts included in the statement of the research focus, rather than a grammatical building block such as a sentence or a paragraph. The qualitative researcher identifies and defines the concept being used to analyze language as well as the rationale for suggesting that a piece of narrative reflects that concept. The combination of guidelines from discourse analysis with rationales for concept identification and explication gives a solid foundation for interpreting qualitative data.

7

Assessment and Engagement— Development of Understanding of the Research Focus and Entrée to the Research Setting

Assessment: Understanding of Research Focus

For the post-positivist researcher, an understanding of the research focus evolves during the study. According to Strauss and Corbin (1990), post-positivist research builds grounded theory that is "discovered, developed, and provisionally verified through systematic data collection and analysis of data pertaining to that phenomenon . . . . One does not begin with a theory, then prove it. Rather, one begins with an area of study and what is relevant to that area is allowed to emerge" (p. 23). Thus the post-positivist does not develop a precise question and hypothesis before starting the study. He or she starts with an interest in a particular area and then gathers information about that area from literature, key players, observations, and personal experience to narrow the focus of the theory being developed. The generic question in all such research is "What is happening here?" Thus specific questions are oriented to understanding action and process. A study of gang life might start with questions such as "How does someone become aware of a gang?" "How does someone choose a gang, or does it choose you?"

"What are the 'joining' rituals?" "When do social workers interface with gangs and how?" Such questions lead researchers to develop sensitivity to the meaning of their data and the capacity to distinguish the important data by comparing conclusions about their data with the literature and the conclusions of key experts. Post-positivist researchers preserve a balance between following the rules of a research methodology and creativity by periodically stepping back from the data to ask themselves and other key informants, "What is really going on here and am I seeing it all?"

For post-positivist researchers, developing the focus of the study, data collection, and analysis are interwoven activities that inform each other. An area of interest is stated, an interview is carried out or an observation is made, the data is analyzed, and the area of interest is refined and focused. This process is repeated throughout the study so that the researcher identifies the components of the area of interest, describes them, and develops explanations for them. Crabtree and Miller (1992) illustrate this process by suggesting that qualitative research aims, questions, and analysis objectives can be categorized into identification, description, and explanation. Each of these aims, according to the authors, suggests associated questions. This idea is applied to a student study of homeless children (Young & Creacy, 1995) in Table 7.1. This is a study of various homeless children living in a temporary shelter and receiving services from M.S.W. students over a period of nine months. The children were individually interviewed and invited to write or draw about their perceptions of their lives in group sessions focused on building self-esteem. Eventually 30 homeless children were included in the study; however, because of the nature of the shelter, very few were part of the study for the whole nine months. Table 7.1 shows the aims, research questions, and analysis objectives that emerged during the study. It starts by identifying the characteristics of the children in the study and then moves on to descriptions of how they perceive their lives, their low self-esteem, and their ambivalence about being in a shelter with rules as opposed to being homeless without rules. Explanations emerge for social work interventions including promoting self-actualization in the face of negative experiences. The guiding framework for developing this knowledge was the identified aims, questions, and analysis objectives. The aim was to identify, describe, and explain. Questions were developed to meet these aims and the emergent analysis did indeed identify and name, give qualitative and normative descriptions, and give an interpretive explanation of appropriate social work practice with these children.

Thus when developing an understanding of the research focus, the post-positivist should consider the research aim, questions, and analysis objective.

Table 7.1   Study of Homeless Children

Aims	Research Questions	Analysis Objectives
Identification Who are the homeless children and what is their experience?	**What?** What are the dimensions of homelessness for single parent, female-headed families? **Who?** What are the characteristics of the children of such families? **What is the main focus?** What helps children survive homelessness and make a success of their lives?	**Identify and Name** 50% of homeless women are between the ages of 17 and 25. They have sporadic employment records. They have experienced family violence. The children are depressed, have behavioral problems, have no sense of privacy.
Description What are homeless children's perceptions about their past and present life styles?	**What is going on here? What do we see?** How are children experiencing homelessness? **What are the dimensions and variations of the concept?** Which parts of the children's lives does homelessness affect (personal, social, school, and leisure) and how? **What meanings/practices occur in lived experiences?** How do homeless children gain food and shelter, make friends, or make progress at school? **What is the value of the phenomenon?** How can social workers learn more about such children so that they can promote success?	**Qualitative and Normative Description** Homeless children tend to have fragmented support networks. They see life, people, places, and schools as temporary and out of their control. They have low self-esteem. If they live in a shelter, they consider themselves not homeless. The children experience ambivalence about the freedom of living on the streets versus the rules of living in a shelter. The children are preoccupied with getting money. The children wish they had a stronger family and more friends. The children took a long time to trust the researchers and some of the older ones never did.

(Continued)

Table 7.1 (Continued)

Aims	Research Questions	Analysis Objectives
Explanation Generation What can we do to change children's perceptions about their future and promote a positive vision for their future?	*What is happening here?* *What patterns exist?* Are older children more pessimistic about their situation than younger children? *How do phenomena differ and relate to each other?* *How does it work?* How does moving from living in a car or on the streets to living in a temporary shelter impact children's ability to understand and cope with their situation? *How did something occur/happen?* How did the children get here? What do they need? How can they move forward with their lives?	*Interpretative Explanation Generation* The children need to achieve self-actualization in the face of low self-esteem and ambivalence about the shelter and their life experiences so far.

Tutty, Rothery, and Grinnell (1996) offer a structure to this preparatory stage that includes the following:

- Defining your general problem area
  - Reflecting on the personal interest in the problem. Who are the people affected by the problem? For example, Young and Creacy (1995) carried out a study of homeless children because they were in a field placement setting at a homeless shelter and noticed an increase in families living at the shelter.
  - Narrowing down the group to be studied. Is it children? Is it homeless children? Is it homeless children in a particular shelter? Is it the children of single parents? In the example study, it was the children of single parents living in one particular shelter.
  - Exploring the problems of the people to be studied. What do you know about homeless children at this shelter? What does the literature say about the reasons for their homelessness and their experiences of homelessness? What do you want to focus on in particular? In the example study, the

focus was the children's experiences of the homeless shelter and their wishes and dreams for the future.

- Reflecting on the significance of the study
  - Why is this an important study? What contribution is being made to knowledge about social work practice? What will social work practice gain from your study? Why would we want to know about homeless children's perceptions of their physical, emotional, and social well-being? In the example study, the importance of the study was seen as giving social workers insight into homeless children's realities to improve sensitivity and competency when working with these children.

- Thinking through preliminary groundwork to be done
  - What is your definition or articulation of the problem? What is your conceptual map of the problem? Can you articulate this to study sponsors, research sites, and research supervisors? In our example study, the authors identified a series of circumstances that led to single mothers' homelessness and the characteristics of children's understanding and responses to their plight, and used Mazlow's hierarchy to identify homeless children's needs.

- Clarifying the essential concepts that are the focus of the study
  - In our example study, these were children's perceptions of being homeless and how this perception affects their understanding of self and world.

- Deciding who will supervise the project
  - Has a synopsis of the study been written to help the supervisor understand the study and the chosen approach?
  - What do you need in a supervisor (in terms of knowledge, areas of your weakness that you need help with, level of independence you need)?
  - What is the understanding you have with the supervisor regarding which parts of the study he or she will help you with and how this help will be given? Are you asking for advice or clear direction? How will you address disagreements with the supervisor over the direction of the study?

- Identifying resources needed in terms of time, access, equipment and supplies, space, and social support
  - In our example, the shelter provided the supplies needed for the groups, and other students who were also completing research projects offered social support.

- Deciding on the site of the study
  - How will you choose the site? Who is the contact? How will contact be made and maintained? In our example, the site was a field placement site, but without such an infrastructure to support the study, considerations discussed below under "Engagement: Gaining Entrée" should be addressed.

- Addressing ethical issues of your study
  - In our example study, children were the focus of the study and they were vulnerable. Informed consent was gained from parents, and the feelings of the children regarding the intrusiveness of intense collaboration with the researchers regarding personal issues was continually revisited. Children were informed that they could leave the study at any time, and some of the older children chose not to participate fully in the study.

- Writing the proposal
  - The qualitative research proposal is difficult to write because there is the assumption that both the focus and the methods of the research will change and emerge as the study progresses. Thus the proposal gives a description of the anticipated study and notes areas of potential change. Areas to be addressed in the proposal include:
    o Focus of inquiry. Describe the problem area, the people who will be the participants in the study, rationales for these, and significance of this focus for social work practice. Discuss the literature on the focus of inquiry. Explain the aims, research questions, and analysis objectives.
    o The fit of the focus to the post-positivist paradigm. Why is this the appropriate approach to this topic? Why are you building this theory and how will this approach address your interest in the topic?
    o Where and from whom the data will be collected. Explain the research site, the potential interviewees, and the pragmatics of moving forward with data collection at this site.
    o How data will be collected and recorded. Strategies and procedures for gathering and recording data are discussed in Chapter 2. Which of these will you use and why?
    o Proposed analysis procedures. These are discussed in Chapter 2. Again, how do you plan to use these procedures in your study?
    o Ethical issues. Which of the ethical issues discussed in Chapter 17 have the potential to emerge in this study? How will they be addressed?
    o Diversity issues. Which of the diversity issues discussed in Chapter 18 need to be addressed in this study? How will they be addressed?
    o Resource needs. What are the practical constraints of time and resources that will affect this study? How will you make sure you carry out a credible study within these constraints?

- Gaining human subjects clearance
  - Having thought through the above issues and written the proposal, the research project must obtain approval from a human subjects committee or institutional review board.

The role of the literature review at this initial stage of the project is to inform the researcher's evolving "theoretical sensitivity." Strauss and Corbin (1990) in the past have used this term to describe the researcher's awareness and understanding of the meaning of the data. Since the interpretation of the data will be a mixture of the science of synthesis of information and the art of intuition, the researcher needs to consciously develop a mature understanding of the topic by not only reviewing the literature but also consulting with experts. Strauss and Corbin (1998) suggest that the researcher need not read all the literature before the project starts but simply use reading as a stimulus for thinking about the topic. This reading will continue during the study and will also influence data collection and interpretation of data. The literature can offer concepts that can be compared to concepts emerging in data collection. It can help with formulating questions before and during the study. The same is true for consulting with experts. They can offer insights, concepts, and questions that challenge the researcher to take a fresh perspective.

Berg (1995) offers an approach to the literature review for qualitative researchers that he calls the "two card" system. This is a reference to using an old-fashioned paper system of index cards, but the idea can also be used with word processing programs. This author suggests that when doing the literature review, one should invent words and phrases that describe aspects of one's research interest that are likely to be used in information search engines and indexes such as the university library's Web site. For example, using homeless children as our topic, we might come up with phrases such as "homelessness," "homeless families," "women and homelessness," "income maintenance," "food and shelter," "services to the homeless child," and so on. These phrases can be typed into the search engines to find relevant articles and books. To record the content of each reading, two referencing systems are used. First, there is the "author index" that lists the author(s) and all citation materials on one reference "card" or word processing page of a document. These entries can be sorted alphabetically using the "sort" function of the word processing program. The second, parallel indexing system is the "topic index" that is organized by putting the topic at the top of a page and then reproducing verbatim quotes on that topic with associated authors' names. Again, this would be on pages of a word processing document that is searchable using the "find" function and can be sorted according to specified criteria using the "sort" function. Thus the qualitative researcher has a flexible, synthesized resource that is organized under topics and authors and can be used throughout the research project.

Engagement: Gaining Entrée

Since, for the post-positivist, the research site is not only the source of the data from which theory will emerge but also the place where the metamorphosis of the research focus will be seen, entrée to the research site goes beyond formal agreements and arrangements to gather data. Participants in the study will be interviewed and perhaps observed over extended periods of time. Thus gaining entry includes both formal contracting and the more informal interpersonal permission to build an intensive relationship with study participants. Gaining entrée to the site begins with engaging the gatekeepers to that site. There are various kinds of gatekeepers: those who have the authority to give permission for the research, those who are respected opinion leaders for members of the study sample, and those who have the credibility to obstruct or facilitate the study. The researcher needs to approach the site with all of these gatekeepers in mind. The site may be a private home, an agency or program setting, or a community setting. Initial contact with the site is most often successful through an intermediary or through the researcher's own relationship with the site. In the student project on homeless children, the student researchers had built a relationship with the shelter and its clients through their roles as student interns. A researcher without such an established role would need to use intermediaries such as professional colleagues to negotiate meetings and initial contact so that various gatekeepers can be convinced to endorse the project. This usually includes exploration and acknowledgement of the gatekeepers' priorities and needs for the research setting. If the researcher's study can address these priorities and needs as well as his or her own research focus, progress towards gaining entrée to the site is smoothed a little. Thus, specific steps of engagement of the research site include

- Networking with friends and colleagues to find out whether there is anyone you know who has a current relationship with a potential research site
  - If you do have a contact, ask that person to be an intermediary and let a site gatekeeper know that you would like to talk to him or her about the research project. Set up a meeting and prepare well for the meeting so that you do not waste anybody's time by not being clear about the purpose of the project. Discuss the study focus, timelines, the potential impact of the study on the site, the benefits to the site, and the fit of the study with the needs and priorities of the site.
  - If you do not have a contact, gaining entry is harder. Gatekeepers to agency and community sites receive numerous research requests. If you write a letter requesting a meeting to discuss the study, show that you have researched the setting and let the gatekeeper know that you have informed yourself about the issues that the site values. Try to make the potential project an attractive idea rather than a time-consuming burden for the site.

- Once you have actually gained a meeting to discuss the project, use your micro practice skills when engaging the person. Use active listening and effective interviewing skills.

- Once you have gained entry to the site, remember that entrée to the site includes effectively engaging every participant in the study. Treat everyone with respect, make sure you explain the project clearly, ask for permission to interview and observe, and check and address any concerns that you become aware of. Be vigilant about building and maintaining a positive relationship with everyone who is affected by your presence at the site.

To sum up this section on assessment and engagement, the post-positivist researcher identifies research aims, questions, and analysis objectives and develops a flexible plan for concurrent data collection, analysis, and synthesis. The researcher's major task at this stage is to develop sensitivity to the focus of the inquiry, not to develop "correct" design. The post-positivist researcher uses a combination of art and science to focus understanding of the research problem. At the same time, the researcher builds a relationship with the research site and its gatekeepers so that the intense engagement required by post-positivist research can be accommodated.

Main Points

- Understanding the focus of the inquiry is an ongoing process throughout the study
- At the beginning of the study, clarity of thinking can be achieved by outlining the research aim, the research questions, and the analysis objectives
- A proposal can be written outlining anticipated study procedures; however, the post-positivist is open to adjustments in procedures as the study is implemented
- Engagement of the research site is a critical research skill both at the beginning and throughout the study

Learning Assignments

1. Think of a research aim, question, and analysis goal for an area of social work practice that interests you.

2. What would be a potential site for that study and how would you gain entry to that site?

3. Discuss these ideas with your partner and present them in a group discussion. Role-play the conversations you might have with key players at the research site. Note the approaches that make people feel comfortable with being engaged in a research project.

8

Planning, Implementation, Evaluation—Rationales for Gathering Data, Data Gathering, and Developing an Understanding of the Data and Its Meaning

Planning: Rationales for Gathering Data

Moustakas (1990) notes that "there is no exclusive list of tasks and procedures that would be appropriate for every heuristic investigation, but rather each research process unfolds in its own way. Initially, methods are envisioned and constructed that will guide the research through the preparation phase and facilitate the collection and analysis of data" (p. 43). This is a good time to begin the research journals. Post-positivist researchers, and qualitative researchers in general, keep two journals. The first is a journal recording the researcher's rationales for the research plan as well as sampling, data collection, and analysis decisions as the study proceeds. This journal includes not only a clear articulation of the chosen approach to data collection but also an account of rationales for the theory that emerges from the study. The second journal is the narrative account of the data collected in interviews, observations, and document reviews, with their accompanying analysis. These journals are revisited below as the process of data collection and interpretation is described.

When planning data collection procedures, the post-positivist researcher develops strategies that will uncover as many meanings as possible. The plan includes sequences of interviews, observations, and document reviews that comprehensively discover data addressing the research focus. In a study of gang life, for example, the researcher may decide that participant observation is the most appropriate starting point for immersion in the topic. This might be intertwined with interviews with professionals who intervene with gangs, including law enforcement officials and various human service professionals. In time, in-depth conversations with family members and other members of the neighborhood might be the sampling and data collection strategy. Such intensive experiences will, of course, require periods away from the gang experience for reflection and input from other experts. Thus the key to the planning phase is immersion in the topic to be studied, reflection on the most appropriate ways to gather data, and continual reappraisal with the self and with other trusted experts.

To clarify and solidify thinking about the rationale for data collection, Michael Quinn Patton's (1990) division of research foci into three types is useful. He suggests that research can be basic, applied, or a formative and summative program evaluation. Basic research is grounded theory development, as described by Strauss and Corbin (1990, 1998), that requires lengthy intensive fieldwork. Applied research takes the findings of basic research and applies them to real-world problems. Applied researchers are trying to understand how to intervene in and solve a problem, in contrast to basic researchers who are trying to understand why that problem happened in the first place. Finally, evaluation research assesses both the operations and the impact of the solutions to problems that have been implemented through policies and programs based on the results of basic and applied research. The inductive, exploratory nature of post-positivist research offers fresh approaches to each of these kinds of research. If we return to our example study of homeless children, we can illustrate hypothetical post-positivist approaches to each of these research modes, as shown in Table 8.1.

The type of research, purpose, and the research question identified in Table 8.1 are fairly self-explanatory. They identify stages of a process: understanding an issue, identifying interventions with that issue, evaluating the impact of the intervention, and maintaining the quality of that intervention. After a research purpose has been decided, the data collection strategies that accompany the research purpose can be developed. These are discussed below in terms of units of analysis and purposive sampling.

Table 8.1 Types of Research and Their Associated Methodologies

Type of Research	Purpose	Question	Data Collection Strategies	Impact of Findings
Basic	To discover knowledge, to discover the truth	What are the variations in food and shelter experienced by family units in poverty and how do those variations affect the family unit? (this could be a local, national, or international study)	A combination of interviews, field observations, literature reviews, and review of documents with a purposefully selected sample of families in poverty.	An in-depth statement about variations in food and shelter for the sampled range of families in poverty.
Applied	Understand the nature and sources of human and societal problems	How can we intervene in family units in poverty to reduce homelessness among children? (this could be a local, national, or international study)	A combination of interviews, field observations, literature reviews, and review of documents with a purposefully selected sample of families and children living in poverty, as well as human service practitioners who intervene with homeless children.	An in-depth statement about the needs of the sampled range of families and children in poverty, and services to address those needs.
Summative Evaluation	To determine effectiveness of interventions in a societal problem	What is the impact of this shelter program on homelessness among children in its service area?	A combination of interviews, field observations, literature reviews, and review of documents with a purposefully selected sample of shelter personnel, clients, and other key informants identified by data gathering and analysis.	An in-depth statement about what is and is not working in a specified shelter program.
Formative Evaluation	To improve the performance of interventions in a societal problem	How does this shelter program deliver services (qualifications of employees and volunteers, content of services, timelines of services, focus of outreach, budgetary constraints, etc.)?	A combination of interviews, field observations, literature reviews, and review of documents with a purposefully selected sample of shelter personnel.	An in-depth statement about the quality of services in a specified shelter.

SOURCE: Adapted from Patton, 1990, pp. 160–162.

Units of Analysis

In post-positivist research, ultimately, the unit of analysis is the whole entity being researched. However, while the study is being carried out, various units of analysis are identified. In our example study in Chapter 7, the unit of analysis was the children themselves. In Table 8.1, the unit of analysis varies between families, children, and human service practitioners. In our hypothetical example of basic research families in poverty, the unit of analysis and data are reported using families as the organizing entity. In our example of applied research, both families and children are the units of analysis. The researcher may well hold an interview with the family, but he or she can report data from the family as a group and specifically highlight the data from children as a subcategory of data, since he or she is primarily aiming to make a statement about children in general but is acknowledging the family context of children. In our example of summative evaluation, the shelter program is the unit of analysis and a holistic approach is taken to gathering data on that program from shelter personnel, clients, and other appropriate key informants. For our summative evaluation example, the same holds true. Thus the goal here is not to enumerate and compare findings for a class of people so that tested generalizable statements can be made. Rather, the goal is to make an in-depth statement about a particular research issue that enriches our understanding and offers general theoretical statements about the phenomenon. For qualitative researchers, units of analysis go beyond human units and can be particular kinds of events; times of the day, week, month; or season of the year for a particular program. Patton (1990) suggests that "the key issue in selecting and making decisions about the appropriate unit of analysis is to decide what it is you want to be able to say something about at the end of the study" (p. 168). Is it individuals, families, groups, organizations, communities, or all of the above?

For example, in our student study of homeless children, our unit of analysis was the children. The researchers not only wanted to describe children's experiences of homelessness, but they also wanted to offer social work practitioners some guidance on how to intervene with such children. Thus the level of practice being studied was micro practice interventions with individuals.

Purposive Sampling

Having decided on the type of research and the unit of analysis, the post-positivist researcher will now need to decide on a method of sampling. Who will be the participants in the study? As a reminder, the post-positivist accepts the notion of an objective reality in which the mechanics and patterns of human behavior can be identified, but does not try to understand those mechanics by testing preconceived hypotheses with representative samples. They see their research as discovering theoretical statements about those patterns of behavior and verifying those statements through rigorous qualitative analysis. Thus the most appropriate approach to sampling is not random sampling but "purposive" sampling, in which the researcher looks for study participants who will give the most complete data about the study focus. To further illustrate, as Patton (1990) says, for example,

> if the purpose of an evaluation is to increase the effectiveness of a program in reaching lower-socioeconomic groups, one may learn a great deal more by focusing in depth on understanding the needs, interests, and incentives of a small number of carefully selected poor families than by gathering standardized information from a large, statistically representative sample of the whole program. (p. 169)

Patton (1990) and Strauss and Corbin (1998) talk about purposive sampling in different ways. Patton talks about various strategies to gather purposive samples of people, whereas Strauss and Corbin discuss sampling in terms of "representativeness of concepts and how concepts vary dimensionally" (p. 214). They discuss sampling of the data that is being collected. This sampling of the data leads to the development of an understanding of the data and reveals the necessary direction for further data gathering. This is where we see the integration of data gathering and data analysis. For the purposes of clarity, Patton's approach to sampling will be discussed here. Strauss and Corbin's approach to sampling will be discussed in relation to data analysis with reference to "understanding the data and its meaning" below. However, to repeat, both approaches to sampling lead to data gathering.

Patton's (1990) approach to sampling identifies a group of people who have particular experience of a social phenomenon and a range of strategies for selecting a purposeful sample from that group of people. His approach assumes that one sample is selected according to the stated purpose of the study. He offers 15 possible sampling strategies.

1. *Extreme or Deviant Case Sampling.* The logic of this sampling procedure is the notion that if we already know the range of experience of a particular social phenomenon and we have time and resource limitations, in-depth understanding of the extremes of that range of experience will give us insight into its manifestations and appropriate interventions. For example, in the homeless children studies identified in Table 8.1, for the basic research project, samples of poor families who have permanent housing and those who live on the streets would be selected; for the applied research project,

samples of those who have experienced chronic homelessness and those who have experienced acute episodes of homelessness would be selected; and for the summative and formative evaluations, samples of successful and unsuccessful client cases would be selected.

2. *Intensity Sampling.* This uses the same logic as extreme case sampling but chooses to identify cases that are good examples of the phenomenon being studied and offer rich information on its manifestation. Extreme cases might be dismissed as distortions of the reality, but less extreme, information-rich cases can offer in-depth understanding. In Table 8.1, for the basic research question, samples of homeless families that have experienced neither chronic nor acute homelessness but nonetheless have had an intense experience of homelessness would be selected; for the applied question, samples of families and practitioners that have experience with various aspects of homelessness would be selected; and for the summative and formative evaluations, practitioners and clients who have had in-depth contact with the program would be selected.

3. *Maximum Variation Sampling.* This sampling strategy identifies the diversity of experiences with a social phenomenon and gives in-depth descriptions of unique cases as well as any important shared patterns that are common to diverse cases. In all of our example studies, families and case records from various ethnic groups would be sampled as well as cases from various age groups of parents, geographical areas, and any other pertinent dimensions of diversity.

4. *Homogeneous Samples.* This sampling strategy uses the opposite logic of maximum variation sampling and identifies a subgroup for in-depth study. This could be, in our examples, for the basic research question, all homeless families at one particular income level; for the applied study, all homeless families that received one particular intervention such as a work training program; and for our summative and formative evaluations, all cases that have been in the program for more than a year.

5. *Typical Case Sampling.* This would be used to describe an issue or program to those who are not familiar with it. It would give a profile of what tends to be regular or routine, not a generalizable statement about experiences of the program or issue. In our example studies, for the basic research question, it would be all families who have experienced homelessness for the average time period; for the applied research question, it could be all families and practitioners who have experience of the typical homeless program providing shelter and work assistance; and for the summative and formative evaluations, it could be all client cases that stay in the program for the average length of time.

6. *Stratified Purposeful Sampling.* This strategy is a combination of extreme case sampling and typical case sampling. In our sample studies, for the basic

research question, the sample could be a selection of families who have experienced chronic, acute, and episodic periods of homelessness; in our applied research study, it could be a sample of practitioners from various kinds of homelessness programs; and for the summative and formative program evaluations, it could be a sampling of clients with, perhaps, below average and above average characteristics of poverty and homelessness.

7. *Critical Case Sampling.* This sampling strategy would be used to select people or cases who tend to be "markers" of the key events included in the phenomenon being studied. In our example program evaluation studies, if we are evaluating whether an afterschool program in the shelter will assist homeless children, we might select children who are doing particularly badly at school in the sample. The rationale for this sample would be to test whether the program works for those most in need of it. This is a useful approach if resources are limited and the study must be completed in a short period of time.

8. *Snowball or Chain Sampling.* This sampling strategy is a way of under-standing and utilizing the networks between key people in relation to the study focus. In our example studies, members of homeless families or prac-titioners who work with the homeless would be invited to participate in the study. After they were interviewed they would be invited to identify other people they knew who are experiencing homelessness or who are practi-tioners who work with the homeless population.

9. *Criterion Sampling.* This would be sampling based on a particular charac-teristic of the population that potentially can be included in the study. It is generally useful in formative evaluations. For example, if a homeless shelter had an employment program for parents that lasted six weeks, then all par-ticipants who were not employed at the end of six weeks would be included in the study sample so that service delivery to tougher cases could be improved.

10. *Theory-Based or Operational Construct Sampling.* This is the kind of sampling that Strauss and Corbin (1998) rely on and is explained in more detail below in the discussion of "bottom up" interpretations of data and its meaning. Data is gathered that illustrates a particular concept or theory that is emerging in the data. The researcher samples events, time periods, or people for their potential to exhibit the concept or theory. In our example study, the theory that lack of education combined with family and friends who are substance abusers leads to single parent homeless families might be emerging from the data. The researcher might then choose to spend some time sampling participants in substance abuse programs to further explore this pattern. It is explained in more detail below.

11. *Confirming and Disconfirming Cases.* Again, this is much like the "standing back" strategy that Strauss and Corbin describe in analysis procedures

described below. If a researcher is developing a theory, he or she should also be looking for data or cases that not only confirm the theory but also those that contradict the theory.

12. *Opportunistic Sampling.* This is simply deciding to sample a particular person, event, or document because something important seems to be happening. It is an on-the-spot decision to gather data that might be important.

13. *Purposeful Random Sampling.* The post-positivist researcher may well decide to gather a small random sample, not with the goal of generalizing findings to a larger population but more with the intention of systematizing data. Patton (1990) describes an agency that would regularly report case histories to the legislature to illustrate the need for funding. They would report, say, 10 cases out of a client group of 300. To give the presentation more credibility, they systematized the selection of the cases, not to make generalizations about their clients but to reduce suspicion about biases when selecting cases for presentation.

14. *Sampling Politically Important Cases.* This is blatantly using the politics of the situation to decide on a sample. For example, if the chair of the legislative committee that funds homeless shelters sees a study of a shelter in his or her district, the issue may gain more attention.

15. *Convenience Sampling.* This is a common technique in qualitative sampling and the least desirable. It has no rationale and no clear function. As Patton (1990) says, "it is neither purposeful not strategic" (p. 181). Other strategies described here meet more rigorous standards and are as easy and inexpensive as this approach.

The underlying rationale for choosing any of these approaches to sampling will depend on the type of research, the purpose of the research, the questions being asked, and the resources available. Researchers may well use a combination of these sampling strategies in the same study depending on the concepts and theories that are emerging from the data. The size of sample will be driven by data collection. One rule is to stop when redundancy sets in. However, in truth there are no rules regarding sample size for post-positivist research. The sample can be one, a case study, or several hundred if resources and time allow. The quality of the sample is judged by whether it addresses the purpose of the research. In the study of homeless children in Chapter 7, the sample was all children housed in one particular temporary shelter over a nine-month period. This was a total of 30 children who lived in the shelter for various periods of time during the course of the study. This sample was a criterion-based sample since the focus of the study was to understand children's experience of homelessness in one shelter over a period of time.

To sum up this discussion of planning that develops rationales for gathering data, the post-positivist researcher needs to decide on the aim of the research, the unit of analysis, and the strategy(ies) for selecting the sample of participants. This is all driven by the original research focus and the intention of the researcher. Having developed this rationale, the researcher can begin implementation and gather the data.

Implementation: Data Gathering

Data gathering, for the post-positivist, includes interviews, observations of settings, and review of documents and social artifacts. Skilled questioning, active listening, focused observation, and disciplined reading will all facilitate the collection of valid data. There are various ways that researchers can organize their thinking to begin the data collection phase. Some use the core questions Why, What, How, When, and Where while others use foci such as meanings, practices, episodes, encounters, roles, and relationships. Or, they might use case study structures or ethnographic frameworks. As they begin data collection, though, they will also need to develop skills in recording, interpreting, summarizing, and synthesizing data. The following discussion of data gathering is organized in terms of the most frequently used procedures to gather qualitative data: interviews, observation, review of documents, and recording of social artifacts.

Interviews

Post-positivists approach interviews in a different way than the positivists, critical theorists, and constructivists who are discussed in other parts of this book. Unlike the positivists, they acknowledge the inevitability of the impact of their own values and biases on the interview and data collection in general. Unlike the critical theorists, they aim to minimize the impact of these values and biases on the interview. And, unlike the constructivists, they aim to uncover an objective reality in spite of the influence of these values and biases. The post-positivist is searching for regularities and patterns that will emerge from the data and be assembled into a theory. Thus the post-positivist interviewer is comfortable with preparing a structured set of questions before the interview, since this will ensure that all interviewees experience the same or similar interview and common patterns regarding similar research foci will be addressed. Ongoing data analysis may lead to changes in this interview schedule, but since the post-positivist has looked to previous knowledge in the form of readings and the opinions of experts to identify the topics and questions to be addressed at the beginning of the study, incremental rather than radical changes are anticipated.

The topics addressed in the interviews are not seen as variables to be identified, measured, and tested but rather foci to be explored, reexamined, perhaps redefined, and eventually connected with each other. Thus this interviewer uses strategies aimed at identifying patterns and regularities. Crabtree and Miller (1992) suggest three categories of questions that explore a person's understanding of a research focus and assist in the process of sorting data for later analysis. These are descriptive, structural, and contrast questions. *Descriptive* questions are overarching questions, such as "What is your day-to-day experience with homelessness?" "What do you do in a typical day spent in the shelter?" More focused descriptive questions might be "What things do you like about the shelter?" "How do you spend your weekends at the shelter?" "Who are your friends there and what do you do together?" "What is your vision for your future?" *Structured* questions expand understanding of a particular topic. They can be inclusion questions, verification questions, or substitution frame questions. Inclusion questions expand a particular topic, for example, "How has the shelter helped your family?" Verification questions assess a researcher's understanding of a topic, for example, "Since you live in the shelter, do you even see yourself as homeless?" Substitution frame questions remove a piece of information from a question and invite the respondent to replace the piece of information with his or her understanding or reaction, for example, "When I think of the future of these homeless children I feel ..."*Contrast* questions develop criteria for inclusion and exclusion for a category of knowledge. For example, the interviewer might ask, with reference to the shelter, "What is it about the shelter that makes you feel like you have a home and family?" "Is there anything about the shelter that makes you feel like you do not have a home and family?" These are "pile sorting" and "set sorting" questions where various topics are labeled as respondents report agreement on information that should be included in each topic. Topics are then grouped into sets and labeled as concepts. For example, children may repeatedly report that shelter life makes them feel like they are not homeless anymore but does make them feel deprived because they can't invite friends over to their house. This might be used to build a definition of a continuum of homelessness, ranging from being on the street to having a home, where being in a shelter is at a midpoint of that continuum. At this midpoint on the continuum, the shelter and basic food needs are met but developmental and social needs are not met. However, the "being on the street" point of the continuum is a point where none of these needs are met, and the point of the continuum where the family has its own home is a point where all of these needs are met. This continuum might then be combined with other continua, which

Table 8.2   Posible Synthesis of Interview Data

	Living on Street or in a Car	Living in Homeless Shelter	Living in Permanent Home
Basic Food and Shelter Needs Met	No	Yes	Yes
Developmental Needs of Children Met	No	Sometimes	Yes
Social Needs of Family Met	No	No	Yes
Level of Children's Self-Esteem	Low	Low-Medium	High
Level of Family Functioning	Dysfunctional	Stable but not yet Functional	Functional

address feelings of self-esteem at various stages of homelessness and family functioning at various stages of homelessness, to form a rough draft of the set of homelessness continua that will guide further thinking and question development (see Table 8.2). All of this synthesis of data is built from descriptive, structured, and contrast questions that are used throughout the interview process as appropriate.

As well as deciding on questions for the interview, the interviewer anticipates the various stages of an interview. Tutty et al. (1996) suggest the following steps in the interviewing process.

Preparing for the Interview

Preparing for the interview includes preparation for both the interviewer and the interviewee. Post-positivist interviewers prepare themselves by being knowledgeable about the topic and having a set of prepared questions. They also work on developing a consciousness of their own biases and values regarding the research topic and "controlling" the influence of these biases and values on the data gathering process. The earlier the habit of recognizing and controlling the influence of the interviewer's values and biases on the research project is begun, the more credibility the data and findings will have as post-positivist research. One place where this process takes place is in the research journal as the researcher records his or her thought processes and reasoning as the study is implemented. This journal writing also facilitates the reflection on, and stepping back from, the data so favored by Strauss and Corbin (1998).

When preparing the interviewee, the interviewer makes sure that he or she is properly oriented to the research study and this interview. The participant's informed consent is secured, ensuring privacy and confidentiality, ensuring that no harm will come to the interviewee, and answering any questions the interviewee might have. Formal Human Subjects approval for the study, as described above, will have included a sample informed consent letter. However, since qualitative interviewing for post-positivist research purposes involves a more intense engagement with the interviewee, phone calls and letters offering extra explanations about the study are important. The researcher's aim is to put the interviewee at ease so that reliable, valid, and comprehensive data is collected during the interview.

Choosing a Recording Mode

Having completed preparation tasks successfully, the post-positivist interviewer must now establish a method of making accurate records of data collected during the interview. Videotaping or sound recording would offer the most fidelity but may well, even with the miniaturized cameras and microphones we have today, make an interviewee uneasy. Taking notes during the interview may be distracting, and taking notes after the interview may result in the omission of important data that is simply forgotten or ignored. Every method has its strengths and drawbacks. The post-positivist is aiming to get the most accurate record of everything that is said during the interview and thus would favor a form of recording. However, note taking assists the researcher in processing and clarifying responses during the interview. Whatever the decision, it is important to negotiate the recording mode with the interviewee before, or at the start of, the interview and establish a comfort level during the interview that facilitates valid data gathering.

If recording or note taking during the interview is not an option, then a record of the interview must be developed immediately after the interview, and Neuman and Kreuger's (2003) advice on how to recall important information is useful:

- Make notes as soon as possible after the interview; a laptop computer or PDA with a keyboard would be the most efficient mode for doing this
- Make sure you have included identifying information: time, place, interviewee name, role, etc.

- Record the conversation in the order it happened; include everything that you can remember, even if it seems irrelevant right now
- Record your reactions and feelings at this point and any insights that come into your mind as you write
- Make diagrams, charts, or tables if they explain ideas
- Try not to evaluate what was said; simply record without commentary
- Make sure you have a backup copy of the record you develop

Conducting the Interview

Generally, like any conversation with another person, the interview is divided into phases that build comfort and familiarity. These are usually engagement, development of focus, maintaining focus, and termination. However, it would be useful to be aware of various individuals' reactions to these stages. Some people or cultures may not see the need for the engagement stage, given the informed consent process. Others may need a long period of engagement. And still others may be conscious of the gender and ethnicity of the researcher and need to take time to react to and process the prospect of being interviewed by a particular interviewer. Regardless of order of stages of the interview, or the interview questions, Berg (1995) notes that in order to obtain the most complete data from an interview, four types of questions to assist the interview process should be included:

Essential Questions. These are questions addressing the specific research topic; they can be grouped together or scattered throughout the interview. (What is it like to live in the shelter? What are your three wishes for the future? What would your dream home look like?)

Extra Questions. These are questions that are similar to essential questions but worded slightly differently to check on the consistency of responses to the same inquiry. (Do you enjoy living in the shelter? What do you think you will be doing in five years' time? Where would you like to live?)

Throw Away Questions. These may be demographic questions or general questions used at the beginning of the interview to establish rapport. They may also be scattered throughout the interview to assist a change in focus or to calm things down if a sensitive topic has been broached. Berg refers to this as "cooling out the subject" (Where were you born? Did you like it there? What do you remember about that place? What is you favorite food? Who is your best friend?)

Probing Questions. These are simply requests for elaboration, such as "Tell me about that," or minimal encouragers such as "uh-huh" or "I see." Again, these might be scattered throughout the interview depending on need for clarification and elaboration.

Berg (1995) describes the interview as a drama or a scene from a play where one person has a script and the other does not. He suggests that interviewers should be aware of their changing roles as actor, director, and choreographer. He also suggests that the more practice or "rehearsal" that you have, the better interviewer you become. In time, the interviewer starts to sense which role to play and how to sequence questions.

The interviewer signals the termination of the interview by offering a summary of his or her understanding of what has been said. This is a time to ask the interviewee for feedback on the interview and to address any concerns that might be voiced. It has been an intense "conversation," and it is important to ease out of the interview in the same way that it was eased into. It is a good idea to gradually reduce the intensity of questions and include nonthreatening throwaway comments as the exchange ends. The interviewee should know how to contact the interviewer if he or she has further questions. The likely use of the data should be clarified as well as the source of information about the findings of the study.

Reflecting About the Interview

After the interview it is important to take time to write in the research journal about reactions, both thoughts and feelings, to the experience. The researcher should decide whether the data gathered was important or irrelevant to the study. This is the time to evaluate the interview; what worked and what did not work? Was there a functional balance between types of questions? How did interviewer values and biases affect the interview, and how were these values and biases challenged by the interview? What can be improved next time?

To summarize guidance for interviewing, the checklist below combines Berg's (1995, p. 57) ten commandments of interviewing with other important reminders to give you guidance on carrying out your post-positivist interview.

1. Never begin an interview cold; make sure there is an initial engagement phase. In addition to gaining formal consent, continually strive to keep the person you are interviewing engaged and interested in the interview.

2. Remember your purpose; don't get distracted by something the interviewee is excited about that has nothing to do with the study. Make a decision about whether a tangent in the interview conversation is an important addition to the development of your theory or a completely different topic.

3. Present a natural front. Jean Giraudoux (1882–1944) said, "The secret of success is sincerity. Once you can fake that you've got it made." You need

not be this cynical, but you do need to put your interviewee at ease by being relaxed and informal.

4. Demonstrate aware hearing. Use nonverbal cues or minimal encouragers such as "I see" or "Is that right?" to communicate that you have heard what has been said and are interested in hearing more. Reflect back what you have heard and check that you have understood correctly.

5. Think about your appearance. What is the appropriate dress in this setting and how will the interviewee react to how you look? Think about the range of possibilities from formal to informal clothing and find out what is appropriate and acceptable.

6. Interview in a comfortable place. Where is the interviewee most relaxed, in your office or at a coffee shop? Find out.

7. Don't be satisfied with monosyllabic answers. Prompt for reflection from your interviewee. You have put a lot of work into organizing this interview; make sure you actually gather quality data.

8. Be respectful. Make sure you are polite and show appreciation for the time and effort the interviewee is putting into your project.

9. Practice, practice, and practice some more. Remember, you have the script; make sure you know it and deliver your lines well.

10. Be cordial and appreciative (see 8 above). This person is doing you a favor; let him or her know you appreciate it.

11. Make sure you prepare well for the interview and follow the stages of the interview identified above.

Observations

Although the usual source of information for a post-positivist researcher is the interview, this has its limitations. The interview data gives a report of the interviewee's perceptions and knowledge but it is a secondhand report, filtered by the interviewee, of the context and activities associated with the interviewee. Since accurate collection of data on an objective reality is the goal, the post-positivist may also need to make his or her own observations at the site of the research project and directly observe the context and activities at the study site. The ethics of some approaches to observation have been questioned and these are addressed in more detail in the critical theory section of the book. However, for the post-positivist, the opportunity to observe objective data is a powerful motivation to proceed with this approach to data gathering.

The discipline with the most experience of direct observation of human phenomena is anthropology, and generally anthropologists refer to the practice of such observation as "ethnography." Wolcott (1973) defines ethnography as "the science of cultural description." Berg (1995) notes that it "places researchers in the midst of whatever it is they study" and suggests that a new ethnography has emerged in the last 20 years that has "highly formal techniques designed to extract cognitive data" (pp. 86–87). Like interviewing, ethnography has stages.

Accessing a Field Setting: "Getting In"

Like the interview, the beginning of observation has an engagement phase. The observer needs to remember that this is an imposition on people and an intrusion into their daily lives; appreciation and thanks should be offered. The researcher's personal motivations need to be faced as well. Is there some personal agenda for choosing to observe this situation? Is there some theoretical reason that makes this observation necessary or is it simply convenient? The purpose of the observation should be thought through. Since the post-positivist does not want to influence the situation being observed, he or she must find ways to "become invisible." Berg (1995) offers six insightful strategies for doing this:

a. Dis-attending by becoming invisible, or just being present in the setting over a long period of time so that eventually people do not pay any unusual attention to you
b. Dis-attending by making no symbolic attachments to activities being observed
c. Dis-attending by making symbolic attachments so that after initially being noticed as a new member of the group, the observer becomes less important
d. Dis-attending by personalizing the ethnographer-informant relationship so that people simply just like having the observer around as a friend and colleague
e. Dis-attending by masking the real research interest; thus, the ethnographer pretends to be studying one thing but is actually studying another thing
f. Dis-attending by not revealing the ethnographer as a researcher and pretending to be simply a new member of the group

The last two options, of course, would need to be thoroughly justified to a human subjects committee so that no harm follows such deception and debriefing is carried out. In addition, the impact of any deception being identified and bringing harm to the researcher would need to be evaluated.

Watching, Listening, and Learning

Having entered the observation site, the researcher can begin to gather data. While in the observer or ethnographer role, the researcher must be a disciplined onlooker. This discipline includes:

- Taking in the physical setting, which includes mapping it out, deciding on the most significant places in the setting for the research focus, and developing a planned timetable for observing various areas
- Developing relationships with inhabitants of the setting, which includes casual conversations as well as conversations that may later be revisited for interview purposes
- Tracking people, which includes observing individuals in a planned way for reasons associated with the purpose of the study, and eavesdropping
- Locating subgroups and key players, which includes noting the opinion leaders, the organizational leaders, and subgroups formed around both informal and formal issues and activities

Throughout this process, record key words and phrases while in the field, make notes about the sequence of events being observed, limit the time in the setting so that only short periods of time need to be recalled for note taking, write the notes immediately after leaving the field, and write the notes before discussing observations and conclusions with others.

Disengaging: "Getting Out"

Like approaching the end of an interview, ethnographers must plan the process of terminating the observation period. This can be done by negotiating time lines at the beginning of the study but will still need the researcher's personal attention at the end of the study. People have been observed and are aware of the researcher; they will react negatively if the researcher just stops "turning up." Both you and they will regret that. It is important to talk to people about the study coming to an end or, if you have disguised your observer role, about your reasons for leaving. Both participants and the researcher must be prepared for an ending and exit.

Handling Documents: Historical Research

A third source of data for post-positivist researchers is documents and social artifacts such as symbols or rituals that are talked about or observed in the research setting. These sources are recorded and analyzed like any other data. They are reviewed and then synthesized through codes and connections that build theory. However, for the post-positivist there is a warning here. Documents are constructions of events. Indeed, historical research is the research of those constructions, rather than the research of historical facts. There is a difference between historical data, such as the Declaration of Independence and the Magna Carta, and historical facts, such as the dates of these documents. Thus documents such as reports or mission and goal statements are not really appropriate for post-positivist research because they are data on subjective understandings of an event or entity. They may enrich a concept or theory, but as subjective constructions, for the post-positivist, they are a weak source of data. They are not a record of an objective reality and its regulatory mechanisms. Before using these documents, the post-positivist needs to think about what they represent and how "accurate" the data are for an objective post-positivist scientist. Having chosen to use a document as a data source, the post-positivist uses the analysis techniques discussed below to identify its concepts and theories.

In this discussion of data gathering we have reviewed the three main data gathering strategies for post-positivist researchers: interviews, observations, and review of documents. Each has its own process and requirements, and each offers an opportunity to gather data that builds the research project's theory.

Evaluation: Developing an Understanding of the Data and Its Meaning

For the post-positivist researcher, data collection and data analysis are interwoven. This researcher does not identify measurable variables, gather data on those variables, and then analyze the data at the end of the data collection phase. Rather, this researcher gathers data in an interview, from an observation, or from a document and immediately analyzes that data. The results of this analysis then inform the next round of data gathering. Thus although analysis procedures that allow us to understand the meaning of the data are discussed here under a separate heading, they are, in fact, an integral part of the data gathering procedures described above. This discussion of methods for interpreting the meaning of qualitative data describes two approaches. The first is a "top down" approach in which the same analysis framework is applied to all qualitative data. It is rooted in linguistics and ethnography. This approach to analysis should be used when the researcher is looking for patterns or describing processes. The second is a "bottom up" approach to qualitative analysis, in which the framework emerges from the data. This approach is rooted in sociology. It should be used when the researcher is interested in developing theories about a particular topic.

"Top-Down" Approach to Interpreting Data

The precise analysis and interpretation of meaning in language is rooted in linguistics and ethnography. Brown and Yule (1991), when discussing coherence in interpretation of discourse, note that linguists understand the meaning of language by analyzing sentences, identifying the format in which information is being conveyed, and using sociocultural knowledge to make assumptions about what the speaker or writer is intending to say. We do this by

1. Computing the communicative function. What is both the social and literal meaning of the communication? What is being said and how is the person behaving? Sinclair and Coulthard (1975) identified five categories of discourse: lesson, transaction, exchange, move, act. Sachs, Schegloff, and Jefferson (1974) suggested that a better way to compute the communication function is to analyze "turn-taking" in conversations. Examples of forms of turn-taking include greeting-greeting (First person says, "Hi, how are you?" Second person answers, "Fine, how about you?") and interrogative (First person says, "Did you schedule another appointment for next week?" Second person answers, "Yes, it's on Tuesday at 10:00 a.m.") Austin's (1962) theory of speech acts is another form of computation. The speech itself is an explicit or implicit act, such as asserting, congratulating, apologizing, and so on. All of these approaches give us some guidelines for understanding language. Although they lead us to categorization systems that sometimes appear to be arbitrary, they do give us a framework for our analysis of the interview or observation data.

2. Using general sociocultural knowledge. What is the previously learned knowledge of context that is being used to predict what the next sentence will be and where the conversation is going? We do this using frames, scripts, scenarios, schemata, and mental models. Frames are simply preconceived understandings of a new situation (we have an appointment with a client); scripts are sequences of activities that we associate with particular situations (we have procedures that we follow when intervening with a client); scenarios are the components we anticipate for any new situation that has been given a label that we understand (we have an understanding of who and what should be present during the intervention); schemata are higher-level knowledge that helps us understand a situation (our knowledge of theory and practice with this client); mental models are logical sequences of thought that explain a situation (the client cannot sleep and has a flat affect and is therefore depressed and we have decided to intervene with strategies that address cognition).

There is some overlap between these terms but, again, they do give us a perspective from which to analyze our data.

3. Determining the inferences being made. How do we find the missing link, either automatically or with a conscious thought process, that allows us to make an explicit link between statements? Automatic links would be made when, for example, a client who is depressed enters the room, sits down, and begins to cry. We automatically interpret the crying as part of the depression. Conscious links are made when we step back from a situation and ask ourselves the questions "Who is involved?" "What is involved?" "Where is this happening?" "When is this happening?" We ask ourselves further questions to elaborate and evaluate the situation. "How is this happening?" "Why is this happening?" Again, these ideas give us guidelines for interpreting our data.

Coulthard (1985), in his discussion of the ethnography of speaking, notes that ethnographers for all speech events need to provide data on

1. The structure of the speech event (letter, song, hymn, poem, interview, conversation, meeting).

2. The setting of the speech event, both physical and psychological. That is, a description of the physical surroundings in which the event is taking place and the cultural meaning of the setting.

3. Participants in the speech event, who can include
   a. Addresser or Speaker
   b. Addressee
   c. Hearer or Audience

4. The purpose of the speech event from the point of view of each participant

5. The "key" or the tone or spirit of the speech event as demonstrated by both verbal and nonverbal cues

6. The channels of communication used in the speech event, which can be oral or written

7. The message content giving all topics being addressed

8. The message form, which can be informal or formal

9. The rule breaking being demonstrated in the speech event, where a statement of norms is given and an indication of whether and when any norms are being broken

10. The norms of interaction for the speech event, which includes how much silence is tolerated, the physical distance between people, the gender roles, and the norms for turn taking in any conversation

By combining the above ideas, we can identify a framework for analyzing qualitative data using a consistent approach across all data sets where the framework is used as a template to understand any source of data, whether it be an interview, observation, or document.

Thus if we are analyzing a narrative we can develop an analysis that gives us both an understanding of the meaning of the narrative and suggests further direction for data gathering. Below is an excerpt from a student study of interventions with abusive men in which a probation officer is talking about the process for taking domestic violence cases to court. A top-down analysis of the narrative is shown in Table 8.4.

The process goes as follows: the district attorney reviews the case from the police department, they must then decide if they even have a case. Sometimes there is not enough evidence, or maybe she hit him with a baseball bat before he hit her, or maybe the police officer wrote a lousy report; if the D.A. cannot make a case they send the file over to the person that handles the pre-filing diversions. The person there writes a letter saying "if you go to anger management, the case will be dropped." It's kind of a sucker approach because the D.A. isn't going to try to prosecute anyway. The rates of those who complete the classes as a result of this approach are low. These are called pre-filing diversions. It's frustrating because some of the cases sent for pre-filing are legitimate cases that should be taken to court. If the case is filed and goes to court, they can still be considered for the diversion program if they meet certain criteria. These are: they have no conviction for any offense involving violence within ten years, their record does not indicate that probation or parole have ever been revoked, they have not been diverted pursuant to this chapter within ten years, and they haven't assaulted anyone with a deadly weapon. If they are diverted, I get their probation case and they have to go to 52 weeks of anger management classes. The deal here is that I have the leverage of the court, which is crucial, because if he doesn't go to anger diversion, the threat is that criminal proceedings will be reinstated. Let's say he doesn't fit into one of these categories, the case may be tried and he may go to jail. I'm afraid those cases are few and far between. (Walters, 1995, p. 45)

This framework for analysis of qualitative data gives us a set of dimensions that can be used to understand any piece of qualitative data, whether it is an interview narrative, an account of an observation, or a document. The specific analysis in Table 8.4 shows how the framework clarifies the meaning of what we have (a system that does not work effectively from the probation officer's point of view) and what we need (specific data that will show whether this perspective is correct and how others are experiencing the process). It shows us what we have and what we need in future rounds of interviews or observations. It gives us common dimensions that we can

Table 8.3   Framework for Data Analysis Using a "Top Down" Approach to Analysis

Dimensions	Interview	Observation	Document

Setting
  Physical
  Psychological
  Cultural/Social			

Participants
  Addresser
  Addressee
  Audience			

Purpose of
  Addresser
  Addressee
  Audience			

Key (tone)
  Verbal
  Nonverbal			

Channels of Communication
  Oral
  Written
  Other			

Message Content Topics (list)			

Message Form
  Formal
  Informal			

Norms of Behavior Rule Breaking			

Norms of Interaction
  Turn Taking Rules
  Category of Discourse			

Communication Function
  Literal
  Social			

Relevant Sociocultural Knowledge Being Used
  Frames
  Scripts
  Scenarios
  Schemata
  Mental Models			

Inferences
  Automatic
  Constructed Consciously (Who? What?
  Where? When? How? Why?)			

Table 8.4   Analysis of Excerpt from Text of Probation Officer Interview

Dimensions	Interview Narrative
Setting Physical	Courts, anger management settings, probation officer's office
Psychological	Abuser's denying guilt, court officials feeling inadequate, unable to prosecute or enforce law
Cultural/Social	Notion that although abuse is illegal and prohibited, there will be no punishment for this offence since it is not serious enough *Need more data on settings for the abusive male and probation officer, perhaps through observation*
Participants Addresser	District Attorney, Diversion Officer, Anger Management Trainer, Probation Officer
Addressee	Abusive Male
Audience	Victims of crime *Need more data on audience*
Purpose of Addresser	To punish male abusers
Addressee	To avoid being punished
Audience	To see that punishment happens? *Need more data on times when the victims do not want to see abuser punished*
Key (Tone) Verbal	There is an attempt to be firm with the abuser and suggest that punishment will happen, but there is also a kind of tired cynicism, a regret that more is not done
Nonverbal	*Need data on this, perhaps observation of exchanges between participants*
Channels of Communication Oral	All participants have written and oral communication
Written Other	*Need more detailed data on this, specific modes of communications between specific participants*

(Continued)

Table 8.4 (Continued)

Dimensions	Interview Narrative
Message Content Topics	Process for taking domestic violence cases to court 1. DA decides if they have a case, usually no case 2. Diversion officer threatens legal action if noncompliance with anger management 3. Labels diversion as "sucker approach" 4. Completion rate low 5. Process and criteria for diversion after pre-filing 6. Probation's role in diversion 7. Requirement for anger management 8. Comment on rarity of jail time for offenders
Message Form Formal Informal	There are various formal messages between court and probation officials and the male abuser. There is the formal requirement for completion of anger management and the informal knowledge that the threats of punishment cannot be carried out.
Norms of Behavior Rule Breaking	The official social norm is that all these men have broken the law and that abuse of women is wrong. There is the unofficial norm that not much is done in terms of punishment and the crime is not taken very seriously. This suggests that the norm is in fact only theoretical and not real. *Need more data on whether anyone ever breaks these norms and insists on prosecution and punishment*
Norms of Interaction Turn Taking	*Need data on how abuser interacts with other participants, perhaps direct observation or written accounts of interviews*
Communication Function Literal Social	Communication between participants will involve legal mandates and required responses The social function of these communications is to deter male abusers from continuing to abuse; however, it appears that such a deterrent does not exist *Need more data on repeat offenders*

Dimensions	Interview Narrative
Relevant Sociocultural Knowledge Being Used	
Frames	The probation officer is describing a sequence of activities that leads to minimal jail time or prosecution
Scripts	A sequence of actions is described regarding the processing of male abusers
Scenarios	There is an official expectation that punishment will be carried out, people have roles, the offender moves through the stages without experiencing too much punishment
Schemata	Participants have a knowledge of the legal mandates and procedures and the anger management treatment
Mental Models	The overall assumption is that male abusers are committing a crime and are punished. Pragmatic descriptions tell us that this is not happening *Need more data on the abusers' sociocultural knowledge of this process*
Inferences Automatic Constructed Consciously (Who? What? Where? When? How? Why?)	The automatic inference is that this process is not working and needs to be addressed. The constructed inference is that we need to know more about the participants, the constraints on the legal professionals, where and when the system breaks down, how it breaks down, and why. *Need more data on each to the topics in message content*

use for analysis for all our data, and it gives us a structure for describing the meaning of our data.

"Bottom-Up" Approach to Interpreting Data

A second, "bottom-up" approach to analyzing qualitative data is a much more inductive, open-ended approach and is rooted in sociology. Glaser and Strauss (1967), in their book *Discovery of Grounded Theory: Strategies for Qualitative Research,* talk about a need to generate theory from empirical data. They suggest that research can be used to both test theory and create theory, and they offer approaches to theory creation. Strauss and Corbin (1990) later offer guidelines on the art of interpreting qualitative data when carrying out such theory creation. They suggest that various stages of synthesis should be applied with increasing complexity. Thus a narrative text is transformed from a series of words to a theoretical statement about regularities in nature. These stages of synthesis are described in a sequential fashion, but in reality the researcher moves back and forth between them as the theory develops. They begin with *open coding*. Here the narrative of the interview or observation is broken down into themes or categories. Such categories guide refinement of future questioning and observation. At the next stage, *axial coding*, relationships between themes or categories are proposed; these relationships are tested in further rounds of data gathering. The third stage, *selective coding*, is when a theoretical statement is developed. The conditions of the relationships between categories and themes are identified and included in a comprehensive statement. The last stage is the *conditional matrix*, where the theoretical statement is put in the context of current knowledge about human interaction. In a study of gang life, for example, a theoretical statement might have been developed linking "joining rituals" to acculturation for young people from immigrant families. This might then be included in the theoretical knowledge on acculturation for individuals, families, and communities. This might also be added to social work practice knowledge on interventions with gang members.

Strauss and Corbin (1998) talk about this analysis process as sampling data. The researcher decides upon a type, purpose, and question for research and then chooses a research site. The researcher then immerses himself or herself in the research focus at the site through interviews, observations, and review of documents so that emerging concepts can be identified and sampled from the data being gathered. Sampling for these authors is sampling of concepts to identify regularities that lead to theoretical statements. Sampling the correct group of people is not the major design issue for these authors; it is the sampling of observations, interviews, artifacts, and documents to explore emerging concepts and categories that is important when deciding whom to include in the study. In our example study of homeless children, discussed above, researchers using this approach would identify a shelter or larger community and seek out key players who have something to say about homeless children. These key players would be interviewed and the resultant data analyzed. The selection of further study participants would then continue, guided by all stages of the grounded theory analysis procedures. During open coding an inclusive process of gathering data from several key players, so that all relevant concepts are identified, would be carried out. Then, during axial coding, where relationships between categories or concepts are being identified and articulated, the relationships that are emerging from the data would dictate further data gathering. The same is true at the stage of selective coding where the core theme is being identified. When the conditional matrix is being built, it is assumed that data collection is mostly completed, since this is an overall reflective statement about where the newly created theory fits in the grand scheme of things.

Open Coding

In the early stages of analysis, grounded theory researchers carry out micro-analysis. This initial process is used to develop a routine practice of analyzing data with a frame of mind that is open to all potential interpretations. The researcher may scan a narrative of an interview, for example, and pick an interesting segment. Then that segment is analyzed in detail. To do the analysis, the researcher takes chunks of the narrative that seem to hang together. This could be a word, a line, a sentence, or a paragraph. For example, the researcher may find a statement such as,

I'm glad we came here, cause before I was running the streets with hoods and going nowhere in life but now that I'm here, the rules are too strict and you can't go to the mall or 7–11 without your parents being with you. (Young & Creacy, 1995, p. 21)

This might be divided up into chunks such as,

- I'm glad we came here
- before I was running the streets with hoods
- and going nowhere in life
- now that I'm here,
- the rules are too strict
- you can't go to the mall or 7–11
- without your parents being with you

The researcher then uses analytical tools to develop concepts, their dimensions, and their links with other concepts. Analytical tools include asking sensitizing, theoretical, practical, and guiding questions about the chunks of data and making theoretical comparisons. Possible questions include Who? When? Why? Where? What? How? How much? With what results? Questions about the above data might include:

- Where on the range of feelings does glad come?
- What are the range of places they have come to?

- How did they develop their assumptions about the direction of life?
- What rules do they mean?
- What range of rules have they experienced and what is their effect?
- What range of independent activities are they aware of?
- How do they understand parents' authority and its consequences?

Such questions and their answers identify concepts and theories as well as directions for further sampling and data gathering.

Techniques for making theoretical comparisons include the "flip flop technique," "systematic comparison," and "waving the red flag." They make the researcher confront his or her values and assumptions about the data and reassess any interpretations that might be taken for granted. In relation to the above data we might ask,

- What happens to children who have feelings of unhappiness at being in a shelter?
- How do these statements compare to those of any teenager who is not homeless?
- How does the homeless adult react to being in a shelter?
- Is this appropriate developmentally for children at this age?
- Is there a situation where children would be better off homeless than in a shelter?

Usually, there is not enough time for all narratives to be analyzed in this detailed fashion. However, microanalysis should be done extensively with initial data and then later when new themes are emerging or something that is puzzling has been noticed.

Having used microanalysis tools to review and interpret the data, the researcher can proceed with sampling appropriate study participants and gathering data to facilitate open coding, which is the process of identifying the social phenomenon's concepts, categories of concepts, the properties of concepts, and the dimensions of those properties. (See Figure 8.1.)

In Figure 8.1, after microanalysis of the narratives, the concepts of fear, lack of hope, loss of job, and lack of food have emerged, and the patterns in the narratives suggest that these concepts be grouped into the category of loss of shelter. One dimension of loss of shelter has been identified, "type of shelter," and it ranges from none when the family is living on the street, to living in a car, to living in a shelter. To develop this analysis, the researcher would have taken a piece of text or a transcript of an interview and, using microanalysis techniques, reviewed its possible meanings. Writing memos in the research journal to explain the reasoning, the researcher would have concluded that the four identified concepts are depicted in the text and that they

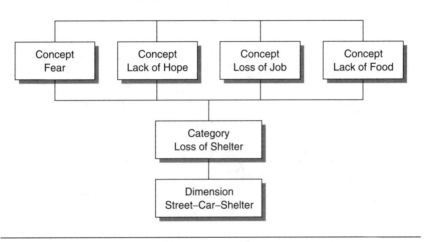

Figure 8.1   Example of Open Coding

can be grouped into a category of loss of shelter. This gives us our dimension of loss of shelter. It is the literal type of shelter and it ranges from no shelter and living on the street, to living in a car, to living in a temporary homeless shelter. This process of open coding is repeated with other data so that a number of categories are identified that are included in the social phenomenon of homelessness. Study participants continue to be sampled according to their knowledge and connection with the open codes that are emerging. The next step is to identify the connections between these open codes or categories, and Strauss and Corbin (1998) refer to this as axial coding.

Axial Coding

Axial coding is a procedure for linking the emergent categories and making statements about the relationship between categories and their dimensions. Moving forward with our example, as well as a category of homelessness we may also have a category of "children's hope for the future" that has the dimension range of "hopelessness—a wish for a toy—a wish for a friend—a wish for a community of family and friends—an optimistic vision for the child's future life." When this is linked to the dimension of the lack of shelter category, we have the relationship illustrated in Figure 8.2.

In Figure 8.2, four quadrants of possible experiences have been identified for homeless children.

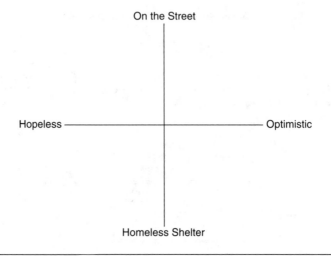

Figure 8.2   Example of Axial Coding

- No Shelter/Hopeless (The child would have nowhere to go and no wish for even a toy)
- No Shelter/Optimistic (The child would have nowhere to go but still had hopes for a toy, a friend, and a community of family and friends)
- Homeless Shelter/Hopeless (Although he or she had shelter, the child still did not have wishes for anything)
- Homeless Shelter/Optimistic (The child had shelter and wishes and dreams for the future)

Such dimensions having emerged from narratives would lead to a collection of more focused data on the characteristics of children falling into each of the four quadrants and why and how they reach those particular quadrants of homelessness.

Selective Coding

Selective coding is the process of integrating and refining the categories and their dimensions to develop theory. According to Strauss and Corbin (1998) this process (1) is not based on romantic inspiration but is based on work; (2) is created, not a solution to a puzzle; (3) will not include everything there is to know about a topic in one version of the theory; and (4) will be brought together differently by different projects. The first step is to identify the core category. This is the unifying theme that emerges from the data and the open and axial coding process. Strauss and Corbin identify the following criteria for a core category:

1. All the categories identified in open and axial coding can be related to it.

2. It is a repeated pattern in the data.

3. It allows the categories to be related in a logical and consistent manner without "forcing" the data.

4. It is sufficiently abstract to be a term that could be used in research in other arenas.

5. It has explanatory power.

6. It explains the main pattern in the data and variations of that pattern. (p. 147)

Strategies for developing the theory by identifying the core category and articulating its integration of categories include:

1. Telling the story by just spontaneously writing a few phrases that explain the findings. The researcher can just give himself or herself the freedom to take a blank piece of paper and write down what comes to mind when summing up the data and its meaning.

2. Using diagrams to explain emergent connections between categories. If summing up findings in words is becoming a struggle, then perhaps drawing diagrams to illustrate major directions of the data analysis will come more easily.

3. Reviewing the research journal for patterns of reaction and decision-making.

4. Exploring patterns identified by a qualitative analysis computer program. These days there are a number of computer programs that can analyze languages and speed up qualitative data analysis. There is detailed discussion of the use of computers for qualitative analysis in Part V of this book.

We now need to refine the theory that has emerged so far. We can do this by using the following strategies:

1. Identifying the properties of the core categories and filling in any dimensions that might be missing. In our example study of homeless children, we may need more dimensions of hopelessness to fully describe the quadrants we have identified.

2. Both filling in poorly developed categories and eliminating categories that now are irrelevant. In our study, the older children were resistant to talking

about hopes and wishes for the future, and it might have been possible, with more of this age group in the study, to develop a more sophisticated category of hopelessness/optimism that was age appropriate.

3. Validating the emerging theory by comparing it with cases in the raw data. In our study there were 30 children; if the study had been on a larger scale with more resources, we could have included other shelters in the study and substantiated it as we studied children from these other shelters.

4. Building explanations for cases that do not fit the data. In our study, we would need to offer explanations for children who were optimistic while living on the street or hopeless while living in the shelter.

5. Building in variations. In our study, with additional resources, we could have looked at families that had been re-housed and moved on from the shelter to develop a broader dimension of the children's hopelessness/optimism.

When building theory the post-positivists not only develop concepts, categories, and their linking statements, but they also describe the process that goes along with development of these statements. An analyzing process, according to Strauss and Corbin (1998), is "purposefully looking at action/ interaction and noting movement, sequence, and change as well as how it evolves (changes or remains the same) in response to changes in context or conditions" (p. 167). To identify the process, the analysis asks the following questions:

1. What is going on here? How does a child move from one stage to another and when? In our study, the process of being in group sessions at the shelter assisted development of self-esteem and optimism.

2. What problems, issues, or happenings are being handled through action/interaction, and what form does it take? Who is involved in the children's transitions to various stages of hopelessness/optimism and what roles do they play? In our study, parents, shelter staff, social work students, and other children all were brought together to promote self-esteem in the shelter's children.

3. What conditions combine to create the context in which the action/interaction is located? Where does the child experience hopelessness/optimism—at school, with friends? In our study, this varied with the age of the child. The older teenage children tended to be pessimistic in all observed settings while the younger children were more open to expressing optimism in the group setting.

4. Why is the action/interaction staying the same? Are the children "stuck" at one stage, and why? Again, in our study, the teenage children did seem stuck at a pessimistic stage, but other arenas of their lives were not directly observed.

5. Why and how is it changing? Are the children changing, and why? In our study, this was related to the opportunity for shelter and the group sessions offered to the children in the shelter.

6. Are actions/interactions aligned or misaligned? Is it appropriate that the teacher, friend, stranger, plays the role he or she is playing in promoting or obstructing the child's hopelessness/optimism? In our study, it appeared that the school personnel were not able to play a stronger role in promoting optimism, since they did not always know the background of the shelter children.

7. What conditions or activities connect one sequence of events to another? Can we identify the usual process of moving from hopelessness to optimism, or optimism to hopelessness? In our study, this process was identified for young children as linked to the shelter and the prospect of a home and a "normal" life where friends can be invited home to play. For the teenage children, the process was unclear, even after nine months of study.

8. What happens to the form, flow, continuity, and rhythm of action/interaction when conditions, or the usual patterns, change? Can we identify breaks in this usual process of moving from hopelessness to optimism, or optimism to hopelessness? Again, in our example study, the process of moving to optimism is speeded up by self-esteem-focused group interventions in the temporary shelter.

9. How is action/interaction taken in response to problems or contingencies similar to, or different from, action/interaction that is routine? How do we intervene with the children's process of moving through this dimension? What seems to be working? Again, we seemed to know how to work with younger children through art work and creative songwriting, but the older children made individual choices about whether they would be part of this. Their process was dictated by their own decisions rather than automatic acceptance of a program offered by a homeless shelter.

10. How do the consequences of one set of actions/interactions play into the next sequence of action/interactions to either alter the actions/interactions or allow them to stay the same? Can we build a more complete picture of the process combining events, players, and interventions? This leads us to the full statement of the theory that is discussed below.

The Conditional/Consequential Matrix

The answers to the above questions assist us in the final stage of analysis where we make a statement about how the newly developed theory fits into its societal context. Strauss and Corbin (1998) adopt social work practice's notion of micro and macro levels of human interaction. The conditional matrix prompts the researcher to state where the theory fits in micro and macro levels of interaction. The researcher traces events identified in the process analysis through their spiral of impact on individuals, families, groups, organizations, and communities at the local, national, and international levels. The matrix reminds researchers to link their findings to the human experiences and is particularly useful to social work researchers because it reminds us to consider not only human interaction, but also practice interventions at the various levels of human interaction. In our example it could look something like this:

Homeless Children

- **Individual level:** Homeless children in our study experience a transition from a feeling of hopelessness to a feeling of optimism as they move from the homeless state to a temporary shelter. Younger children's feelings move more easily along this continuum than those of older teenage children. For the younger children, the movement to a more optimistic frame of mind is facilitated and speeded up by the provision of group sessions encouraging artistic expression of hopes and dreams for the future. For the older children, a personal choice has to be made to engage in such activities, and some will choose not to be part of such programs.
- **Family level:** In this study, single-parent families were the study sample. Children did express the wish for a "normal" family in a "normal" home, but the single-parent nature of the family did not seem to be a factor in developing optimism. The children accepted their family situations as a given and tended to blame problems on their homeless status rather than family issues. The fact that the family could be housed together in the shelter helped the process of building children's self-esteem.
- **Group level:** The homeless children, as a group, tended to take care of each other and "watch out" for each other no matter what the age. The younger children were more adaptable and able to find hope while living in the shelter. The older children missed not being able to bring other teenagers home. They also were more embarrassed about being homeless.
- **Organization level:** The organizations affecting these children were the shelter and their schools. The researchers did not have access to the school setting. A larger scale study in the future could explore this aspect of homeless children's lives.
- **Community level:** At the local level, obviously the presence of homeless children is something that is addressed by shelters such as the one selected for the example study. It was clear that more shelters are needed in the local community, but in addition, more child-centered programs need to be developed in the shelters. At the national level, the phenomenon of homeless children clearly threatens the development of human potential and enrichment of life while making the nation vulnerable to the threats associated with having a class of

alienated youth with low self-esteem. At the international level, the phenomenon of homeless children brings us into the arena of accepting responsibility for developing countries and the newer notion of links to terrorism, where children with no hope see violence against their perceived enemy and martyrdom as the most optimistic vision for their future.

In this discussion of evaluation or interpreting the meaning of the data, two approaches to analysis have been described: a top-down approach and a bottom-up approach. The approach you choose depends on the questions you are interested in. If you want to understand how a process works in general and whether it relates to interventions at the micro or macro level, you probably should use the top-down approach. However, if you simply have an exploratory question about "what is happening here," you will probably find the bottom-up approach more useful.

To sum up this section, there are various strategies for data collection and evaluation of data. They do not lead to a recipe for the one correct way to carry out a post-positivist study. The key issue for the post-positivist researcher is the question to be explored. Once this is clarified then the appropriate strategies can be adopted with a clear rationale for those choices being recorded in the research journal. This is how research is done in the flexible, changing, naturalistic setting understood through words. To assist in making these decisions, a set of questions is offered below to guide planning. They are adapted from Patton (1990, p. 197). When deciding on your plan, ask yourself,

1. What is my research focus and question?

2. Is this research basic, applied, a summative evaluation, or a formative evaluation?

3. What is the unit of analysis: individuals, families, groups, organizations, communities, or all of the above?

4. What kind(s) of purposeful sampling will be used, and why?

5. What types of data will be collected and analyzed (interviews, observations, documents, social artifacts), and why?

6. How will you ensure validity of findings (the rigor of data collection procedures and analysis procedures)?

7. Which analysis procedure will you use, top down or bottom up? Why?

8. What are the time lines for the study?

9. How will the practical and logistical tasks be carried out (access to research site and data, gathering of resources needed)?

10. How will you address ethical issues?

11. How will you address issues of diversity (discussed in Part V of this book)?

Main Points

- Post-positivist research can be basic, applied, a formative evaluation, or a summative evaluation
- The unit of analysis needs to be clear: individuals, families, groups, organizations, or communities
- Various strategies for purposive sampling are available; the choice of strategy depends on the study question and purpose
- Data can be gathered by means of interviews, observations, or review of documents
- Always keep two research journals when gathering data; one includes the data and the other includes rationales for data gathering and analysis decisions
- Both interviews and observations are carried out in stages from beginning to ending the data gathering process
- There are two possible procedures for evaluating the data and understanding its meaning. One is a top-down approach using a common framework and the other is a bottom-up approach where theory emerges from the data.

Learning Assignments

1. Think of a social work practice research issue that you are interested in. Formulate a post-positivist question about that issue. Decide whether your research question is basic, applied, or an evaluation. Identify

- your unit of analysis
- your sampling strategy
- your method of collecting data

2. Start keeping two journals on your research education. In one journal summarize what you are learning about research each week. In the second journal, write down your reactions to what you are learning. What are you enjoying? Which parts are difficult? How are your reactions changing as time goes by and you learn more?

3. In group discussion, share the insights from your journals and find out about other students' insights.

9

Termination and Follow Up—Reporting on Findings and Exiting the Research Setting and Communication and Distribution of Findings

S o now we are almost at the end of the post-positivist study. We have gathered data and we have evaluated its meaning. How do we communicate these findings in an interesting and informative manner, and to whom? In his paper on writing up qualitative research, Wolcott (1990) offers some entertaining, playful, and very useful strategies for getting started on writing as well as making writing a personal habit. He begins by offering some tips for getting started. This process of convincing yourself to get to work might commence with a ritual of having to do other "essential" tasks before sitting down at the desk. These might include washing the kitchen floor; vacuuming the house throughout; or, in one of a colleague's times of resistance, making your own granola from scratch. This ritual of avoidance needs to be recognized, embraced, and compressed as far as possible. With so many games on the computer and your e-mail to pick up, you could get yourself to your computer quickly by intending to have some fun and communicate with friends. You could put out some snacks on your desk. Once there, though, bring up the blank page and start typing some words. However you do it, recognize your human frailty and move forward. Once you have got to the blank page, Walcott suggests the following preliminary writing exercises:

- Write down the plan. Write a statement of purpose. Write the sequence of events. Writing a "pretend" table of contents can help you with this. You can come up with phantom chapter headings and page numbers. Put subheadings within the chapters. The generic structure might be
  - Introduction and Overview
  - Focus of Inquiry
  - Methods of Sampling and Data Collection
  - Approaches to Evaluating the Meaning of the Data
  - Results of Top-Down analysis, using dimensions of framework for headings
  - Concepts and Categories identified in open coding process and rationales
  - Theoretical Statements Developed and overall statement of theory in context of human activity
  - What you discovered about social work practice with individuals, families, groups, organizations, or communities
  - Statement of Strengths and Limitations on the study and its findings
  - Recommendations and Implications, giving statements about the meaning of the study and potential of this study and its findings, without veering into opinion and rhetoric
- Start writing as soon as you start the study. You have a proposal—start rewriting that with a final product in mind. You could start by writing about the methods you are using to carry out the study. Another way to start would be to give a simple narrative description of the project and its setting.
- Write the problem focus. This may require several drafts and turn out to be a thinking and refining exercise for yourself as you figure out what your study is about and talk to other people about what you are trying to say.
- Write drafts of each of the chapters identified in the pretend table of contents. This will go through stages: scattered notes and thoughts at first, then an outline, a rough draft, and finally a polished draft.
- Take a break from writing and draft your acknowledgements and dedications and possible title.

These are ideas for getting started and sticking with it. After this, when the first draft is written, the task is to refine the product and write a paper with a formal structure. To do this you can get feedback from colleagues or those who took part in the study, but be careful, as Wolcott (1990) warns that a little feedback goes a long way.

The final structure should include the following content, but not necessarily all in this order,

- Title
- Dedication
- Preface
- Introduction and Foreword
- Acknowledgments (credit all those who were the source of your ideas, whether orally or in print)
- Table of Contents
- Body of Report (as suggested above)
- Endnotes and Footnotes
- References and Bibliography
- Appendices and Supplements
- Index and Keywords
- About the Author
- Abstract

The headings and subheadings for the discussion of the findings are developed during the evaluation of the meaning of the data. They can either be the headings offered in the top-down approach to analysis or they can be the components of the theory that emerged during the bottom-up approach. There are no strict guidelines for what to include. However, Coffey and Atkinson (1996) report six possible levels of generalization that help organize our thinking. They suggest that we decide whether we are making,

1. Universal statements: An overall summary statement about everything we observed, the people, the activity, the processes

2. Cross-cultural descriptive statements: Comparative statements about individuals, groups, families, organizations, or communities we observed

3. General statements about one specific individual, family, group, organization, or community we observed

4. General statements about the context of the activity we research

5. Specific statements about the concepts and categories and their relationships that we developed

6. Specific statements about one incident

When the report is finished, to check that it is complete, the questions created by Drisko (1997) for assessing qualitative research can be used as guidelines. Has the report described the paradigm being used, rationales for the paradigm, and methodologies for each stage of the research process?

Post-positivists, like positivists, report their findings at conferences or in journals in the form of posters, presentations, and papers as described in Part I of this book. The advice given above is guidance for these kinds of presentations to expert audiences. However, post-positivists also tend to be committed to reporting findings back to the setting that was the focus of the inquiry. In preparing for this very different audience, the researcher needs to think not only about the level of generalization that is being addressed but also the form of the communication with the audience.

A community audience will generally be a novice audience when it comes to knowledge about research methods and tolerance for abstract discussion of their own experiences. They are interested in the presentation because the topic is real and alive for them, thus presentation of findings needs to build on this motivation. Coffey and Atkinson (1996), when exploring alternative forms of presentation, address visual presentation of data and offer some useful thoughts for those who are preparing to present to a community audience.

- Use diagrams and tables to summarize narrative
- Use photographs and images to bring the data to life
- Show social artifacts from the setting (in our homeless children study, reproduction of drawings, poems, and songs written by the children about their experience of homelessness were included in the final report)
- Also, in community presentations it is helpful to give study participants a role in the presentation. At the presentation of the findings of the homeless study to the community and other students, the researchers displayed children's drawings and poems around the walls and invited them to sing a song they had written about homelessness. There wasn't a dry eye in the house.

Not only does the post-positivist need to present findings to colleagues and to the research setting, he or she needs to develop a process for terminating with the research site. The presentation is the formal procedure for noting the end of the study, but since there has been such an intense involvement with the research site, an informal disengagement is needed. This could simply be an informal discussion over coffee about how the study went and plans for the future. It could be a more elaborate event with food and congratulations and thanks given to participants and study sponsors. However it is done, there needs to be acknowledgement of closure at both the formal and informal levels.

Main Points

- Termination involves writing a paper, making presentations, and disengaging with the research site and research participants
- Writing is a habit that needs to be formed from the start of the study using various strategies to get to the "blank page" and then fill it
- Make sure that the intense personal engagement is honored by appropriately saying "goodbye" to the people who have contributed to the success of the study

Learning Assignments

1. With a partner, role-play different ways you might terminate with a study site. How is this different from the termination you carry out with clients in practice situations?

2. Write in your journal about these differences.

Conclusion

This section of the book has described the background, theories, and methods for carrying out post-positivist research. The discovery nature of the approach was explained along with its roots in ethnography, linguistics, and sociology. Assessment was described as a process of deciding the research aim, question, and objective. Engagement was described as a more intense formal and informal process than would be expected with a positivist approach to research. Planning, implementation, and engagement were shown to be interwoven processes driven by each stage of the discovery. Planning involved identifying the type of research being carried out: basic, applied, or evaluative. It also involved decisions about units of analysis and sampling procedures. Implementation focused on interviews and observation, while evaluation was shown to be either a "top-down" or a "bottom-up" process depending on the goal of the research project. Termination and follow up was seen to be not only a formal presentation of findings but also an informal disengagement from the research site and the study participants.

Qualitative research is increasingly included in social work research texts. It tends to be presented as an extension of positivism and is therefore seen as having a weaker methodology and having findings that need to be tested using positivist methods. However, as can be seen here, once the unique paradigmatic view of, for example, post-positivism is delineated, qualitative research becomes an approach to research that is clearly rigorous and significant in its own right. Qualitative exploratory researchers can build scientific knowledge by adopting a post-positivist paradigm and can engage audiences in validating its use by showing how research that uses words as data is so alive and meaningful to the social work field. Research projects that address micro or macro practice questions by using qualitative methods to ask what is happening here or how is this happening give us scientific knowledge and insight into the processes of practice.

PART III

Critical Theory

Introduction to Part III

It is with this paradigm that we make a fundamental shift in our portrayal of the role of the researcher. The critical theory researcher agrees with positivism that there is an objective reality, agrees with post-positivism that values mediate a researcher's understanding of that reality, but disagrees with both paradigms and their focus on the researcher as someone standing outside of the research experience doing research *to* people rather than doing research *with* people. Critical theory is an ideologically oriented approach to studying human phenomena. It includes those who adopt a neo-Marxist, feminist, racialist oppression, or any other ideology that addresses oppression by those with power and empowerment of those without power. The critical theory paradigm assumes that we can never be free of our own values when observing the objective reality around us. Unlike post-positivism, this approach demands that researchers embrace and promote these values when entering the research arena rather than keeping them under control. Critical theorists begin by taking an ideological stance, and more, their research aims to actively address the oppression identified in that professed ideology. The goal of the critical theory research project is to change the participants and their context through eliminating false consciousness and facilitating transformation.

In the *Handbook of Qualitative Research* by Denzin and Lincoln (1994), Kincheloe and McLaren define this approach as follows (reformatted from original for clarity):

> We are defining a criticalist as a researcher or theorist who attempts to use her or his work as a form of social or cultural criticism and who accepts certain basic assumptions:
>
> - That all thought is fundamentally mediated by power relations that are socially and historically constituted
> - That facts can never be isolated from the domain of values or removed from some form of ideological inscription

131

- That the relationship between concept and object and between signifier and signified is never stable or fixed and is often mediated by the social relations of capitalist production and consumption
- That language is central to the formation of subjectivity (conscious and unconscious awareness)
- That certain groups in any society are privileged over others, and although the reasons for this privileging may vary widely, the oppression that characterizes contemporary societies is most forcefully reproduced when subordinates accept that social status as natural, necessary, or inevitable
- That oppression has many faces and that focusing on only one at the expense of others (e.g., class oppression vs. racism) often elides the interconnections among them
- That mainstream research practices are generally, although most often unwittingly, implicated in the reproduction of systems of class, race, and gender oppression (pp. 139–140)

Wow! For a social worker committed to social action, this is an exciting alternative. It positions the researcher as both skeptical realist about people and their motivations and convinced advocate for the downtrodden. This resonates with many people who have been attracted to social work. It can lead to research that is often controversial, may well threaten those who have power, and will certainly empower those who do not.

Kincheloe and McLaren (1994) offer a brief history of critical theory. They note that it developed from a set of ideas formulated by a group of academics who came to be known as the Frankfurt School and who were situated at the Frankfurt Institute of Social Research in the 1920s. Most members of the movement at the Institute were Jewish, and with the rise of the Nazi party in the 1930s they left Germany. Many of them moved to California. In the United States these academics were shocked and offended by the "taken for granted" empirical practices of American social sciences" (p. 139) that assumed that there was no value context for approaching social research but simply a set of methods that were tools for doing the job, in much the same way as a carpenter's hammer simply drives in a nail but has no influence on the kind of nail being driven in and where it is being nailed. Such an assumption clearly ignores the role of the carpenter, as well as her background and skill, let alone the choice of the wood. In responding to this situation, these theorists (Horkheimer, Adorno, and Marcuse) produced major works offering ideological analyses of American society. In the 1950s, Horkheimer and Adorno went back to Germany but Marcuse stayed and became the inspirational philosopher of the student movements of the 1960s. His writings also stimulated a New Left in the United States, preaching political emancipation (Gibson, 1986; Wexler, 1991). This has led to emergent schools of inquiry such as neo-Marxism, post-structuralist deconstruction, and postmodernism.

Popkewitz (1990, pp. 51–63) notes six themes of the Critical Theory paradigm:

1. The methods of science are not separated from their context but actually emerge from a question to be studied. For example, a social worker and a psychologist studying child abuse will ask different questions and use different approaches to understand the topic. The social worker will be interested in studying interventions with child abuse while the psychologist is likely to be interested in cognitions and behaviors associated with child abuse.

2. The methods of science developed in a historical context. For example, psychology emerged in the late nineteenth century to replace philosophy in a religious crisis regarding the mind/body split in the light of Darwin's theories. At that time, the other major emerging school of thought was behaviorism with its focus on experimentation, testing, and measurement. Adoption of behaviorist methodologies gave psychology an ally that brought it the credibility it needed. Social work has emerged as a discipline in its own right during the twentieth century and, needing to gain credibility, has tended to adopt the assumptions of positivist science when considering approaches to research.

3. It is impossible to separate the subjective from the objective. Objective reality is socially formed and subjective reality is the mind's response to that objective reality. For example, there is a tree outside the window and the environmentalist, poet, child, and lumberjack all see and define it differently. Or, there is a homeless person standing on the street corner and the social worker, nurse, police officer, and local politician all see that person differently.

4. There is no such thing as a disinterested science. The pretence of disinterest was a political strategy used by universities in the first part of the twentieth century because of a concern that business leaders would react badly to activist professors and withhold funding. It also grew from a need to project a neutral "professional" image.

5. The production of knowledge is the production of values. For example, the use of statistics expands the number of phenomena that can be studied and quantifying data avoids acknowledgment of the assumptions behind the definitions of variables such as family, child abuse, or dysfunction. The case study method limits the number of phenomena that can be studied but acknowledges an assumption of connection and a negotiated order.

6. Science is a study of the past. By definition, generalizations about the present and the future are based on data about the past. We have no data about the future and, therefore, any generalizations or predictions are statements of rhetoric or ideology.

A paradigm born in postwar loss and nurtured in Nazi oppression and American indifference cannot help but be provocative and challenging. Feminists in particular have embraced this perspective and used it to challenge the research establishment. Liane Davis (1986), in her article on a feminist approach to social work research, suggested that traditional positivist research is a process whereby men oppress women by offering conceptualization and methodologies that ignore relationships and separate phenomena into variables and hypotheses measured through numbers (p. 33). This line of thought has been further developed by Reinharz (1992), who edited a book on feminist approaches to data collection, and McCarl Nielsen (1990), who edited a book discussing feminist concerns with positivist research that offered examples of feminist research projects. Reinharz concluded that feminist research has the following characteristics:

1. Feminism is a perspective, not a research method.

2. Feminists use a multiplicity of research methods.

3. Feminist research involves an ongoing criticism of non-feminist scholarship.

4. Feminist research is guided by feminist theory.

5. Feminist research may be transdisciplinary.

6. Feminist research aims to create social change.

7. Feminist research strives to represent human diversity.

8. Feminist research frequently includes the researcher as a person.

9. Feminist research frequently attempts to develop special relations with the people studied (in interactive research).

10. Feminist research frequently defines a special relationship with the reader. (p. 240)

Neuman and Kreuger (2003) restate this position in pragmatic terms. They propose that the feminist stance declares that positivist research reflects a male emphasis on "individual competition, on dominating and controlling the environment, and on the hard facts and forces that act on the world" (p. 90). Feminist researchers suggest that relationships, the connections between people, and subject experience of the context are the keys to understanding social phenomena. These authors offer a different set of characteristics for feminist research. These are,

- Advocacy of a feminist value position and perspective
- Rejection of sexism in assumptions, concepts, and research questions

- Creation of empathic connections between the researcher and those he or she studies
- Sensitivity to how relations of gender and power permeate spheres of social life
- Incorporation of the researcher's personal feelings and experiences into the research process
- Flexibility in choosing research techniques and crossing boundaries between academic fields
- Recognition of the emotional and mutual-dependence dimensions in human experience
- Action-oriented research that seeks to facilitate personal and societal change (p. 90)

In their book *Research as Resistance,* Leslie Brown and Susan Stega (2005) note that for too long the illusion of neutrality has been fostered by using a positivist worldview to frame the discussion of what constitutes true knowledge. They suggest that critical, indigenous, and anti-oppressive approaches to research that foster social justice need no longer be marginalized but can also be at the center of this debate. Two of the contributors to this book (Potts & Brown, 2005) offer three principles of anti-oppressive research:

1. Anti-oppressive research is social justice and resistance in process and in outcome. Carrying out this research is a commitment to personal reflection on one's own power relationships during the project and on one's personal commitment to taking action for change during the project.

2. Anti-oppressive research recognizes that all knowledge is socially constructed and political. Thus this research is not a process of discovering knowledge but a partnership between researchers and researched to jointly create and rediscover knowledge

3. The anti-oppressive research process is all about power and relationships. There is an assumption that the researcher and the researched may well be starting a lifelong relationship where power and knowledge are shared. (pp. 260–262)

So to sum up, a critical theory researcher brings an ideological commitment to the research arena along with a social action agenda. Research questions and problem statements are not neutral; they are statements and reflections offering polemics on power relationships and remedies addressing inequities inherent in those relationships.

In this section of the book, a methodology for carrying out social work critical theory research is described. It is time consuming and a little complicated but worth the effort for the potential impact on social justice. Put briefly, the process of critical theory research takes the following steps:

1. Problem Development (Assessment and Engagement) through ideological analysis of literature and ideological engagement of the participants in the research.

2. Looking (Engagement) or data gathering from key informants on the ideological consciousness of participants regarding the issue or problem that is the focus of the study. Through a teaching-learning process study participants are engaged in consciousness raising about the identified oppression and potential for empowerment.

3. Thinking (Planning) or conceptualizing the results of the Problem Development and Looking phases of the study in terms of ideological statements about oppression and potential for empowerment.

4. Action (Implementation). A process of developing and implementing actions for empowerment.

5. Evaluation. A process of formally evaluating the impact of the action.

6. Reflection and Celebration (Termination and Follow up). Reflecting on and celebrating the project's contribution to empowerment.

10

Assessment, Engagement, and Planning—Development of Understanding of the Research Focus, Entrée to the Research Setting, Rationales for Carrying Out the Research

The critical theory paradigm requires that researchers first identify and state the ideology that is informing their study. This names the categories or classes of people who are oppressed by the power relationships identified in that ideology and who are therefore the targets of the research project. The core research question is, "How is the oppression identified in the chosen ideology demonstrated in this class of people, and how can they and the researcher be empowered to understand and address that oppression?" If the ideology is neo-Marxism, then the focus of the research is a subgroup of the poor. If the ideology is feminism, then the focus is a subgroup of women. If it is racial inequity, then the focus is members of particular minority ethnic groups who are oppressed. Popkewitz (1990) notes that for critical theorists, the research question addresses contradictions that emerge from the interaction of social, political, economic, and cultural patterns. For example, social welfare is an institution that reflects many contradictory functions. It aims to help the poor, keep the poor content, develop a reserve army of labor, keep the poor poor, and support the continuation of capitalism. The critical theory researcher will systematically inquire into such functions and contradictions by reviewing a history of the functions and contradictions, engaging in a teaching/learning exchange with the poor about this history, and partnering with the poor in developing empowering action strategies to address these contradictions. Thus the initial stages of the study involve reviewing the literature and engaging oppressed groups that are the focus of the study.

Assessment: Researching and Interpreting Ideology in the Literature

The critical theory researcher, in effect, develops two interwoven literature reviews: first, a review of the literature giving an analysis of the chosen ideological position; and second, a literature review of the specific research topic as described in previous sections of this book, which, of course, is interpreted through the chosen ideological worldview. Talshir (2003) suggests that ideologies should be analyzed in three ways: diachronic, discursive, and conceptual. A *diachronic* analysis traces the thematic transformation as the ideology develops over time. For example, in her analysis of the ideology of the Green party in Germany, she notes the following stages of development: unity in diversity (1960s); ecology and politics (1970s and 80s); ecology versus the economy (1990); and multicultural democracy (since reunification of Germany). A *discursive* analysis tracks the evolving ideology that is identified when the evolving themes identified in the diachronic analysis are integrated. In her example, the Green party developed "ecosocialism" with four pillars: ecological politics, social politics, grass roots democratic politics, and nonviolent politics (p. 170). This was a risky expansion of the definition of politics into the domains of family and community that had not been entertained in Germany since the Nazi experience. She states that it has now been reformed into "classical political liberalism" with a focus on the individual and the dignity of each human being, rather than the collective. It stresses the right to self-determination, justice, and democracy. The third analysis, the *conceptual* analysis, gives a rationale for the ideological development that has been described by the first two analyses and synthesizes the progression of thought over time, giving a historical and social context for such changes.

For example, in their ideological analysis of Oscar Lewis's culture of poverty, Harvey and Reed (1996) begin with a review of the history or "career" of the concept and the misunderstandings of the concept that have been perpetrated. They give this review a historical context, noting the controversy over the Moynihan report in the 1960s and the mood of the time where many members of the New Left were competing to be perceived as the "most radical." They then review the career of Oscar Lewis and assess exactly what he was trying to say about poverty. They give a current understanding of the "culture of poverty" as a class analysis, suggesting that criticisms of the concept as racist have been unfair and misguided. They also suggest that with the rightward movement of political and social thought over the last thirty years, discussion of class has been undermined or at least ignored and in its place we have interpretive studies of culture and subjectivity.

Social work critical theory researchers carry out a similar analysis at the start of the study and address the following questions:

1. What is the history of this ideology?
   - How has the ideology evolved over time? What are the themes?
   - What is the current ideology? What are its current name and definitions?
   - Why have these developments taken place?
   - Who are the key authors and spokespeople for this ideology?

2. Which power relations are identified by this ideology?
   - Which group is considered powerful?
   - Which group is to be empowered?
   - What action is favored for empowerment?

3. When this ideology is used to understand the research topic, what does it say about
   - The powerful?
   - The oppressed?
   - Action to empower?

For example, a student's critical theory study of eating disorders in young women, Christopulos (1995), reviewed the literature using a feminist perspective. The problem was stated as follows:

This research project asked how obsession with weight and body image preoccupies women and adopted an ideology that suggests such obsession renders women powerless. The ideological position of this critical theory study is that eating disorders in women, brought on by the oppression of women and confusing messages delivered to women by society and the media, can be eliminated by re-socializing women's perspectives at the high school level. Feminist critical theory suggests that indoctrinating women with the misconception that success is measured only by body size and the worthless pursuit for an unattainable "ideal" body is a method in which the patriarchy attempts to control women. (p. 1)

The author then reviewed literature on women's body image and eating disorders and reviewed the feminist "worldview" addressing unity, diversity, and personal power and responsibility. Each of these principles was linked to eating disorders by

- Reviewing feminist writing on body image and eating disorders (e.g., Charles & Kerr, 1986; Chernin, 1981, 1986; Mahowald, 1992) that reveal the patriarchal emphasis on competition rather than unity and its impact on women who feel they have lost the "race" for beauty
- Revealing the patriarchal lack of appreciation for each person's unique characteristics
- Revealing an action orientation that addresses this patriarchy, acknowledging
  - The value of a masculine appearance or body type in a patriarchal society
  - The denial of nurturing for women, which is compensated for by eating
  - That being large breaks the rules regarding personal space that women occupy. Large women are visible and they take up space!
  - That medical reports stress, inaccurately, that being thin is healthy

Thus, this student developed an ideological position from the literature. A similar analysis was carried out by Rutman, Hubberstey, Barlow, and Brown (2005) in their review of literature on young people transitioning from care. They found that such young people generally come from poor, marginalized families; often live with disabilities; and are expected to live independently sooner than the average young person with fewer resources than the average young person. A third example of such a literature review is Farquhar and Wing's (2003) conclusion that "inequalities in health between gender, race, and class groups are generated by social institutions that create disparities in exposure to adequate nutrition, hazardous agents, safe living and working conditions, educational opportunities and personal medical services" (p. 221). However, such reviews of the literature are carried out in tandem with an engagement of study participants in exploration and discussion of the topic in its ideological context.

Engagement: Researching and Interpreting the Ideology at the Research Site

While engaging in a review of the literature in an ideological context, the critical theory researcher must also engage the individuals, families, groups, organizations, or communities that are the focus of the study in the development of the ideological position. In our example student study of eating disorders, a group of high school girls were invited to participate in this dialogue. These girls were engaged in the project by means of a presentation and discussion session on feminism and eating disorders that was part of a regularly scheduled high school activity. They were a preexisting group who were interested in the topic. This will not always be the case, and the critical theory researcher may well need to spend time finding participants for the study who are willing to engage in a process of consciousness raising regarding the intent of the research. These participants can be the targets of the oppression, practitioners concerned about intervening to address the oppression, or a mixture of both interest groups. Selection into the study follows a purposive process where participants are chosen using the following guidelines:

- Participants are affected by the oppression being studied. They are either "victims" or practitioners who wish to intervene with the oppression, but they are not disinterested observers.
- Participants are willing and able to engage in a discussion of the oppression and empowerment being studied.
  a. They are able to understand the ideas being presented and willing to engage in political discussions.
  b. They have the time to take part in these discussions.
  c. They are willing to commit to action strategies regarding empowerment that will be developed in these discussions.
  d. They are willing to change ideas as the discussion continues and information is shared.

The number of participants will depend on the focus of the study and the time and resources of the researcher. Since the critical theory researcher celebrates empowerment wherever it takes place, a small group is as acceptable as a large group. As an aside on sampling, since critical theory researchers have a sensitivity to power and oppression, referring to participants as a "sample" or as "subjects" starts to sound offensive. Such researchers are concerned with personal dignity and are studying the promotion of self-respect. Thus study participants are chosen because of the knowledge and qualities they bring to the study, and they are partners in data collection. The procedures of random sampling for generalizing findings to a population of interest are considered to be insensitive manipulation of people. As stated above, it is involvement, commitment, and potential to affect empowerment that guide selection of participants in a critical theory study, not their identification number on a table of random numbers.

Having invited participants to take part in the study, a process of engagement commences. Participants are interviewed individually or in groups. In
their book *Just Practice: A Social Justice Approach to Social Work*, Finn and
Jacobson (2003) describe such engagement as "a socio-emotional, practical
and political process of coming together with others to create a space of
respect and hope, pose questions, and learn about one another" (p. 186).
The researcher and the participants collaboratively gather data on the
identified oppression and strategies for empowerment. Thus the researcher
begins with a commitment to engaging people in understanding their problems and within a values context of "Democracy, Equality, Liberation, and
Life Enhancement" (Stringer, 1996, p. 10). Finn and Jacobson (2003) introduce teaching-learning as a stage of social work intervention. Although
their focus is social work practice, this teaching-learning process offers an
approach to data gathering that can be an effective tool for the social work
critical theory researcher. They frame this process as

> a collaborative effort of uncovering information, making it meaningful in the
> context of our concern and creating and disseminating knowledge and possi-
> bilities for action. Each party to the process brings knowledge grounded in per-
> sonal experience and cultural history. Together we begin to map out what we
> know, consider what we need to learn about, seek out knowledge, consider
> underlying forces and patterns that shape experience, and bring our collective
> wisdom to bear in translating data into a meaningful guide for action. (p. 233)

These authors then suggest that the engagement of people using a critical
theory approach needs to be a teaching-learning process where all parties to
the engagement both teach and learn. This includes sharing data, a dialectical process of synthesizing data and experiences, exploration of taboo
subjects such as discrimination, acknowledgment that we are not alone in
these experiences, emotional support that honors difficult emotions and
experiences, acceptance of responsibility, acknowledgement of expectations,
problem solving, rehearsal of proposed action, and acknowledgement of
the strength that comes from awareness of group identity. Thus the critical
theory researcher, whether studying individuals, groups, organizations, or
communities, will promote the formation of groups that can engage in self-
reflection, analysis, synthesis, and the development of action strategies.

This teaching-learning approach is used to gather data about participants'
ideological awareness and to initiate a process of consciousness raising. Hope
and Timmel (1999), in their handbook of transformation for community
workers, offer a process for conducting a listening survey that identifies the
generative themes for communities. This process is described below and

can be used when engaging individuals, groups, or organizations, as well as communities in critical theory interviews. Finn and Jacobson (2003) itemize the process as follows:

- Questions to be asked should include What are participants worried about? What are participants happy about? What are participants sad about? What are participants angry about? What are participants fearful about? What are participants hopeful about?
- Interviewers should be trained to pay attention to gender, race, age, and other dimensions of diversity
- Researchers should gather background statistical information on the participants and the issue that is the focus of inquiry
- Interviews at this early stage of engagement should be informal and unstructured
- Researchers should listen for themes addressing basic needs such as housing, food, shelter, safety, security, love, belonging, self-respect, and personal growth
- Interviewers should make sure the six areas of life that concern people's well-being are addressed
  - Meeting basic physical needs
  - Relationships with people
  - Access to participation in decision-making processes and structures
  - Education and socialization
  - Recreation
  - Beliefs and values

- If the opportunity arises and permission is granted, researchers can observe as well as interview in formal and informal settings. However, data collected in this fashion is seen as secondary data to that being gathered in the teaching-learning process. Such observations are shared and reviewed by participants (this is discussed below in the data gathering section)
- Researchers should inform people of the data being gathered, its purposes, and uses
- Researchers should gather data on facts and feelings
- Researchers should have a colleague or research team with whom they can critically analyze the emerging themes in relation to the six areas of well-being
- Researchers should make an initial assessment of the priority of each theme for those who are being researched and share this assessment with participants (pp. 244–245)

To be able to carry out such an intensive listening process, the researcher needs to establish himself or herself as a trusted person who has participants' interests at heart. Stringer (1996) describes this as "Establishing a Role." He notes that the researcher will have little success "if the researcher is perceived as a stranger prying into people's affairs for little apparent reason or as an authority attempting to impose an agenda" (p. 45). This may well be an issue for critical theory researchers who do indeed have an ideological agenda. If the researcher's ideology does not resonate with those who are the focus of the inquiry, then the study cannot move forward. An important aspect of the listening exercise described above is to note non-response or non-concern about the six areas of well-being in relation to the researcher's chosen ideology. If this is the case, then the researcher may need to find a new research site or new participants for the study. An ideological position cannot be successfully, or ethically, imposed on study participants.

Stringer (1996) notes that establishing a role has three elements: agenda, stance, and position. The critical theory researcher must explain his or her *agenda*. This can be done by taking a *stance* that encourages exploration of ideas rather than insistence on the correctness of those ideas. For example, the label of feminist for many women has become a stigma rather than a simple description. Rather than challenge the feelings of stigma attached to the term, researchers can explore the perceived stigma using the listening procedures itemized above and appreciate how it links to a person's feeling of well-being. With regards to Stinger's third element, *position,* he notes three entities that anyone can make a claim to: physical space, social status, and symbolic territory. The researcher needs to be sensitive to who "owns" the space in which data gathering is taking place. A range of different informal and formal settings would make a statement that the researcher is not "owned" by any one person or group.

To sum up, Assessment and Engagement for critical theory researchers entail an ideological review of the literature and an ideological engagement with study participants using a teaching-learning approach to establish an ideological partnership between researcher and study participants. Examples of such partnerships can be found in Schulz et al.'s (2003) study that engaged women in community-based participatory research for health and Rutman et al.'s (2005) study of youth transitioning out of care. Schultz et al. (2003) set up a partnership in the east side of Detroit that included community health workers, representatives from community-based organizations, health service providers, and academics. This steering committee surveyed the community over a nine-month period to discover community strengths, resources, and risk factors affecting community residents. According to the authors, "the emphasis was on the engagement of community partners in shaping the research questions, determining how those questions would be asked, and interpreting the results and integrating them into the action components of the partnership" (pp. 298–299). Rutman et al. (2005) formed an advisory committee that included the researchers, youth from care, community-based service providers, and government representatives. This group collaborated equally in developing data collections instruments, liaising with various interest groups, carrying out data gathering, developing and carrying out workshops, and developing and implementing action strategies.

Planning: Rationale for Carrying Out the Research

As can be seen from the above discussion, Planning tends to merge with Assessment and Engagement in critical theory research. The plan emerges as the study progresses. It is guided not only by the analysis of the literature on the ideology and specific topic identified as guiding the project, but also by the engagement of the community. The plan will include strategies for identifying participants; engaging participants in the teaching-learning process; recording and analyzing data that describes oppression and empowerment; expanding the circle of research participants, if necessary; jointly developing action strategies for empowerment; taking action; and evaluating, celebrating, and reflecting on action. This research is seen as a circular process of understanding, connecting, empowering, taking action, reflecting, understanding, connecting, empowering, and so on. Stringer (1996), when discussing action research, suggests that the researcher needs to be carrying out three major activities: "Looking, Thinking, and Acting" (p. 16). The critical theory action researcher makes plans to carry out these three activities while integrating the teaching-learning process throughout.

Looking Using Teaching-Learning

Having initially engaged research participants with a discussion of the ideological orientation to the topic to be studied, the researcher now can move forward with implementing a plan for more intensive data gathering. As a result of the listening exercise the researcher will have identified a number of emerging themes. These relate to participants' concerns regarding the topic of inquiry and the power relationships affecting these concerns. They guide further decisions about who should be interviewed and observed. For example, Riech (1994) carried out a student study of "Curanderismo," a Mexican folk healing art. The researcher, after completing a few months of an M.S.W. program, noted that textbooks and journals tended not to address ethnic approaches to practice with individuals, families, and groups. In particular, the practice of Curanderismo was rarely mentioned. Students, field placement instructors, and social work practice educators were not conversant with Curanderismo and did not have an appreciation of its value.

This student researcher was also was aware of concerns among Mexican clients that a Curandero, a practitioner of Curanderismo, could not easily be found when seeking mental health services. After the researcher had discussed this issue with various students and Mexican American clients and friends, certain generative themes emerged:

- The Curandero tends to be dismissed as a charlatan or "quack"
- Definitions of mental health and mental illness are mostly derived from the dominant Anglo culture
- Interventions, such as "limpia" ceremonies that bring mystical messages, are dismissed as subjective interpretations rather than objective occurrences
- Mexican or Mexican American clients of mental health agencies who have traditional Mexican values and prefer traditional approaches to the treatment of illness experience a sense of marginality
- Minority clients in general experience difficulty in receiving adequate mental health services
- There are class as well as ethnic differences between middle class white therapists and working class traditional Mexican clients
- The Latino culture does not make the same distinction between physical and emotional health that the dominant Anglo culture makes
- Social work students need to be empowered to confront and challenge the Anglo culture's definitions of appropriate mental health interventions found in M.S.W. curricula (pp. 15–22)

This researcher, through a process of informal interviews, gathered these themes from students, Curanderos, Mexican friends and colleagues, faculty members, and a review of the literature. To offer another illustration of this process, we can return to the study of eating disorders introduced above. Emergent themes identified after talking to adolescent girls and reviewing the literature included

- Mixed messages to women about the importance of the perfect body: diet, weight, and body image
- The prevalence of eating disorders—5% to 10% of adolescent females suffer from anorexia nervosa and 30% to 60% of adolescent girls suffer from bulimia (Seid, 1989)
- The prevalent conclusion that the media equates female beauty with being very thin
- Knowledge that feminist principles suggest
  - Women should join together rather than compete with each other
  - We should respect individual difference
  - Each individual has the right and responsibility to be and become her or his unique self

- Issues regarding eating disorders:
  - Men are the valued gender in society, thus the more masculine you look the greater your chance of success and respect. Thus being thin is powerful and having curves and breasts reduces power. Many women are almost in denial about having curves and breasts.
  - Women are taught to deny themselves pleasure and take care of others.
  - Being large and curvy and feeding herself means that a woman is breaking the rules of personal power that suggest that power lies with thin women who look like men.
  - "Science" allows misconceptions about the healthiness of being thin to prevail.
- The potential to re-socialize young women about these issues and perceptions (Christopulos, 1995, pp. 1–12)

Our two example studies developed ideological positions, engaged study participants in a teaching-learning process to develop those positions, and thus identified emergent themes. These themes guided further selection of research participants, decisions about further data to be collected, and ideas for action strategies.

Thinking and Understanding

Stringer (1996) suggests various strategies for interpreting or thinking about what the data collected in the Looking stage means. One of these is "Concept Mapping" and another is "Problem Analysis." In concept mapping, a diagram of the connections between generative themes is developed, while in problem analysis a table of antecedents and consequences is developed. In our two sample studies these interpretations were developed in the following ways. In the Riech (1994) study of Curanderismo, the conceptual map was as shown in Table 10.1.

Table 10.1 reveals four options. Option 1 is the situation where the Mexican client with traditional values is confronted with mental health services that are based only on Anglo values and customs. Option 2 is the situation where the traditional Mexican client can find mental health services that incorporate traditional Mexican folk healing. Option 3 is the most common situation, where Anglo clients receive services based on Anglo values and customs. Option 4 is not likely to happen but it is theoretically possible; it is the situation where an Anglo client can only find mental health services offering traditional folk healing. The map suggested that interventions were needed to address Options 1 and 2.

In the Christopulos (1995) study of eating disorders, a table of antecedents and consequences was developed from the literature and from talking to

Table 10.1   Conceptual Map for Study of Curanderismo

	Mental Health Interventions Framed by Majority Culture	Mental Health Interventions Framed by Folk Healing
Mental Health Clients with Traditional, Culture of Origin Values	Option 1 Culturally Inappropriate Interventions (Usually Happens)	Option 2 Culturally Appropriate Intervention (Rarely Happens)
Mental Health Clients with Anglo Values	Option 3 Culturally Appropriate Intervention (Usually Happens)	Option 4 Culturally Inappropriate Intervention (Never Happens)

teenage girls, showing two possible approaches to understanding the female body (see Figure 10.1). One approach rests on feminist values that suggest all women are unique and valued, and that if women cooperate rather than compete they will understand their own strengths and know that the proposition that only one body type is attractive is wrong. If a woman accepts this approach, the study's ideological position suggests that she has more opportunity for learning about a healthy approach to eating and care of her body. The other approach rests on patriarchal values and suggests that since men are perceived as powerful, women must compete with each other and be like men if they want to be powerful. This competition includes looking like a man and having a male-shaped body. The ideological position of the study suggests that in the quest to get this kind of body, a woman will develop eating disorders.

Action

Thus having completed an ideological analysis and an interpretation of data gathered from both the literature and participants, the critical theory researcher now moves on to a plan for action to address the empowerment issues that have been identified. The action is developed and implemented in partnership with study participants. Researchers share the results of the looking and thinking phases of the study with participants and collaboratively review the interpretations, make changes that respondents and the researchers deem appropriate and necessary, and then develop action strategies to respond to these findings. This action planning takes place, ideally, at a meeting of participants, but if this is not possible it can be carried out by

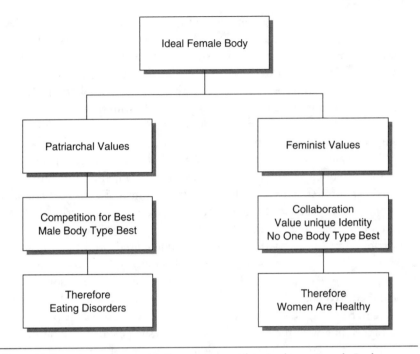

Figure 10.1   Antecedents and Consequences of Attitudes to Female Body

a combination of meetings with individuals, e-mails, Internet discussion boards, and Internet meetings via streaming video. The goal for this process is for researchers and participants to agree with the ideological analysis and commit to action strategies.

Both of our study examples, being authored by students with time and resource limitations, opted for an action strategy where the researcher developed and implemented an educational experience for participants as an action strategy but did not complete an extensive teaching-learning process at this stage. Rather than continuing the teaching-learning dialogue between partners that is at the heart of this approach to research, they developed a time limited one-off exchange of information. This was a compromise where the spirit of the ideological approach guided the Action step, but the time requirements of an extended teaching-learning phase during the action phase was cut short. Thus in the Riech (1994) study of Curanderismo, the researcher developed a videotape explaining Curanderismo and its role in Mexican healing and folk healing in general. The student also developed a survey instrument that addressed knowledge and attitudes regarding Curanderismo. Study participants, who were 77 M.S.W. students and 25 B.S.W. students, completed the survey, saw the video, and then completed the survey again. The same approach was used in the Christopulos (1995) study of eating disorders. The researcher developed an instrument measuring knowledge and attitudes about personal and career goals, perception and satisfaction with own body type, and knowledge of eating disorders and dieting. A small group of 16 adolescent girls in high school completed the instrument and then engaged in an education presentation and discussion regarding eating disorders, feminist perspectives on the role of women, and the impact of male values on the role of women. At the end of the session, the girls completed the survey again. As stated above, these action strategies were not developed strictly in partnership with participants, which the critical theory approach calls for. However, this compromise was a pragmatic solution to the problem of giving students experience of critical theory research in a time- and resource-limited situation. Thus when it came to the evaluation stage, both of these example studies used traditional positivist approaches using pretests and posttests of ideological consciousness to assess the impact of their educational interventions. These studies addressed the critical theorist's goal of empowerment but did not fully utilize the teaching-learning partnership to develop an action plan. In both cases the project was cut short, ending with the presentation of the results of the thinking stage to the study participants. The presentation was evaluated and reflected upon, but there was no cooperative action strategy that was implemented and celebrated.

This situation presents us with a nuance in the critical theory approach that needs to be attended to. The researcher is the source of knowledge about the critical theory and ideology that is informing the study, but he or she is also open to other ideas and committed to engaging in a dialogue with study participants so that a shared understanding of the ideological position is developed. The researcher starts in a "one-up" relationship with participants but moves quickly to a partnership with participants. This raises issues regarding "informed" consent. Initially, participants may well give their informed consent to this approach to research, but at this later stage, when they see and hear the interpretation of the critical theory and ideology as it relates to them, they may become uncomfortable and want to withdraw from the study. This kind of situation is discussed by Johnsen and Norman (2004) in their article describing a conflict between researchers and the community in a community empowerment project in southern Norway. They note that there was

a lack of reflectivity and learning in the RDC (Regional Development Coalition), and a rejection of the mandate of the program and the researchers' goal of radical change. The RDC became a part of or an instrument in the regional strategic power play. The researchers' activities were subsequently recognized not as reflective capacities, but as parts of a political process. (p. 230)

These authors suggest that there is an inherent conflict between the role of practitioner and researcher in the action research approach to carrying out research. They suggest that there is less potential for conflict when the project is simple and incremental rather than complex and radical with many stakeholders involved. They suggest that the action researcher (in this book the critical theory researcher) in the complex radical situation needs to focus on understanding rather than success and deliberation rather than strategy. They also note that such a researcher is playing multiple roles: facilitator, observer and data collector, supplier of relevant knowledge, bridge builder between interested parties, and service provider during action. Indeed, the critical theory researcher is frequently called on to be both outside the project looking in and understanding and inside the project looking out experiencing empowerment in the face of oppression.

In our example student studies, the project ended at this point, and therefore such reactions were not addressed. However, if participants indeed disagree with using the critical theory approach at this stage, then the project is not viable and may well need to be either abandoned or begun again with different participants. To avoid such a situation, it is important to negotiate partnerships for participation in the Looking, Thinking, and Action phases. The steps for building the partnership are as follows.

- The researcher has an ideological position. The study participants may have only a partial understanding of that ideological position but certainly agree to find out more about it (otherwise the study ends right there, since the researcher cannot ethically or pragmatically impose a point of view on anyone). These understandings are negotiated in the initial informed consent process.
- The researcher then imparts his or her knowledge of the chosen ideology to participants in a teaching-learning process where participants respond and a dialogue is developed. Both researcher and participants teach and learn. At this stage, the researcher may add key participants as themes emerge requiring new key informants. For example, in the Riech (1994) study of Curanderismo the researcher began by talking to social work students, and social work students were the targets of the action. However, later Curanderos, social work faculty members, Mexican clients, and other students were added to the group of participants who gave input during the Looking phase of the study.
- The ideological analysis is reformulated through a synthesis of the researcher's knowledge and the data collected from respondents during the Looking phase. This reformulation is shared with participants at the beginning of the Action

phase. The participants respond to the new ideological analysis, evaluate it, and decide whether it applies to them. They also decide whether they are committed to taking action to address the oppression and empowerment included in the reformulated ideological analysis.

- The democracy of the critical theory approach, and the explicit acknowledgment that we are always engaged in some form of power relationship with each other, allows us to assume that any differences of interpretation are highly likely to be resolved. There is a fundamental truth being addressed here and a liberating process being experienced.

- When agreement is reached, an action plan is developed that includes implementation, evaluation, reflection, and celebration. If agreement cannot be reached, the researcher and participants may well need to terminate the study at this point. Researchers will need to review where the spirit and process of the critical theory approach to problem solving was lost. They would need to reflect on whether a teaching-learning process had been honored. They would also need to assess whether the ideological approach was simply too threatening for study participants.

In our sample studies, the pretest/posttest process implied that the synthesis was a foregone conclusion. Neither researcher entertained the notion that their perceptions would be changed at this point, thus action was implemented with minimal consultation. With more time and resources, a synthesis for the Reich (1994) study of Curanderismo might have been reached where it was agreed that there are times when the Curanderismo approach is harmful given modern knowledge about mental health. Likewise, a synthesis for the eating disorders study might have been an agreement that the inclusion of girls in more team sports, as a result of role modeling from college sports activities for women that have developed in response to the requirements of Title IX, has changed the body image favored by girls to a more muscular body type showing strength, not a thin type mimicking men.

Rutman et al. (2005), in their study of youth transitioning out of care, addressed this issue by using a process of reflection and evaluation. During the first stage of the study the project team carried out data collection and analysis. They then carried out an evaluation of stage one. They individually and collaboratively identified what worked well in stage one, the challenges faced in stage one, and strategies for doing things differently as they proceed to stage two action strategies. Schulz et al. (2003) similarly describe a process of building consensus in the context of differing individual visions for women's community health in Detroit. They noted that,

In 1999, Village Health Workers and representatives from the steering committee gathered to determine priorities for the partnership for the next four years. Based on results from the community survey, descriptive data indicating the extent to which women living on Detroit's East Side reported a range of stressors and partial correlations indicating the strength of the relationships between stressors and mental and physical health outcomes were incorporated into the dialogue . . . . as all worked together in this process, an opportunity was provided for members of the partnership to act on their commitment to shared power and influence within the partnership itself. (pp. 308–309)

Organizing for Implementing Action

If we have successfully reached agreement on the shared ideological analysis, then our next step is to organize and implement a pragmatic action plan to address empowerment. Stringer (1996) suggests that this phase is built on the foundation of productive working relationships that have grown throughout the project. It consists of four phases: planning, implementation, evaluation, and celebration. Priorities are set with stated goals and objectives for action using the following questions adapted from Stringer (1996, p. 99):

- What activities are required?
  - In the Curanderismo study, if there had been time and resources, there could have been a plan to campaign for the introduction of folk healing into local social work education and training curricula. Specific objects might have been to develop a one-day workshop on folk healing and Curanderismo in a mental health setting or to develop an elective course on this topic in the local M.S.W. and B.S.W. programs.
  - In the eating disorders study, specific objectives might have been to start a self-help group in the high school that was the site of the study and then network with other high schools to set up other such groups. There could have been a plan to develop local self-help groups for adolescent girls focusing on body image, dieting, and eating disorders.

- How are these activities to take place? What is the sequence of tasks?
  - In the Curanderismo study, contacting the local universities, training contractors, NASW, and other training providers would have been the first step, followed by negotiation of curriculum development procedures.
  - In the eating disorders study, tasks would have included engaging the administration of the high school in the project, training facilitators, setting schedules, advertising the self-help groups, and generally networking with adolescent girls.

- Who is to carry out each task?
  - In the Curanderismo study, a task group of Curanderos, social work faculty, students, and potential clients would have been brought together to take on the organizational roles associated with developing a curriculum and steering it through a curriculum acceptance process.

- In the eating disorders study, high school administrators, parents, and other high school female students would have been recruited to campaign for, organize, and run the groups.

- Where will the action take place?
  - In the Curanderismo study, the action would have been implemented in a university.
  - In the eating disorders study, the action would be taking place in the high school.

- When will the action take place?
  - In the Curanderismo study, the timing of the annual curricula development processes would have dictated the action timelines.
  - In the eating disorders study, negotiation with high school administrators and scheduling of the school year would have dictated the timeline.

- What resources are needed and who will acquire them?
  - In the Curanderismo study, this would have been negotiated with training and education providers and would probably have led to applications for grant funding.
  - In the eating disorders study, this would have been negotiated with high school administrators.

- Should people who have not yet participated in the study be asked to help with the action?
  - In the Curanderismo study, more Curanderos and social work academics would need to have been brought into the process to advocate for the curriculum change and manage the curriculum change process.
  - In the eating disorders study, those with expertise in building self-help groups would have been needed as well as experts in group work to train the group facilitators.

- Is the plan realistic?
  - In both our sample studies, the study participants and additional key players would have reviewed these plans for feasibility.

For the critical theory researcher, both the process and the outcome of the study are important. Throughout the development of the plan, researchers need to ensure that the project is empowering participants and that study participants feel that these activities will improve

- pride and feeling of self-worth
- dignity and feeling of autonomy
- sense of social identity (women are not doing "women's work")
- sense of control over what is happening to them
- sense of responsibility and sense of unity

- sense of comfort with the place where both the activity and the planning are taking place, and
- sense of connection to locations with which they have a historical, cultural, or social tie

Since much of the organizing and assignment of tasks will take place in task group settings, the researchers must continually carry out self-assessments, asking themselves whether the group processes they are using to develop action strategies are promoting the empowerment described above. Again we return to our practice colleagues for guidance on such self-assessments. While group work skills that interpret personal behavior or offer reflective responding to personal issues are not so important in this situation, building relationships through warmth, empathy, and genuineness is crucial. The task group facilitator needs to use listening skills and be able to summarize, clarify, and provide information (Kirst-Ashmen & Hull, 2002). Stringer (1996) lays out these skills under the following headings:

Relationships: promoting equality, handling conflicts, acceptance of group members, promoting cooperation, sensitive to diversity

Communication: understandable, truthful, open, sincere, socially and culturally appropriate, open to comment and change

Participation: everybody has a meaningful role, participants supported in role, have direct access to researchers

Inclusion: all stakeholders included, all stakeholders' issues addressed, cooperation with other relevant entities, all relevant groups benefit from action (p. 103)

Keeping participants committed to implementation, if they are not being paid or this is not part of their job, is a challenging process. Even with all the personal investment that has been described so far, volunteers over time develop other priorities or just run out of energy for a project. Thus critical theory researchers need to have a plan to support participants as they move forward with implementation of action and face any obstacles. They need to keep in touch with participants via phone calls, e-mails and meetings. They need to reassure participants that they are doing well and help them reflect on and assess their progress or lack of progress. They need to keep people connected and share any information they may be discovering that will help with the action. They also need to facilitate a support network that is not focused on the researchers but allows each study participant to feel that he or she can get help from several members of the group. All of this will help participants to stay committed to implementing the action plan as well as successful evaluation and celebration. Rutman et al. (2005) give an example of how hard this can be when they discuss the difficulty of keeping the young people involved in their study. They took an egalitarian approach and thus unconsciously assumed that all team members would be comfortable taking initiatives and would have a high level of interpersonal skills. This was not always true, and a lack of structure and hierarchy sometimes was confusing for the young people involved in the study.

To sum up this section, it is clear that for the critical theory researcher, Assessment, Engagement, and Planning are intertwined. While developing an ideological position, this researcher engages both the literature and research participants. Planning emerges from Assessment and Engagement and includes looking, thinking, and acting. A teaching-learning approach that facilitates a partnership between the researcher and study participants is the core of these initial stages of the critical theory research project where the final product is action. This does not look like the research described in Parts I and II of this book. It is definitely not neutral and it definitely has an agenda that includes more than simple data gathering and analysis of findings. These research strategies promote change in power relationships that empower the oppressed.

Main Points

- The initial stages of a critical theory involve simultaneous assessment, engagement, and planning
- Assessment includes reviewing the literature on the chosen ideology as well as the chosen research topic
- Ideology is analyzed in three ways: diachronic, discursive, and conceptual
- The ideological position is developed through a combination of literature review and engagement of study participants at the chosen research site using a teaching-learning approach
- Engaging the research site also requires "establishing a role" through the agenda, stance, and position
- The plan for critical theory research emerges as the study progresses. Phases of this kind of research are "looking," "thinking," and "acting"
- Looking includes a teaching-learning dialogue with study participants guided by emerging ideological themes
- Thinking includes developing a concise statement of the ideological position using strategies such as concept mapping or problem analysis
- The ideological position is shared with the study participants and an action plan is collaboratively developed
- Throughout these stages it is important to pay attention to building and maintaining the researcher-participant partnerships

- The action phase includes planning, implementation, evaluation, and celebration
- During the action phase the researcher is both gathering data and facilitating a task group. These two roles require research and group work skills

Learning Assignments

- Choose an ideology that identifies an oppressed group, a process of oppression, and those with power to oppress. Think of a group locally that is experiencing the consequences of that oppression. Together with your partner develop an action plan to address that oppression. Who would you need to talk to? What would you need to know?
- How would you measure the impact of the action on empowerment? How would you plan to prove that the project empowered the identified oppressed group?

11

Implementation—Gathering Data

Critical theorists can gather quantitative data to support their ideological positions and proposed action plans. They can use the methodologies described in Part I of this book to gather data on needs or to evaluate the effectiveness of a particular action plan. However, such approaches, while gathering data to support empowerment, do not build the researcher partnerships required for an authentic approach to empowerment. This chapter focuses on the collection of qualitative data, since the collection of such data is the primary vehicle for developing teaching-learning relationships between researchers and study participants. So to begin data gathering, like the postpositivist researcher and the constructivist researcher described in Part IV of this book, the critical theory researcher should keep two journals. The first contains the actual data being collected at each phase of the study and the second contains rationales for ideological statements, action strategies, and evaluation decisions. The second journal should also contain reflections on the teaching-learning exchanges and the action taken. Indeed, this journal should include reflections on each stage of the project, since there is so much potential for controversy and loss of clarity about the direction of the project. This section focuses on data to be included in the first journal. The Assessment, Engagement, and Planning strategies discussed above require three major stages of data collection:

Data Collection for Looking and Developing the Ideological Analysis

Data Collection for Action

Data Collection for Evaluation of Action

Data Collection for Looking and Developing the Ideological Analysis

At this stage, the critical theory researcher is refining his or her ideological position as it relates to the focus of the study. Data for this analysis is collected from the literature as well as from interviews with key informants and any supporting observations. The literature on the ideology is reviewed using the synthesis techniques for any literature review, as described in Part I and Part II of this book. It is also reviewed using the process described above in the discussion of "ideological analysis." The researcher may be addressing a topic at the micro or macro practice level. Thus the literature of the ideology and the research topic should be reviewed with this in mind. What do the readings tell us about social work interventions with individuals, families, groups, organizations, or communities and their relationship with power and oppression? In our example studies, the Riech (1994) study of Curanderismo alerted us to a strategy for being culturally sensitive when intervening with a particular population of individuals and families. The Christopulos (1995) study of eating disorders alerted us to an aspect of human development that affects women and may well need to be included in a client assessment protocol.

The interviews with key informants carried out during engagement and initial implementation are aimed at gaining an understanding of the interviewee's perception regarding the ideology and its relevance to him or her. Just to clarify, key informants are "individuals who possess special knowledge, status, or communication skills, who are willing to share that knowledge and skills with the researcher and who have access to perspectives or observations denied the researcher" (Crabtree & Miller, 1992, p. 75). Interviews can be with individuals alone or with groups of participants. When carrying out one-on-one interviews the best practice techniques, according to Evans, Hearn, Uhlemann, and Ivey (2004), include the following skills:

- Listening skills to draw out experiences, issues, and problems
  - Attending behaviors (listening, eye contact, appropriate verbal and non-verbal responses)
  - Effective questioning (timing open and closed questions appropriately and using minimal encouragers appropriately)
  - Reflecting content (hear and clearly describe to the interviewee what you are hearing)
  - Reflecting feeling (identify and reflect emotions)

- Helping interviewees to understand and expand their experiences
  - Communicating and sharing the interviewer's own immediate feelings and reactions.
  - Confronting. In a therapeutic interview, this relates to client behavior. In the critical theory interview, this relates to labeling and exploring power relationships that affect the interviewee.
  - Self-disclosing. Again, this is not the same as a therapeutic interview. It relates to interviewers appropriately disclosing the oppression they have identified and their reasons for adopting the ideology that is guiding the study.
  - Information giving. This includes the results of the ideological analysis of the literature and preliminary analysis of interviews with other key informants.

When interviewing was discussed in the post-positivist part of this book, specific planning and process stages were identified. The critical theory researcher should follow these stages as well (see Chapter 8). Similarly, the data recording options discussed previously can be used. Additionally, the data recording technique will depend on the negotiated comfort that is developed while talking about sensitive political issues. Videotaping or recording an interview may well inhibit the interviewee's willingness to explore power relationships and oppression. The same may be true for taking notes during the interview. Thus the researcher may well need to develop notes after the interview. Since this is an ideological analysis, below are some questions that will help the interviewer to recall what was said about oppression and structure this process.

1. What was the interviewee's personal experience of the power relationship and its oppression? What is his or her history with this?

2. What is the interviewee's perception of the group awareness and experience of this power relationship and oppression?

3. What did the interviewee say about how this power relationship and oppression affects his or her ability to
    - Meet basic physical needs
    - Relate with people
    - Participate in decision-making processes and structures
    - Experience a full formal education
    - Reflect on how he or she was socialized
    - Have access to recreation
    - Develop trust, acceptance, and belief in the society he or she experiences

4. What are his or her demographic characteristics?

Table 11.1   Types of Groups

Type	Setting	Role of Interviewer	Question Format	Purpose
Focus Group	Formal-Preset	Directive	Structured	Exploratory Pretest
Brainstorming	Formal or Informal	Nondirective	Very Unstructured	Exploratory
Nominal/Delphi	Formal	Directive	Structured	Pretest Exploratory
Field, Natural	Informal, Spontaneous	Moderately Nondirective	Very Unstructured	Exploratory Phenomenological
Field, Formal	Preset, but in Field	Somewhat Directive	Semi-structured	Phenomenological

As well as interviews with individuals, critical theory researchers can carry out interviews in group settings. Fontana and Frey (1994, p. 365) offer a typology of such interviews, as shown in Table 11.1.

Critical theory researchers in this early phase of the study are pretesting an ideological position. Thus they should choose either the focus group or nominal/delphi group. With the focus group, all group members address a preset list of questions developed by the researcher. With the nominal/delphi method, there is a preset list of questions, but there is a chance to respond to other participants' answers to the questions. With these processes in mind, the researcher as facilitator needs to apply his or her group work skills. Such researchers need to watch for those who are playing potentially positive roles (information seeker, collaborator, energizer, encourager, tension reliever, listener, etc.) and those who are playing potentially negative roles (dominator, blocker, aggressor, recognition seeker, etc.) (Kirst-Ashman & Hull, 2002). Obviously, the best strategy is to encourage the positive behavior and ignore the negative behavior. Since critical theory research addresses sensitive political topics, the facilitator may well need to deal with group conflict. Kirst-Ashman & Hull suggest that when a conflict emerges, the facilitator can adopt the following strategies:

- Ask participants to listen and then paraphrase what they heard
- Role play a participant's behavior so that they can see how they are being perceived
- Use a board or butcher's paper display to list areas of agreement and disagreement
- Remind participants of the common goal of addressing oppression
- Move the discussion to a discussion of facts rather than opinions and emotions
- Negotiate agreements and concessions for the common good (p. 102)

Thus the researcher, in this context, is the facilitator of a discussion that should not deteriorate into argument but also should not be constrained.

During this ideological analysis stage, a third source of data beyond individual interviews and groups is formal or informal observation. Observation, whether in person or by means of small unobtrusive cameras, can be at least uncomfortable and at most an imposition, no matter how much informed consent is given. In these days of heightened security and various antiterrorism measures, we have all become more accustomed to being observed in public places. Beyond public safety, though, critical theory researchers must ask themselves what gives one person the right to observe and interpret another person's behavior. To simply answer by saying that the observations are necessary for research purposes is not good enough. Not only is the data that is collected using this method subjective, it is a demonstration of power, since it usually does not take into account the perceptions of those being observed. Also, it would be inappropriate, since it suggests that the observer is somehow outside the experience in which he or she is participating. The critical theorist, especially, would argue that none of us is outside social experience. Critical theorists engage study participants rather than observe them from afar.

Given this orientation, the only ethical observation that is possible is in settings in which the observation is obvious and consensual and the report of the observation is shared with participants for feedback, interpretation, and comment. For example, at family events, group meetings, organizational meetings, or community events, the researcher could be identified as an observer and the focus of the enquiry explained. Informed consent would be given with the condition that there is a commitment to share the record of the observations with participants and partner with participants to interpret the meaning of the behaviors that were observed. In this context, the critical theory researcher could carry out participant observation and use the following stages of observation adapted from those offered by Adler & Adler (1994):

1. Select the setting.

2. Gain entrée.

3. Decide on how to record (camera or personally).

4. Develop structure for recording observations.
   - Where are you and what is the name and purpose of the activity?
   - Who is present?
   - What are their power relationships with each other (formal and informal)?

- What incidents happened that illustrate their understanding of the ideological focus of the study?
- What are your conclusions about their understanding of the ideological focus of the study?

5. Decide how and when observations will be shared with participants for joint interpretation.

6. Present the interpretation of the observation to participants in an easily understood format.

7. Engage in a discussion of the interpretation using the teaching-learning philosophy. Modify the interpretation in light of the consensus reached on its meaning during the discussion.

8. Decide how this interpretation will inform the thinking and the action stages of the project.

To sum up, this section on data collection for Looking and developing an ideological analysis has reviewed strategies for discussing oppression with individuals and groups as well as the role of observation and its constraints. We can now move on to a discussion of data collection for action.

Data Collection for Action

The Action phase will be a time when key players are engaged in action for empowerment. Thus at this stage, presentations and materials that will communicate the analysis and alternative action strategies are developed. This could happen in a task group meeting. However, if scheduling such a meeting becomes difficult, then these materials can be posted on a Web site and key players can respond individually or in internet "chat rooms." Also, the materials could be distributed through e-mail and, again, individual reactions could be given. However the process is set up, the key is a learning conversation rather than an expert to non-expert lecture. The goal of this process is to engage key players in an ideological discussion that will result in appropriate action strategies to address oppression.

Data gathering, at this stage, is a process of minute taking and organization. Stringer (1996, p. 100) suggests developing action plans with objectives and organizational charts, as shown in Table 11.2. The researcher, in collaboration with key informants, reviews plans to address strengths, weaknesses, opportunities, and threats.

Using this chart, the task group can identify the action tasks, the steps to be taken, who will be responsible for tasks and steps, where and when the action will happen, and the resources that will be needed. For example,

Table 11.2   Action Planning Chart

Tasks	Steps	People	Place	Time	Budget
1.	a.				
	b.				
	c.				
2.	a.				
	b.				
	c.				
3.	a.				
	b.				
	c.				

in our study of Curanderismo, the task would have included negotiations with the local social work program(s), development of a curriculum on folk healing, negotiating the curriculum review process, and ensuring implementation of the curriculum in social work education and training. Steps for the task would have included identifying the people to be negotiated with and timelines. The people responsible for identifying and implementing these steps would have included students, academics, and experts in Curanderismo. The time would have included scheduling of meetings, and the budget would have included travel and expenses. This is illustrated in Table 11.3.

For the eating disorders study, the tasks could have been negotiating with high school administrators for inclusion of eating disorder groups on high school campuses, development of program, and organizing the groups. The steps could have been meetings with principals and female students as well as contacting experts in group facilitation; the people could have been the researcher, students, parents, and teachers. The timeline could have been for implementation of the groups at the end of one year, and the budget would have been travel to meetings and the cost of materials for the group sessions. This is illustrated in Table 11.4.

Both plans identify tasks so that action for empowerment is carried out as well as assignment of responsibilities and thinking through costs and scheduling. When considering action plans in general, it is necessary to be clear about the level of human organization that is the focus of the action. Is it individuals, families, a particular group, an organization, or a community? The target will dictate data gathering for action. For example, van Olpen et al. (2003), in their description of a policy change campaign to promote community reintegration of drug users leaving jail in Central and East Harlem in New York City, conclude that such reintegration would be facilitated by targeting

Table 11.3   Action Plan for Study of Curanderismo

Tasks	Steps	People Responsible for Task	Place	Time	Budget
1. Negotiate with social work program	a. Contact program head b. Contact faculty members c. Contact students	a. Researcher and experts in Curanderismo b. Students c. Students	At the program's offices	In the fall at the beginning of the academic year	Travel
2 Develop curriculum for training and education	a. Experts in Curanderismo work with key faculty b. Experts in Curanderismo work with key trainers	Curanderismo experts, faculty and students	At any place where participants are comfortable	During fall and winter depending on complexity	Travel
3. Guide curriculum through curriculum review process	a. Find schedule of committee meetings b. Identify key faculty member who will sponsor the curriculum c. Identify someone to check how the process is progressing	a. Social work faculty b. Social work faculty and students c. Researcher and Curanderismo experts	Wherever meetings are held	As scheduled by process	Travel

Table 11.4   Action Plan for Eating Disorders Study

Tasks	Steps	People Responsible for Task	Place	Time	Budget
1. Developing program for eating disorder groups	a. Contact experts on eating disorders b. Search for current programs c. Consult with parents and students and teachers	a. Researcher b. Students and teachers c. Researcher, students, and teachers d. Researcher, administrators, and teachers	At school or in homes	Start in fall at beginning of academic year	Travel
2. Negotiating for groups in high schools	a. Meet with school administrators b. Develop plan for number of groups and when to be implemented c. Negotiate resources for groups	a. Researcher, students b. Researcher, students c. Researcher, students, teachers, administrators	In schools	First groups to start midyear	Travel
3. Implementing groups	a. Scheduling b. Advertising c. Evaluation	a. Administrators b. Researcher, students, parents c. Researcher	In identified school sites	Monthly	Supplies Payment for facilitators and organizers

167

- Policies and programs within prisons so that a comprehensive discharge plan is developed that links offenders to support services and treatment in the community
- The communication between prisons and community health care centers so that medical records are shared
- Medicaid policies so that waiting periods are waived
- Housing policies so that shelters do not refuse to accept people coming out of prison
- Individual employers who discriminate against former inmates so that strategies of rewards can be developed to change these practices
- Employment training programs so that they are encouraged to work with former inmates
- City government entities so that a coordinated community re-entry program is developed

Data Collection for Evaluation of Action Plans

The time for ending and evaluating the project should be set during the planning phase of the project. The evaluation can follow either the constructivist approach described in Part IV of this book or traditional positivist approaches to evaluation described in Part I. Constructivist evaluation, or "fourth generation" evaluation, as identified by Guba and Lincoln (1989), is an approach that requires key players to collaboratively identify claims, concerns, and issues regarding a program and its effectiveness. The group then decides together on the appropriate assessment of the program and any future program development. The traditional positivist approach assesses the process and efficiency of a program through a formative (process) evaluation and the impact of a program by means of a summative (outcome) evaluation that generally uses a pretest/posttest assessment of change. The audience for the evaluation and the function of the evaluation will guide the decision about which evaluation approach to take. In our example studies, our student researchers had an academic audience with certain curriculum prerequisites that were tangential to the project. They opted for positivist outcome evaluations of their presentations of the ideological analysis using pretest/posttest comparisons. Funded projects may also opt for a positivist evaluation, since it generates statistics indicating progress that administrators can easily understand in charts or tables. However, if the evaluation is for study participants or members of the general public who have an interest in the project, then the fourth generation constructivist approach will probably offer more findings that resonate with this audience's perceptions.

This approach will offer participants meaning, a process of reflection, and a future action strategy for the project that requires participant "buy-in" to the proposed action.

Positivist Evaluation

The most rigorous form of outcomes evaluation is the outcome/impact evaluation using the experimental design described in Part I of this book. This is extremely directive and creates artificial groups and power relationships between the researcher and study participants that would not be feasible in a study that operates within the critical theory approach and culture. A non-experimental outcome/impact design would be more feasible. According to Neuman and Kreuger (2003), non-experimental evaluations begin with a description of the ideal situation and then proceed to an assessment of how far the activity has progressed towards that ideal. For a critical theory evaluation of action, the steps are to

1. Describe the ideal empowered power relationship for this topic.

2. Explain the activity, why it was chosen, and how it will affect empowerment.

3. Describe the target organizational entity of the activity.

4. Report progress of activities.

5. Report whether the activity achieved the desired outcome.

In our sample studies, if the action proposed above in the previous discussions had been carried out then the following approaches to evaluation of that action may well have been taken.

Table 11.5 suggests that the ideal outcome is students empowered through knowledge of folk healing and young women empowered by consciousness of healthy decisions regarding body image. The activities to achieve this involve curriculum development and self-help groups in universities and high schools respectively. The action planning tables are used to show activities and progress, and pretest/posttest data is gathered to identify whether the desired empowerment was achieved.

Constructivist Evaluation

In this approach to evaluating the critical theory activity, the circle of key informants is interviewed separately after completing the activity and asked about their claims, concerns, and issues regarding the activity. They are

Table 11.5   Potential Assessment Plan of Action Resulting from Example
Student Studies

	Riech study of Curanderismo	*Christopulos study of eating disorders*
1. Ideal Situation	Social work students know about Curanderismo and can refer to a Curandero when appropriate	Young women make their own decisions about body image and eating habits
2. Activity	Infusion of folk healing in social work curriculum to inform students	Self-help groups in high schools to promote women's "healthy" body image and eating habits
3. Target	University	High School
4. Report on Progress	Identification of achievements using action planning tables	Identification of achievements using action planning tables
5. Did activities achieved desired outcomes?	Comparison of scores on students' knowledge of folk healing before and after curriculum intervention	Comparison of female high school students' scores on measures of body image before and after participating in self-help groups

asked what they liked about the activity and what they did not like about the activity. As these "constructions" are shared, a joint construction emerges noting areas of agreement and issues of disagreement. When all stakeholders have been interviewed separately and been given the opportunity to respond to others' constructions a "member check" meeting is held to finalize the joint construction of the impact of the activity. As a group, the key players decide what worked, what did not, and what further action needs to be taken. A detailed description of this approach to evaluation is offered in Part IV of this book.

To sum up this discussion of implementation, when implementing research critical theorists gather data and take action. Thus the implementation needs are data gathering for ideological analysis, action, evaluation, and organizing for action. The data gathered both reports on the progress of the study and facilitates the action steps to address oppression.

Main Points

- Implementation consists of three types of data gathering: data gathering for the ideological analysis, data gathering for action, and data gathering for evaluating action
- Data gathering for ideological analysis, beyond the literature, includes individuals and groups and observational data collected under clearly defined conditions
- In the Looking phase, researchers carry out interviews that not only follow the usual phases of an interview but also address the interviewee's experience of oppression and empowerment
- In group interviews, as well as using the usual group work skills, researchers should adopt strategies to address conflict
- Observational data can be collected under specific circumstances of full disclosure
- Data gathering for action includes development of work plans with assigned tasks, timelines, and budgets
- Data collection in the evaluation stage will follow either the traditional positivist techniques described in Part I of this book or constructivist techniques addressed in Part IV of this book

Learning Assignments

1. Form small discussion groups. Imagine you are a community group discussing the ideology you identified at the end of Chapter 10. One group member should take on the role of the researcher and the others are community members who are not clear about the ideology or are not sure whether they are oppressed by it. Have a discussion with the goal of coming to a consensus about the impact of the ideology.

2. After the discussion, make notes on the discussion. Record data that was gathered and your rationales for any ideological statements, action strategies, and evaluation decisions. Then get together with the other members of the group and compare notes. Did you manage to remember everything?

12

Evaluation—Developing an Understanding of the Data and Its Meaning

The critical theory researcher has three sets of data to analyze: the first is the data for developing the ideological position, the second is the data for developing the action plan, and the third is the evaluation data regarding the effectiveness of the action. Positivist researchers interpret and explain the meaning of their data using quantitative analysis procedures, as described in Part I of this book. Post-positivist researchers interpret and explain the meaning of their data by carrying out qualitative analysis procedures, as described in Part II of this book. Indeed, the evaluation data gathered by critical theory researchers is analyzed using one or both of these approaches. However, to discuss the analysis of the meaning of the bulk of the data collected by critical theory researchers we need to explore the meaning and function of the term analysis in more detail. The word "analyze," according to the Oxford dictionary, means "examine minutely the constitution of . . . ascertain constituents of (sample of mixture or compound); find or show the essence of structure of (book, music, etc.)," and "analysis" is defined as "resolution into simpler elements by analyzing; statement of result of this . . . use of algebra and calculus in problem-solving." Thus positivist and post-positivist quantitative and qualitative analysis techniques are simply two of many strategies for analyzing or evaluating the meaning of data. For the critical theory researcher the analysis of the data focuses on interpreting the power relationships being revealed. Three kinds of analysis are discussed here that are most useful for understanding the meaning of empowerment and action. These are emergent, ideological, and action analyses.

Emergent Analysis

John and Lynn Lofland (1995), in their book *Analyzing Social Settings,* suggest that in research based in a social setting, analysis is conceived as an "*emergent* product of a process of gradual induction" (p. 181). Such analysis must be worked at and is not simply the creative fictional product of the frustrated novelist! These authors identify six aspects of carrying out emergent analysis (pp. 181–203). They are not all adopted or experienced by everyone, but they are all potential approaches to revealing the meaning of the data. Thus through this analysis the critical theory researcher finds ways to reveal the ideological meaning of the data and the meaning of the action data.

Social Science Framing. With this approach the analysis aims to formulate generic propositions that summarize and organize the data. According to Lofland and Lofland (1995), a proposition can be a hypothesis, a thesis, a concept, an assertion, an idea, a theme, a problem, a story line, general principles, or general interpretations. Dimensions for structuring of propositions include type, frequencies, magnitudes, structures, processes, causes, consequences, and agency (the strategies that people use who are participants in the proposition). In the study of eating disorders, the feminist proposition that eating disorders result from patriarchy is being formed. The researcher looked for examples of this oppression in both literature and the feedback from the high school students. This analysis led to the conclusion stated in the study question regarding magnitudes, structures, processes, causes, consequences, and agency:

> eating disorders in women, brought on by the oppression of women and confusing messages delivered to women by society and the media, can be eliminated by re-socializing women's perspectives at the high school level. Feminist critical theory suggests that indoctrinating women with the misconception that success is measured only by body size and the worthless pursuit for an unattainable "ideal" body is a method by which the patriarchy attempts to control women. (Christopulos, 1995, p. 1)

Socializing Anxiety. In carrying out emergent inductive analysis, researchers allow their data to interact with their intuition and sensibilities. Such an open-ended process can create anxiety and uncertainty since it is not a mechanical, lock step process. It is important to recognize this anxiety as normal and persistently move forward with the analysis process believing that propositions will emerge. In both our example studies, the students were aware that they were taking political positions regarding their research topics, but they built those positions through data and showed that there was a foundation for being concerned about the oppression they had identified.

Coding. This is the core physical activity in emergent deductive analysis. Such analysis develops codes by asking questions about the data, such as "What topic is this data an example of?" "What question about that topic does it suggest?" "What answer to, or proposition about, that question does this data suggest?" Strategies for coding have been described in the post-positivist and constructivist sections of this book under the headings of "open coding" and "building and modifying units," respectively.

Memoing. This is included in the narrative that is written in the research journal where rationales for ideological statements and action steps are recorded. Memos explain the codes and their connections with other codes. They can be a sentence, a paragraph, or several pages. To guide the critical theory memo writing, we return to the questions noted above in ideological analysis and refocus them for analysis. The questions become:

- What does the data say about these study participants' experience with this form of oppression and their potential for empowerment?
  - How has this oppression and potential for empowerment evolved over time with these participants? What are the themes?
  - What are the participants' current understandings of this oppression and potential for empowerment? How do they name and define it?
  - Why have these developments taken place?
  - Who are the key articulators of this oppression and potential for empowerment?
- Which power relations do participants identify as examples of this oppression and potential for empowerment?
  - Which participants or outside stakeholders are considered powerful?
  - Which participants or outside stakeholders are identified as needing to be empowered?
  - What action is favored for empowerment?
- What does the data say about these participants' overall experience of this oppression and the potential for empowerment, including the action strategies to empower?

Diagramming. This is the use of visual displays to succinctly display the relationships between concepts. A diagram is a product of analysis. Lofland and Lofland (1995) identify four kinds of diagrams: typologies, matrix making, concept charting, and flow charting.

- Typologies are the cross-classification of two or more ideas (e.g., Table 10.1 in Chapter 10)
- Matrix making is the construction of more complex typologies where lists of categories are cross-referenced (e.g., the power analysis chart in Table 12.1 below)
- Concept charting takes place when researchers are able to display separate concepts and then move them around as connections between concepts emerge. Lofland and Lofland (1995) quote Carol Stack's comment about analyzing data for *All Our Kin: Strategies for Survival in a Black Community* (1974). To keep her notes and data safe from her active child, she would pin them to the walls throughout her apartment. This practice prompted her to display the data in configurations and to order and reorder them as she thought about them and looked at them over time.
- Flow charting is a development of concept charting where the concepts identified in the data are displayed visually over time or in a connected process (e.g., Figure 10.1 in Chapter 10)

Thinking Flexibly. This raises the question that is crucial for any researcher interested in research methods that are alternatives to those offered by the positivist worldview. Namely, can any analysis be reduced to mechanical, structured, routines? This is even more of a pressing question with the software programs for qualitative data analysis that have become so popular. These authors suggest that such software programs do the initial storage and categorizing of qualitative data efficiently and effectively. However, the latter stages of synthesis and interpretation should not be left to the unknown rules and machine code created by a computer programmer. Critical theory researchers, in particular, are interpreting problems in data with a mindset that cannot be captured by mechanical routine. It is their knowledge and understanding of a particular ideology that is guiding the process of understanding the data. Thus flexible thinking strategies will allow them to recognize the power relationships, potential for empowerment, and favored action strategies in their data. Loftus and Loftus (1995) suggest various strategies for flexible thinking: rephrasing questions, changing diagrams, constantly comparing concepts being identified, thinking in extremes and opposites when making propositions, discussing interpretations with colleagues, standing back to assess the whole picture, and withholding judgment about conclusions for as long as possible.

Analysis for the critical theory researcher is not only the emergent inductive analysis of primarily qualitative data from interviews and observations, as described above. There is another level of analysis of this data where the focus is the ideological reality revealed by the data.

Ideological Analysis

Procedures for analysis of an ideology in the literature at the beginning of a critical theory study are offered in Chapter 10. However, an additional ideological analysis is carried out when interpreting the data gathered from key informants during the teaching-learning process of "Looking." The goal of this analysis is to offer a synthesis that describes the oppression and empowerment experienced by study participants. For example, Hope and Timmel (1999), in their handbook for community workers, offer an instrument that can be used to carry out individual power inventories. This instrument can be given to study participants during the Looking phase. Data collected in these inventories can then be aggregated to give a description of the power position of individuals, families, groups, organizations, or communities that are the focus of the study. The instrument has been adapted below and basically it asks the following groups of questions.

1. What job do you have? What jobs do your relatives have? What jobs do your friends have? The answers to these questions can be categorized into socioeconomic groupings and used to describe the class position of study participants, their families, and their social networks. In our example studies, this question would have been asked in relation to school and university rather than workplace. In the Riech (1994) study of Curanderismo, such questions would have shown the collaborating researcher and study participants who was best placed to effect change in the university and practice setting. The Christopulos (1995) study of eating disorders could have used this information to strategically negotiate with school districts.

2. What organizations do you belong to? What organizations do your relatives belong to? What organizations do your friends belong to? This data can be aggregated to show community links to power and action. In both our example studies, such information would have shown who was a member of a university or high school committee or organization that could have influence to effect change.

3. What businesses do you use? What businesses do your relatives use? What businesses do your friends use? This data can be aggregated to show

the economic power of study participants. This data would not have been a priority in our example studies but may well have shown the limited economic power of those seeking empowerment.

Data collected from these three questions can be used to develop a narrative description of study participants' power positions. The narrative would be subdivided into discussion of individual participants, their families and relatives, the organizations represented by the study participants, and the community links represented by the participants.

In relation to work, organizational memberships, and business use:

a. What are your, your relatives', and your friends' roles?
    i.   Formal Employed Leader
    ii. Elected Leader
    iii. Member/Worker/Customer

b. What is your, your relatives', your friends' influence?
    i.   Formal
    ii. Informal (explain)
    iii. None

Data from question 4 can be tabulated as shown in Table 12.1. Three tables could be created giving totals for the interviewee, relatives, and friends. This would give a numerical description of the power positions of study participants. In our example studies, these numbers would have

Table 12.1   Power Analysis Chart I

	Workplace, School, or University	*Organizational Membership*	*Business Use*
Roles			
1. Formal Employed Leader			
2. Elected Leader			
3. Member/Worker/Customer			
Influence			
1. Formal			
2. Informal			
3. None			

Table 12.2   Power Analysis Chart II

Your Power Over	Workplace, School, or University	Organizational Membership	Business Use
People			
Money			
Physical Property			
Various Skills (give list)			
Introducing New Ideas			

(1 = low; 2 = medium; 3 = high)

shown clearly the power position of study participants and the arenas in which they could most effectively work for empowerment.

What kind of power do you (your relatives, your friends) have? Is it

a. Power over:
   i. People
   ii. Money
   iii. Physical Property
   iv. Various Skills
   v. Introduction of New Ideas

For the above three functions give a score of 1 (low), 2 (medium), 3 (high).

This data would be tabulated as shown in Table 12.2. In our example studies, university students and high school students would have been able to identify their power positions with more precision and understanding.

For the above three affiliations, give a rating of 1 (low), 2 (medium), 3 (high), and/or give examples of the entity's

b. Power over:
   i. People
   ii. Money
   iii. Physical Property
   iv. Various Skills
   v. Introduction of New Ideas
   vi. Something Else?

Table 12.3   Power Analysis Chart III

Entity's Power Over	Workplace, School, or University	Organizational Membership	Business Use
Power over (people, money, property, skills, introduction of new ideas, other)			
Representation in Other Groups			
Representation in Gov. Groups			
Influence with Members			
Influence with Other Groups			
Influence with Media			
New Ideas, Intro. and Control			

   c. Representation in other groups
   d. Representation in groups established by government
   e. Influence with its members
   f. Influence with other groups in the community
   g. Influence with the media
   h. Ability to introduce or control the introduction of new ideas

This data can be tabulated as shown in Table 12.3. In our example studies, we would now have a numerical description of the power of not only our study participants but also their affiliations.

This complete set of data can be combined with Hope and Timmel's (1999) definition of power when, in their case, they were discussing racism (pp. 126–127). In this definition they noted that those who have power

- Set the standards by which they and others are judged; that is, they set the standards for appropriate behavior
- Have the capacity to make and enforce decisions that affect the lives of other people
- Have access to resources and control the distribution of resources
- Define the parameters of a discussion and determine the ideological framework within which debate takes place; that is, they define the problem and therefore determine the solutions that will be considered

These four dimensions can be labeled normative power, hierarchical power, resource power, and conceptual power. Thus data from a survey of the items in the above instrument can be summarized and analyzed, using this definition, to show the power of the individual, family, group, organization, or community that is the focus of the study. Charts can be developed aggregating the four kinds of power, as shown in Table 12.4, for participants in the study and their relatives and friends. In each of the blank spaces would be a numerical score as well as a reference to qualitative examples written up in narrative form as case studies. Such a power analysis of participants would develop further consciousness of the ideological message of the study. It would also suggest content for the teaching-learning phase and arenas for action strategies to promote empowerment.

For example, in our study of eating disorders, the adolescent girls could have identified school-based organizations in which they and their friends could or should have normative or conceptual power to influence development of school-based programs to address female eating disorders. They may have also become aware of their lack of power in institutions that create their role models for eating and body types, such as the media. In the Curanderismo study, the students, likewise, could have identified campus-based organizations and faculty with whom they had influential relationships who could lead initiatives to develop curriculum on folk healing. The students may also have become aware of their lack of power over curriculum development.

Action Analysis

In considering change strategies that emerge from ideological analysis, the critical theory researcher uses a conceptual matrix to categorize each strategy and therefore understand the significance of the activity. Both dimensions of the matrix are the same: levels of human organization we intervene with as generalist social workers. The intent of the action is empowerment. Table 12.5 illustrates this approach. If the target of action is an organization and the instigator of action is an individual, that individual should have scored high on the power inventory to able to carry out an activity that achieves empowerment for an identified disempowered group in the organization. Likewise if a community plans to intervene with an organization, the aggregate power inventory for that community should be high on all four dimensions so that they can indeed empower an identified target. When an organization intervenes with an individual to address

Table 12.4   Framework for Reporting Power Analysis

	Normative Power	Hierarchical Power	Resource Power	Conceptual Power

Job, School, or University:
  Your Role
  Your Influence				

Organization:
  Your Role
  Your Influence				

Business:
  Your Role
  Influence				

Job Site's, School's, or University's:
  Power over (people, money,
  property, skills, introduction
  of new ideas, other)
Representation in Other Groups
Representation in Gov. Groups
Influence with Members
Influence with Other Groups
Influence with Media
New Ideas, Intro. and Control				

Organization's:
  Power over (people, money,
  property, skills, introduction
  of new ideas, other)
Representation in Other Groups
Representation in Gov. Groups
Influence with Members
Influence with Other Groups
Influence with Media
New Ideas, Intro. and Control				

Business's:
  Power over (people, money,
  property, skills, introduction
  of new ideas, other)
Representation in Other Groups
Representation in Gov. Groups
Influence with Members
Influence with Other Groups
Influence with Media
New Ideas, Intro. and Control				

Table 12.5   Chart Clarifying Instigators and Targets of Action for Empowerment

		Targets of Action				
		Individual	Family	Group	Organization	Community
Instigators of Action	Individual					
	Family					
	Group					
	Organization					
	Community					

empowerment, for example county social workers addressing spousal abuse of women, it generally has normative, hierarchical, resource, and conceptual power.

The actual action strategies will depend on the results of the action planning. Much will rest with the social work researcher's practice skills. If the plan is for an individual to intervene with any of the targets of action, then that individual will need to have not only the appropriate power scores but also the skills to intervene at the micro or macro level. If a family is to intervene with any target, this is most likely to be a result of power and affiliation scores, but they will still need guidance and support as they move forward with action. For example, in our example studies an influential family may have intervened with an individual or other family that they knew well who had power in the university or school setting. In addition, such a family may have influence on the school board, with the university trustees, or in local government. While taking action to enact empowerment, though, family members would need support and guidance on appropriate strategies. When the instigator of action is an organization or community, the leaders of those entities will be using micro and macro practice skills to move action forward. Again, support and guidance are needed.

To sum up this analysis section, it has been acknowledged that critical theory researchers will carry out the usual qualitative and quantitative analyses of data identified in Parts I and II of this book when appropriate. However, the critical theory researcher also carries out additional analysis that more clearly identifies the substance and structure of ideology and action: emergent analysis, ideological analysis, and analysis for action.

Main Points

- When understanding the power relationships being revealed in the data, the critical theory researcher can use three possible approaches: emergent, ideological, and action analyses
- Emergent analysis uses various strategies to inductively identify propositions
- Ideological analysis facilitates a more specific statement of power relations and arenas for potential empowerment
- Action analysis clearly identifies instigators and targets of action. It also illuminates the practice skills needed to carry out action

Learning Assignments

- Think about your situation as a student. Either individually or in a group, carry out an ideological analysis and an action analysis of your situation. Share your analysis with other members of your class.
- Decide how you would carry out your action plan.

13

Termination and Follow-Up—Reporting on Findings, Exiting the Research Setting, and Communication and Distribution of Research Findings

For critical theory researchers, this final stage of the project includes not only reporting and distributing findings but also reflection and celebration. The first audience for reporting findings is the people who were the targets of empowerment. The researcher and study participants jointly develop a statement on the progress made on empowerment. This might be a statement to the media; a community meeting; a more personal private communication at a group or individual meeting; or individual letters, e-mails, and phone calls to those for whom empowerment was promoted. A further formal report is given to the sponsors of the project. Like any other researcher, the critical theory researcher will also publish research findings to the audience of professional colleagues, generally in academic settings. One function of reporting, for the critical theory researcher, is not only communicating findings but also exiting the community. The project would not have been successful if the community was not now able to carry on the work that had been started. Disengagement, termination, and celebration are carried out in a thoughtful, careful manner where control of the product is ceded to the study participants.

Reporting to Participants and the Target Entity

The primary responsibility of the critical theory researcher is to ensure that study participants and the target entity (whether it be individuals, families, groups, organizations, or communities) are informed about the study and its impact. Thus the results of the study need to be packaged in ways that communicate most effectively with these entities. For communication with individuals, families, and groups, informal phone calls, e-mails, and personal conversations may be enough. However, if formal communication is expected, then the critical theory researcher has the responsibility to organize meetings and develop presentations and handouts that explain the study and its impact. In addition, key informants should be invited to contribute to the presentation and give their perceptions of the impact of the project. This is an important phase of disengaging with the participants in the study, since the goal is to convince the participants to lead future empowerment activities. Formal methods of presentation include developing a PowerPoint presentation, distributing handouts summarizing the project, and organizing joint panel discussions with researchers and participants. Media representatives may well be invited to such presentations as well as appropriate organizational leaders. The presentations should include the following items with variations in sequencing as seems appropriate:

- Summary of problem and ideological orientation to problem
- Description of teaching-learning engagement with community and key player participation (if confidentiality is requested, then the role can be listed, e.g., a local teacher, various representatives of clients of the department of children's services)
- Summary of analysis of data from key informants
- Overview of action plan
- Description of action taken
- Review of impact of action
- Statement of celebration and reflection on action and suggestions for future action

Reporting to Participants, Funding Sources, and Academic Settings

The critical theory researcher will also need to formally report to sponsors of the study and communicate the findings to the wider social work academic and practice community. This raises the question of who would fund such challenging, and perhaps controversial, research. In this era of poverty action centers and empowered women, minority action groups and gay rights groups, the infrastructure is developing that can sustain such projects. Given a clear proposal and methodology, such projects have the potential to be sponsored by various action groups. For such groups, as well as the academic audience, a traditional report or article should be written. Lofland and Lofland (1995) offer helpful guidelines for structuring the report. These are modified and reorganized here for the critical theory need.

1. Title. This should reflect the overall ideological orientation and the topic that is the focus of the study. For example, "Psychotherapy Encounters Curanderismo: Implications for Clients Treated in the United States by Culturally Insensitive Social Workers" or "Oppression through Obsession: A Feminist Critique of Eating Disorders."

2. Abstract and Table of Contents that give an overview of the content and organization of the report.

3. Introductory paragraphs that lay out the ideological orientation, the topic or issue being studied in the form of a proposition about power relations, and the need to promote empowerment. For example,

The United States is made up of many races, creeds, cultures, and ethnic groups that have come together, each with their own social constructs. Therefore, social workers involved in direct practice need to be aware of their clients' or patients' worldview. This study examined the worldview of the Mexican immigrant living in the United States, or Mexican Americans, who participate in the phenomenon of folk healing. The particular type of folk healing addressed in this study was Curanderismo, which is the folk beliefs about illness, herbal medicine, curative practices, and psychiatric therapy. The preceding is a positive definition . . . the actual dictionary definition of a Curandero is, "Quack, Medicaster, an artful and tricking practitioner of physic." (Riech, 1994, p. 1)

or

This research project asked how obsession with weight and body image preoccupies women and adopted an ideology that suggests that such obsession renders women powerless. The ideological position of this critical theory study is that eating disorders in women, brought on by the oppression of women and confusing messages delivered to women by society and the media, can be eliminated by re-socializing women's perspectives at the high school level. (Christopulos, 1995, p. 1)

4. Early Overview. As the nuns taught me at convent schools when drilling me on how to write an essay, "Say what you are going to say, say it, and then say you

have said it." This is the essence of the summary given in the overview. What was the study intended to do? What did it do? What was its impact?

5. Literature Review. Give an integrated review of both the review of the ideology, as noted in the critical theory engagement section in Chapter 10, and the literature on the specific issue or problem that is the focus of the enquiry. This means that the literature is organized in terms of themes that are used as headings. It is not an annotated bibliography in which a series of readings are summarized.

6. Describe Data Sources. In this section discuss the selection of the key informants, approaches to gathering data from them, the sources for action strategies, and the approach to evaluating the action. Talk about the partnerships with participants, strategies for engaging participants, and the practical details of interviewing and observing.

7. Subdivided Main Body. Organize discussion of the study under the stages that have been discussed here.
   a. Assessment, Engagement, and Planning
   b. Implementation
   c. Evaluation
   d. Termination and Follow-Up

8. Summary and Conclusions

9. Bibliography

Of course, when writing the report or article it is important to follow appropriate conventions regarding style and layout. In social work this is usually the American Psychological Association (APA) style and sometimes *The Chicago Manual of Style*. Make sure the report flows logically and the reader can easily understand the organization of the report.

Alternative Forms of Presentation

There are many critical theorists, particularly feminists, who have challenged the traditional methods of reporting to the academic community as simply an arbitrary set of rules that have been accepted as the correct way to represent reality (Wolf, 1992; Mascia-Lees, Sharpe, & Cohen, 1989; Clough, 1992). Mulkay (1985) has experimented with different forms of presentation including presenting the results of data analysis as conversations between ideal type characters discussing the concepts and categories being developed, in the form of a one-act play or sketch. For some authors, this has gone as far as developing drama and theatre out of data (Mienczakowski, 1994, 1995).

Such dialogues have been presented to study participants with the aim of giving them a voice regarding the issue of oppression being addressed in the study. Such approaches combine both the written and oral presentation of information. This approach to reporting by combining the arts with research has been expanded into writing fictional stories and poetry based on the data that has been collected and analyzed (Krieger, 1984; Richardson, 1992).

Reflection and Celebration

In his article on self-reflection in research, Bell (1998) suggests that critical theory researchers need to reflect on their personal context, their social context, and the complex environmental context of the research setting when understanding and reflecting on a research project. He concludes that researchers are fallible and vulnerable people who, rather than impose their view of the world on the research setting, can partner with others to develop an understanding of a particular research project and its findings and mistakes. He advises that the nonreflective researcher will experience unrealistic quality standards, doubt, a fear and need for self-preservation, incessant self-expression, undue self-assertion, and a feeling of being out of his or her depth. A reflective practitioner will experience realistic expectations, tolerance, humility, self-giving, listening, and a feeling of being part of the project rather than outside the project. The overall idea of reflection is to establish a norm that no research project is the perfect project and that we can all learn to do better the next time. Such a norm frees us to approach a research project with the idea that we will do the best that we can but always assume that we will make unanticipated mistakes. Thus when our study is found to have shortcomings, as all studies are, we celebrate our learning rather than apologize for our incompetence.

For both Stringer (1996) and Finn and Jacobson (2003), an important part of evaluation, reflection, and termination of a project is "celebration" of the project and its accomplishments. Finn and Jacobson note that celebration of achievements keeps us focused on our vision for the project and for a just world (p. 359). They suggest that celebration includes

- Celebrating learning, not just winning
- Creating a celebratory spirit by, for example, decorating a meeting room and providing food and snacks
- Celebrating our adversaries as well as our allies
- Including personal touches during the research project such as remembering peoples' birthdays or celebrating project milestones

- Celebrating symbols of and milestones in resistance to oppression, such as taking time to celebrate national women's day or a cultural holiday in the middle of a project
- Celebrating to bring joy into work

To sum up this discussion, for the critical theorist there are both internal and external audiences for the final report of the project and there are many dimensions to terminating a project that include not only communicating information but the spirit in which information is communicated. A democratic partnership is essential and reflection and celebration are mandatory.

Main Points

- For the critical theorist, the goal of the final stage of the project is to give the study participants ownership of the project
- This is done by reporting findings in user-friendly modes, reflecting on the strengths and weaknesses of the study, and celebrating both the achievements of this project and the potential for future empowerment

Learning Assignments

- Plan a presentation and celebration for the project you identified at the end of Chapter 10.
- Discuss with your group how you would report and celebrate the student empowerment you identified at the end of Chapter 12.

Conclusion

This discussion of critical theory research has offered rationales and methods for carrying out value-laden research that is driven by an ideological position and inspired by empowerment and social justice. This approach is political and addresses power. It requires both analysis of a research focus and action. The critical theory researcher must be skilled at engaging people at the micro and macro level and willing to partner with research participants, be open to new ideas, and share power. The ideological position evolves from both the literature and data gathered from research participants. Action plans are focused, organized, and formally evaluated. The impact of the study is reported, reflected on, and truly celebrated. This is an exciting approach to research that can sometimes be controversial but is always dynamic and challenging.

PART IV

Constructivism

Introduction to Part IV

This is the paradigm that presents the biggest challenge to traditional positivist approaches to research and is most likely to resonate with social work students interested in working with individuals, families, groups, organizations, and communities. To start off our discussion, here is a quick quiz to see whether you are a constructivist or at least a person who wants to do a constructivist study:

1. Do you love your social work practice courses, especially micro?   Y___   N___

2. Do you have *no* idea what your research instructor is talking about?   Y___   N___

3. Do you have an emotional tie to a topic that you would like to do research on but are completely overwhelmed by the research methods that you should use?   Y___   N___

4. Do you enjoy talking to people . . . and listening to them?   Y___   N___

5. Do you like to write?   Y___   N___

6. Do you find that the world makes much more sense when you read or hear about it than when you are presented with statistics about it?   Y___   N___

7. Are you comfortable with uncertainty?   Y___   N___

8. Do you like to work collaboratively?   Y___   N___

9. Are statistics an absolute mystery to you?   Y___   N___

10. Is your favorite color blue?   Y___   N___

If your answer to at least nine of these questions is "yes," then this is the section of the book for you. The constructivist paradigm is the only one of the four that does not assume an objective reality but instead proposes that human experience can only be understood as a subjective reality. It recognizes that we all understand the world from our own points of view and supposes that nobody can stand outside the human experience to observe laws and regulatory mechanisms independent of situation and person. Thus the only way we can understand a human phenomenon is to completely and thoroughly understand the perceptions, or constructions, of those people who are engaged in that human phenomenon. Constructivists propose that researchers gathering new knowledge about the human experience must gather subjective data. To do this they collaborate with those involved in a particular human experience to create a valid, authentic, shared construction of the human experience being researched. Such a collaboration and construction is termed a "hermeneutic dialectic." It is hermeneutic because it seeks out individual interpretations and it is a dialectic because individual interpretations are compared and contrasted and may well change during the hermeneutic dialectic.

This constructivist approach to knowing is rooted in the works of Nelson Goodman, Ernst von Glasersfeld, Kenneth and Mary Gergen, and Egon Guba and Yvonna Lincoln. Nelson Goodman (1984) talked about "irrealism." Schwandt (1994) explains this constructivist theory as

> pluralistic and pragmatic. Through our nonverbal and verbal symbol systems we create many versions of the world in the sciences, the arts, and the humanities. Our process of inquiry is not a matter of somehow getting in touch with the ready-made work; rather, "worldmaking as we know it always starts from worlds already on hand: the making is remaking" (Goodman, 1978, p. 6). These "remakings" are not simply different interpretations of the same world, but literally different world versions. (Schwandt, 1994, p. 126)

Ernst von Glasersfeld (1991) developed the notion of "radical constructivism." Schwandt (1994) characterizes this position as one where "we cannot know such a thing as an independent, objective world that stands apart from our experience of it. Hence we cannot speak of knowledge as somehow corresponding to, mirroring, or representing that world" (p. 127). Kenneth Gergen (1985) further developed the constructivist worldview by developing "social constructionism," which is the study of shared constructions and focuses on the joint development of worldviews by groups of people. His position is that reality is not some stand-alone entity but is shared constructions rather than an objective knowable truth. As well as these writers, when discussing constructivism, Schwandt (1994) includes the philosophers and theorists of "interpretism" from the German tradition of hermeneutics and the Verstehen tradition of sociology to complete an explanation of the intellectual background of the constructivist paradigm and its approaches to gathering knowledge.

Guba and Lincoln (1989) approach the constructivist paradigm from the perspective of program evaluation. In their book *Fourth Generation Evaluation,* they give a brief history of approaches to program evaluation that offers a rationale for adopting a constructivist approach to research in general. They note that the first generation of evaluation stressed measurement. Evaluation consisted of measuring individuals on, for example, IQ tests or other objective tests. The second generation of evaluation acknowledged the person's context and stressed the need for description or formative evaluation of program materials, intervention techniques, and organizational patterns. The third generation of evaluation stressed judgment and introduced the idea of measuring progress towards previously stated objectives. Each of these three generations demonstrated an increasing sophistication in understanding program evaluation. However, even at the third generation, approaches to evaluation had some limitations. They tended to disempower the perspectives of stakeholders who are the subjects of evaluation and empower the perspectives of managers of the program who sponsor the evaluation and adopt a stand outside the evaluation, even though they are the program's leaders and managers. Also, using third generation evaluation, the evaluator usually measures objectives that are developed by the program leadership rather than the array of stakeholders. Finally, the evaluator using these approaches, whether consciously or unconsciously, assumes that he or she is carrying out "science" and is therefore revealing the "truth." This is problematic given the contextual influences on evaluation such as the avoidance of politically sensitive questions or the potential for the misuse of evaluation results to penalize program personnel or clients.

Such developments illustrate the tensions that have led some researchers to explore the constructivist approach not only to evaluation, but to research in general. Many find that when they adopt the traditional positivist approach to research, the problem that they were originally interested in mutates from an exciting idea that energized their imagination to a sterile question and hypothesis that includes precisely defined independent and dependent variables that must be accurately measured but are an anemic depiction of the original focus of research. For example, someone with a commitment to undocumented immigrants and their resettlement experiences can see the life taken out of her project when the research focus is narrowed down to a question about "length of time to employment" or "indicators of acculturation." Or, someone with a personal commitment to understanding HIV-AIDS must step outside the experience of the issue to identify "factors that affect service delivery" or "factors that facilitate community education regarding HIV-AIDS." Such neutral statements are a long way from the emotion and personal insight that sparks a question like "I care about people living with HIV-AIDS; what's more, I love them. I have a family member living with HIV-AIDS and I want to do a study that may enrich his life. How can I understand and express this and make it happen?"

So, what exactly is research? A positivist researcher confronted by the HIV-AIDS question above would conclude that clearly this is not a research question but an emotional commitment to practice that will at best distort "scientific" research. The Oxford dictionary defines research as "careful search or inquiry after or for or into; endeavor to discover new or collate old facts, etc., by scientific study of a subject, course of critical investigation." This definition rests on facts and science. It does not state that only variables measured quantitatively are facts, or that science is positivism. Constructivists argue that subjective constructions are facts and that the constructivist approach is science. A subjective description of living with HIV-AIDS is something that is known to have occurred or be true; it is precise, its existence cannot be ignored, and it is real. All these are criteria for deciding whether something is a fact according to the same Oxford dictionary. The constructivist approach develops knowledge that is systematic, deduced from self-evident truths, and follows consistent principles. Constructivist research thus builds a legitimate body of knowledge using a methodology that is scientific.

14

Engagement, Assessment, and Planning—Entrée to the Research Setting, Development of Understanding of the Research Focus, Rationales for Gathering Data

The guiding principle of this subjectivist approach to research is that data are unique to their time and place. For example, a researcher studying HIV-AIDS in California is assumed to be studying a different phenomenon than a researcher studying HIV-AIDS in Wisconsin. The constructivist researcher starts with a topic or focus of research and an understanding of his or her construction of the topic, not a specific research question and hypothesis addressing causality or correlation. Thus the goal is not to arrive at research findings that can be generalized to other settings but rather to gather valid data about a problem or issue in its context. Consumers of the research make their own judgments about the validity of the findings and their applicability to other settings. Constructivists refer to such decisions as assessments of "trustworthiness" and "transferability."

A number of authors (Guba, 1981; Lincoln & Guba, 1985; Erlandson, Harris, Skipper, & Allen, 1993) offer criteria for evaluating whether constructions are trustworthy. Trustworthy constructions must have credibility, transferability, dependability, and confirmability.

Credibility refers to the need for written constructions to be accurate descriptions of study participants' perspectives. The researcher achieves this by means of prolonged engagement with the research setting; ongoing analysis of and reflection on data in the form of written accounts of interviews and observations; compilation of constructions from key players with diverse points of view; reporting on artifacts, such as pictures and documents, that enrich understanding of the research context; peer debriefing during data collection; and checking with project participants that the written accounts of their constructions are accurate.

Transferability refers to the accuracy with which the findings from one study can be applied to another setting. Since constructivist researchers do not assume that there is a reality with demonstrable and immutable laws and mechanisms, they must give the consumer of the research guidance for deciding whether the study findings are transferable to other settings. This guidance is offered by means of comprehensive descriptions of settings, participants, and constructions.

Dependability and Confirmability is the validity of the data and the reliability of the interpretations of the data. Put pragmatically, it addresses two questions: how was this data collected and how were the interpretations of data made? Was the collection of data exhaustive and did the reasoning behind developing constructions reflect accurately the evidence provided by study participants? To address these questions the constructivist researcher, like the post-positivist researcher and the critical theory researcher, documents all processes of data collection and steps of data analysis used to build constructions in journals. These journals are subjected to external audit, where the auditing trail from initial conceptualization of study through accounts of interviews and observations to the final agreed joint constructions is reviewed by, and justified to, an outside research specialist or faculty advisor.

Assessment and Engagement—Understanding the Research Focus and Entrée to the Research Setting

According to Erlandson et al. (1993), a constructivist problem statement should be broad enough to include central issues and narrow enough to serve as a data collection guide. Such a problem statement, for example, might address HIV-AIDS in a particular community and ask a general questions such as, "What is this community's experience of social work services for people living with HIV-AIDS?" The researcher would then explicate "what?" and "where?" questions, which are exploratory; "how?" and "why?" questions, which are explanatory; and action questions to address interventions with the issue. In this example, such questions might be,

- What services are available in this community for people living with HIV-AIDS?
- Where and in what agencies are these services housed?
- How do these services meet the needs of people living with HIV-AIDS?
- Why were these services developed rather than other possible services?
- What action needs to be taken to address the concerns of people living with HIV-AIDS?

Like any other researcher, the constructivist researcher will begin with his or her expertise on the subject to be researched. This researcher will also review the literature on the research focus. However, both the researcher's expertise and the literature are seen as two constructions of the topic to be researched. These constructions have equal value with those collected from participants in the study. Indeed, while developing the research focus the researcher also contacts and engages a research site that is accessible physically and can offer access to key players who are willing to cooperate with a constructivist study. The gatekeepers of the research site are made aware of the inherent requirements of constructivist research. Such research is demanding of time and energy and requires a more intensive commitment than traditional research. Guba and Lincoln (1989) itemize these demands by describing the following conditions for conducting constructivist research:

All participants must make a commitment to work from a position of integrity. Participants agree to genuinely try to tell the truth and be honest. If participants knowingly give misinformation, the various feedback sharing opportunities built into the paradigm's methodology are likely to discover and challenge such data.

All participants must have minimal competence to communicate verbally and in written form. Thus young children, those who are severely developmentally delayed, and those who are severely mentally ill could not be participants in a constructivist study.

All participants must have a willingness to share power. If the leadership or high status representatives of a particular program either sponsor or simply participate in a constructivist study, such key players need to be aware that their perceptions of the program will be seen as constructions that are equal to all other participants' constructions. Their views are not more important or less important than anyone else's.

All participants must have a willingness to reconsider their perspectives. During the constructivist data collection process, participants' constructions are shared and discussed. Each participant, on hearing another person's construction of the topic, may hear a perspective that challenges his or her own construction. In the face of such challenges, it is assumed that participants will be open to changing their ideas if persuaded by another point of view.

All participants must have a willingness to reconsider their value positions. For most of us, this is a tougher commitment to make. Our value positions have guided our lives, and for many, values are objective, not changing subjective propositions. However, the constructivist orientation includes a relativist assumption regarding values. That is that values are dictated by life experience and social context, not an objective, never-changing set of laws. Participants in a constructivist study need to be able to accept this position, at least in relation to the topic that is the focus of the research project.

All participants must have a willingness to make the time and energy commitment needed in constructivist research. Accurately recording every study participant's complete construction of a research topic is time consuming. The initial interview will be lengthy, and the follow-up exchanges of written accounts of the interview between researcher and study participant to gain agreement on validity are additional conscientious commitments.

The above conditions need to be communicated to the gatekeepers of the research site during initial negotiations for a constructivist research project. Since, at this stage, the constructivist researcher is considering possible research sites, he or she will also integrate input from gatekeepers of the site(s) into initial development of the research focus. Thus problem formulation, or the assessment phase, will be the integration of the researcher's construction, the literature's construction, and the constructions of those who are contacted at the initial stages of the project. To illustrate these early stages of the constructivist research project, two examples are offered below. Both are M.S.W. student projects. One is a study of service to people living with HIV-AIDS, and the other is a study of services to homeless children.

Study of HIV-AIDS: Engagement and Assessment

The researcher who initiated this study, Hogan (1995), was a social work student who had ten years' experience in the HIV-AIDS arena and a family member who had died of AIDS. In her professional and personal experience of HIV-AIDS, she had noted a reticence among social workers to intervene with HIV-AIDS clients. She decided to look more deeply into her perception. A review of the literature at that time confirmed that although there had been social work pioneers fighting discrimination against HIV-AIDS, the social work profession had been slow to respond to this client population's need for services. At the same time, she identified a research site; it was a place that she lived in and was familiar with: the Coachella Valley in southern California, a desert community 100 miles east of Los Angeles. Thus in her report of the study, she states her research focus as

> What are the factors that may inhibit and facilitate social work practice in the HIV-AIDS arena in Coachella Valley? The study was conducted in the Coachella Valley, a region of eastern Riverside County in Southern California. There is a disproportionately high incidence and prevalence of HIV-AIDS in this area. According to Congressman Sonny Bono the Coachella Valley has a rate of incidence of diagnosed AIDS nearly equal to areas such as San Francisco and New York. . . . The objective is to gain an awareness of thoughts, beliefs and feelings of social workers and other key professionals working in agencies and organizations serving HIV-AIDS affected communities in the Coachella Valley . . . to facilitate action and policies that will increase and enhance a social work response (to the needs of people living with HIV-AIDS) in all arenas of social work practice. (Hogan, 1995, pp. 11–14)[1]

Having developed her focus, her next step was to identify a circle of stakeholder groups regarding services for people living with HIV-AIDS in this geographical area. This was developed by means of a preliminary survey and the researcher's knowledge of the region. Agencies that specifically served such clients as well as those serving the general population, who most likely also served HIV-AIDS clients, were initially included. In addition, faculty representatives from the local M.S.W. programs were invited to participate. Thus the stakeholder groups included in the initial circle of key informants were

1. AIDS-specific agencies
2. Medical clinics
3. County substance abuse programs
4. Charitable organizations
5. Universities' social work departments
6. The county Department of Social Services
7. Hospice agencies
8. Local hospitals
9. Persons living with HIV-AIDS

10. Professional social workers

11. The researcher

12. Those who have developed the literature on social work practice with HIV-AIDS

Study of Homeless Children: Engagement and Assessment

A second example of a constructivist study is a student project focusing on the educational needs of homeless children that was carried out over two years by successive students in the same area as our HIV-AIDS study, the Coachella Valley (Becker, 1994; Kelly, 1995). One student developed the study and conducted the first round of interviews. Another student picked up where the first had left off and continued it in the second year. Both students lived in the geographical area and had experience working with homeless children. The initial research focus was as follows:

> Coachella Valley is comprised of several desert resort cities (Palm Springs and the like) located in the southern tip of California . . . . Income levels within the valley vary from the extreme poverty of migrant farm workers to those whose economic status exceeds the highest national level. Although once a retirement community . . . the valley has experienced a demographic shift resulting in the growth of families. Estimates of the number of homeless families within the valley [show] one shelter reporting 110% increase in demand for shelter space. . . . It is, therefore, the purpose of this research to explore the educational as well as social needs of homeless children within the Coachella Valley. And it is hoped that through a greater understanding of the needs of these children, existing services may be strengthened, or new services developed, which may forestall, or even eliminate, future negative consequences. (Becker, 1994, pp. 4–5)

Becker (1994) used her knowledge and the advice of other professionals to select the initial circle of stakeholder groups in the region:

1. Homeless shelters

2. Counseling centers

3. Riverside County Department of Social Services

4. Area hospitals

5. Local Head Start Program

6. Those who have developed the literature on homeless children

7. Local school districts

8. Local Department of Children's Services

However, when data collection began and agencies were contacted, the initial circle was reduced to the listing below because either the agency felt that they had little contact with homeless children, or the agency did not have a representative willing to take part in the study:

1. Homeless shelters

2. Homeless families

3. School districts

4. Public Health Department

5. Those who have developed the literature on homeless children

6. Researcher's own construction

In our two examples of constructivist research, the researchers were personally aware of a problem to be researched and lived in the region chosen for the research study. They were familiar with the service structure and knew some of the key players in the initial circle of informants. However, when the researcher does not yet have a research focus or is not familiar with the research site, what are the procedures to be followed? According to Lincoln and Guba (1985), a naturalistic (constructivist) inquiry can be research, evaluation, or policy analysis. The focus of each of these respectively is a problem, an evaluand, and a policy option. A problem is defined as "state of affairs resulting from the interaction of two or more factors . . . that yields (1) . . . a conceptual problem; (2) . . . an action problem; or (3) an undesirable consequence (a value problem)" (p. 226). An evaluand is a program, organization, performance, material, or facility to be evaluated. A policy option is a proposed or existing policy "the utility of which is to be determined" (p. 227). Our two examples described above are studies of problems that are both action problems and value problems: (1) the factors that inhibit and facilitate social work practice in the HIV-AIDS arena in Coachella Valley; (2) services for a growing population of homeless children in the Coachella Valley.

Erlandson et al. (1993) suggest a number of strategies for selecting and engaging a research site. These include personal contact; surveys of similar sites, for example, social service agencies with the required client group or geographical communities with high incidence of the problem to be studied; and professional referrals. In making the selection the researcher needs to be sure that he or she will be able to gain access to the site and all likely key players with pertinent constructions regarding the research focus. In our example studies, initial approaches were made to key players who were all very busy people. There was an interest in the research topics, but the researchers needed to be persistent to actually gain access and carry out interviews. The fact that they were known to most of the key players, or referred by somebody they knew, helped with access. In other situations where the researcher is new to the site, it is essential that the researcher builds rapport and trust with the gatekeepers to the site. These gatekeepers are not only the institutional heads of the agencies or officials of the community but also the opinion leaders and trusted members of the agencies or community. When initially contacting the site, the researcher needs to be alert to indicators of who the formal and informal key gatekeepers are and how to engage their interest in the project.

Constructivist projects require intensive interaction with participants, sometimes over a long period of time. The researcher does not enter the site as a data gatherer who will report back his or her findings at the end of the study, but as a facilitator who will assist participants in reporting and interpreting their own data. Not only this, a successful constructivist study leads to action by the key players to address the issues raised during data collection. Such a project requires an equal partnership between researcher and study participants. To build this partnership, constructivist researchers can take a leaf out of the book of micro practitioners when engaging clients. Namely, start where the client is and respect his or her perceptions of the proposed project; use listening and attending skills to draw out the participants' experiences, issues, and concerns with the project; develop effective questioning skills using open- and closed-ended questions appropriately; and reflect back not only your understanding of the content of the exchange with the participant but also your understanding of their feelings about that content (Evans et al., 2004). Assuming that these initial contacts have gone well and the researcher is encouraged to continue engaging the research site, the project can now move forward with planning.

Planning—Rationale for Carrying Out the Research

The constructivist researcher is the most distinctively different of all four kinds of researchers that are described in this book. Constructivists are so attentive to subjective data that they even count their own constructions of reality as one of the data sources. When setting up the research plan, therefore, the researcher devises a strategy for finding all possible constructions. Methods of identifying and engaging key players are thought through as well as a strategy and timeline for participants to develop and share their constructions of the problem, evaluand, or policy being researched. To do this, the researcher identifies a "hermeneutic dialectic" circle of key informants who will jointly build a construction of the research issue to be studied. As noted above, the circle is hermeneutic because each person brings his or her own construction to the research project and dialectic because each person is informed of other participants' constructions and given the opportunity to further develop a construction as a result of reflecting on another perspective. The framing of the issue and the membership of the circle will constantly change as the study progresses. Thus this is a planning stage rather than a mapping stage. To offer an explanatory metaphor, the positivist researcher develops a map before embarking on the journey of the research project, assuming that a good researcher's map will exactly portray the territory to be covered during the journey. The map is not changed once the project begins. In contrast, the constructivist researcher develops a plan for the journey, assuming that a good researcher will change the plan once the journey starts because the territory that is encountered will probably be different from territory that was anticipated when the map was made before the journey started. Thus according to Erlandson et al. (1993), when designing a research project, the constructivist researcher plans for negotiating conditions of entry, purposive sample selection (as described in Part II), data collection, data analysis, strategies for assessing the quality of the study, and dissemination of findings. However, all of this can change when the subjective experience of study participants is engaged. For example, let us return to our two example studies.

Study of HIV-AIDS: Planning

Hogan, the student researcher, planned to use purposive sampling to identify stakeholder groups in the community. She decided that maximum variation sampling would be used within each stakeholder group to identify individuals with contrasting constructions regarding services to people living with HIV-AIDS. However, once data collection began, this plan proved impractical. Because of the stigma and possible harm linked with being identified as HIV positive, many agencies that served the general population including people living with HIV-AIDS did not know which of their clients were living with HIV-AIDS. Also, such agencies admitted that should they identify a client who is a person living with HIV-AIDS, they would refer this client to a specialist agency that intervenes with those clients only. Also, some respondents who initially agreed to be interviewed for the study, on reflection, decided that for reasons of personal or professional confidentiality they should withdraw from the study.

Thus the final circle of participants as listed above was the circle of those remaining after this fallout. Some stakeholder groups were represented by one person while others were represented by two or three people. The final circle of participants for the first stage of the study, therefore, totaled 22. Because of the sensitivity of the topic and requests for confidentiality, some participants were simply identified with a grouping name rather than personally identified. The plan was to gather data in two phases: first individual interviews and then a meeting of all participants to review the joint construction. However, the sensitivity of the topic and the limited time frame for the student researcher meant that only the first round of data was collected. The accuracy of these constructions was checked by sending the written account of the interview to participants in the mail and then following up with phone calls to discuss any modifications. The final report was sent to each stakeholder separately.

Study of Homeless Children: Planning

The plan for the homeless children study was more ambitious than the HIV-AIDS study, and in the end, more successful in achieving a shared construction of the problem and action needed to address the problem. As noted above, successive students planned to carry out this study over two years. One student developed the study and conducted the first round of interviews. After she graduated, the second student in the next year of the M.S.W. program continued the study, did a second round of interviews, and held a meeting of all participants to review the joint construction and develop an action plan. For the student in the first year of the study, an initial circle of stakeholders was identified and interviewed, as noted above. In the second year of the study, this circle was expanded and constructions were revisited and further developed. This new circle included:

1. Homeless shelters
2. Domestic violence shelters
3. School districts
4. Public Health Department
5. Local church-based soup kitchen
6. Transportation and food distribution center
7. One member of the Board of County Supervisors (an elected official)
8. A member of city government (an elected official)
9. The Sheriff's Department

10. Child Protective Services

11. The Regional Child Abuse Council

12. The County Department of Social Services

13. A mental health, substance abuse treatment agency

14. Mental Health Department

At the end of the second year of the study, this group met, reviewed their shared construction, and developed an action plan to address the needs of homeless children in the Coachella Valley.

According to Erlandson et al. (1993), the plan for the study at this stage should be intertwined with Engagement and Assessment and include

- *Plan for engagement.* How is the researcher to engage the setting? It could be through a letter of introduction into a formal setting or through personal contacts with trusted key informants in a more informal community setting. In our example studies, the researchers were already living in the community, so they already had a relationship with some participants and were referred to participants they did not know.
- *Plan for renegotiation of terms of engagement with the research site.* As the project starts and people start talking, unexpected issues may surface and the researcher needs to be alert to any need to revisit the terms that were agreed at the beginning of the project. In our HIV-AIDS study, prejudices against people with HIV-AIDS were surfacing within the social work community and this client group was expressing unexpected anger with the profession. The researcher needed to revisit the comfort of the gatekeepers with these conversations, and this changed participation in the study.
- *Plan for purposive sample selection.* As far as possible, the researcher needs to anticipate those who are likely to have constructions of the research focus. In addition, the researcher needs to have a plan for including a wide range of differing constructions of the research focus. As can be seen in both of our example studies, either the sensitivity of the topic or pragmatic time constraints can make some stakeholder groups reluctant to participate in the study.
- *Plan for data collection.* The combination of interviewing, observation, and review of additional artifacts that will most comprehensively address the research focus should be thought through at this stage. Of course, as data gathering progresses this will change, but a starting point where as much has been thought through as possible is important. In our example studies, data was gathered by interviews only. This was partly due to the students' time constraints but was also the result of a plan where various entities needed to be brought together to plan action. At the planning stage of each of these studies, additional sources of data were not considered to be a priority.

- *Plan for analysis.* As with post-positivist and critical theory research, data collection and analysis are parallel processes. The constructivist researcher needs to think through a process and timeline for both that is realistic and fruitful.
- *Plan for trustworthiness and authenticity.* In a large scale, fully-funded constructivist study, there would be funding for an outside auditor to check the researcher's journal on data gathering and the steps of data analysis. Usually, the student researcher does not have funding and must turn to the research advisor for auditing. Such an auditing process needs to be negotiated at the start of the project.
- *Plan for dissemination.* The constructivist researcher needs to anticipate the likely audiences for the project findings. Of course, the members of the circle of informants are the first audience, but are there others? Will there be a wider community meeting? Is the media interested? Is there an academic setting where results must be displayed? For our studies, the HIV-AIDS study was too sensitive for dissemination beyond sending the report on the joint construction back to individual participants for their own reflection. In addition, a summary of the findings was displayed at an on-campus poster session for social work student research. The study of homeless children was able to move further forward with the constructivist process. It included a meeting of all stakeholders where findings were reported and action plans were developed. It, too, was reported at an on-campus poster session for student projects.

The planning identified in the steps above facilitates thoughtful entrance to the research setting and appropriate invitations into the circle of informants, whether the research site is a formal agency setting or a more loosely defined community. Thinking through this plan helps researchers understand the dynamics of the setting and answer questions from participants such as why they should participate in the study and what they may gain from the study. It also helps researchers be aware of the agendas of participants and their motivations for taking part in the study, ranging from airing grievances to an interest in improvement and change.

However, as can be seen from our example student projects, without resources and time, sometimes such a plan can only be approximated. Even with the approximated plan, though, our example studies show that useful research that impacts service delivery in the research site can be carried out. Constructivist research is a process and an outcome. The process of being engaged in developing constructions, although truncated in the HIV-AIDS study, still brought a meaningful review of this issue to a community that was being heavily impacted by this client population. The study of homeless children both engaged key participants in building a joint construction and resulted in action to improve service delivery.

Main Points

- Each constructivist study is considered unique to its time and place
- The quality of a constructivist study is measured by its credibility, transferability, dependability, and confirmability
- Constructivist studies ask exploratory, explanatory, and action questions
- A constructivist study demands an intensive commitment of time and energy
- Constructivist studies focus on problems, evaluands, or policy options
- Initial engagement of research sites needs to be thoughtful, well-planned, and persistent
- The plan for a constructivist study includes strategies for collecting all possible interpretations of the research topic
- The research plan identifies a "hermeneutic dialectic" circle of key informants. In addition, the researcher plans for negotiation of conditions of entry, purposive sampling, data collection, data analysis, assessment of quality of the study, and dissemination of the findings
- The research plan will change once the project begins and the reality of engaging the research site and gathering data is encountered. Constructivist researchers anticipate such changes and build flexibility into their approach to research

Learning Assignments

1. Think of a topic that you are interested in. How would you study it using a constructivist approach? Where and when would you carry it out? Who would be included in your hermeneutic dialectic circle?

2. In pairs, discuss your possible projects. How would you engage the circle of key informants?

Note

1. This study was completed before Sonny Bono's death.

15

Implementation and Evaluation—Gathering the Data and Developing an Understanding of the Data and Its Meaning

D ata from interviews, observations, and review of social artifacts can be used to build constructions. During interviews each participant in the hermeneutic dialectic circle of stakeholders is asked for his or her construction of the research focus. In addition, the constructions of other interviewees are shared so that participants have an opportunity to refine their constructions after hearing other points of view. Participants are asked to identify any other relevant and important contributions to the joint construction such as social artifacts, reports, and documents. At the end of initial interviews, participants are asked for the name of key players who are likely to have a completely different perspective on the research focus. Thus the hermeneutic dialectic is set in motion. Participants build their own initial constructions and also engage in a dynamic process of developing and refining the joint construction over time with additional input from others and as a response to any events that may be happening during the study. Initially interviews take place separately; then after each study participant has been interviewed once, the circle of study participants is brought together to review the group's current joint construction and to give feedback on any further development of that construction that might be needed.

Having gained initial trust and agreements with the gatekeepers of the setting, the researcher builds the hermeneutic dialectic circle of study participants. The gatekeepers are asked to nominate stakeholders who should be invited into the circle. This is a starting point; as the study proceeds, each participant in the study is asked to nominate other stakeholders who should be included in the circle. Guba and Lincoln (1989) suggest that stakeholders can be divided into agents, beneficiaries, and victims of a particular research focus. In the Hogan study of HIV-AIDS, the agents of services were the human service professionals, the beneficiaries were those who successfully received services, and the victims were not only those who did not successfully receive services but other members of the community who were opposed to services to HIV-AIDS clients and perhaps prejudiced against this population. Michael Quinn Patton (1990) suggested 14 types of sampling, besides random sampling, which is explained in detail in the post-positivist section of this book. These are sampling extreme cases; sampling data rich cases; maximum variation sampling; sampling a homogeneous subgroup of cases; sampling typical cases; stratified purposive sampling of above average, average, and below average cases; sampling critical cases; snowball sampling; criterion sampling; theory base sampling; confirming and disconfirming case sampling; opportunistic sampling; sampling politically important or sensitive cases; and convenience sampling (pp. 182–183). The constructivist researcher, while keeping all these possibilities in mind, tends to use a combination of maximum variation and snowball sampling. The researcher aims to get a diverse set of perspectives and develops the sample by means of recommendations of interviewees.

Implementation: Gathering Data

Interviews

Theoretically, the stance of the constructivist researcher is to enter an interview with a blank sheet of paper and no preconceived questions. The first question to a participant in this ideal world of constructivist research would be, "What do you think are the key questions regarding this research topic and what do you consider the answers to those questions to be?" However, to actually do this would not only be anxiety-generating for the researcher but a little disconcerting for the participant. Thus the constructivist researcher has this "blank page" notion in mind when starting the interview but also has some general questions prepared so that the ice can be broken and both the interviewer and interviewee can start to relax with each other. Erlandson et al. (1993) divided the constructivist research interview into four stages: preparing for the interview, beginning the interview, maintaining productivity during the interview, and closing the interview.

The researcher, not the questions on a piece of paper, is the interview instrument in this kind of research. When preparing for the interview, he or she needs to hone all five senses as well as anticipate the need to use intuition and thought during the interview. Again, the constructivist research interviewer can learn from micro practitioners' interviewing skills when preparing to gain a valid, comprehensive account of a study participant's constructions. It is important to learn the vocabulary and terminology of the setting. It is also important to think about the likely situations for open-ended questions and those for closed-ended questions (Evans et al., 2004). It may well be useful to spend some time in the interviewee's setting to gain an experiential understanding of how he or she may perceive the research topic. Preparing for the interview also includes developing a pool of questions. Patton (1990) lists several types of questions that can be prepared:

1. Experience/Behavior Questions. What is your experience with this topic? What do you do each day in relation to this topic? If I were to follow you around, what would I see you experiencing in relation to this topic?

2. Opinion/Values Questions. What do you think about this topic? What do you believe is happening with this topic? What would you like to see happening with this topic? What is your opinion about all of this?

3. Feeling Questions. To what extent do you feel pleased, confident, satisfied, unhappy, or dissatisfied with this issue?

4. Knowledge Questions. What is your understanding of this topic? Which parts of it do you know most about? What do you know about those parts?

5. Sensory Questions. When you are engaging in this topic, what do you see? What do you hear people saying?

6. Background/Demographic Questions. What is your age, education, occupation, mobility, residence, ethnicity?

When asking any of these questions, the focus can be on the present, the past, or the future. In addition to deciding which types of questions to have in the pool of possible questions, the researcher will think about presentation of self. What style of dress is appropriate? What is the level of formality? Also, the study participant needs to be prepared for the interview. The participant should be contacted, told about the study, and informed about what to expect in addition to any formal informed consent procedures. If possible, the study participant should choose the setting for the interview. When beginning the interview, the researcher should orient the interviewee once more to the aim of the project as well as its approach, noting that it entails open sharing. Any concerns, such as need for anonymity, should be addressed and honored. The logistics of the project should be explained, including any possible follow-up contact, other interviews, any possible meetings, proposed length of data collection period, any payments, and who has final control over the data and research report.

Having completed these initial negotiations and understandings, it would be best to begin with some broad experience/behavior questions that put the interviewee at ease and keep the conversation in familiar territory. The aim is to establish a relaxed rapport between interviewee and researcher. The researcher, at this point, will be asking general questions about the interviewee's background and experiences in general and with the study topic in particular. These are "getting to know you" questions rather than data gathering questions. When the researcher senses that the interviewee is ready, the data gathering questions can be asked. The researcher should be alert to any tangents that the participant seems to be interested in at this point, and encourage exploration of those tangents. For example, in the HIV-AIDS study, focus questions included

- What is your experience of HIV-AIDS?
- How would you define AIDS?
- In your opinion, what causes AIDS?
- Have you ever worked with social workers?
- In your opinion, how might the social work profession best make a contribution to the field of AIDS in this region?
- What factors might facilitate this involvement?
- What factors might inhibit this involvement?

For Kelly's (1995) homeless children study, these questions included

- In your opinion, what are the key issues in meeting the social and educational needs of homeless children in this region?
- How do you think these needs are being met?
- How do you think these needs are not being met?
- What, in your opinion, can be done to improve services aimed at meeting these needs?
- What do you see as barriers to successfully meeting the needs of homeless children in this region?

As the interview proceeds, the interviewer can explore tangents by using probes and prompts and being as natural and relaxed as possible. Prompts or "minimal encouragers" (Evans et al., 2004) let the interviewee know that you are interested and would like to hear more. Lincoln and Guba (1985) suggest encouragers such as a wave of the hand, sounds such as "umm" or "uh-huh," or simply reflecting back by restating your understanding of what has just been said. Interviewees need to get the message that the focus is on them and that you are genuinely interested in making sure that they say all they have to say and that it is understood correctly.

The usual and most effective way of closing the interview is to review and summarize what has been said. This may lead to further clarification and conversation, but it also starts the process of ending the interview. One last question for the constructivist researcher is to ask whether there is anyone else who might have something to say about the topic. Also, the interviewee should be thanked both at that time and with a follow-up note. Always leave the door open for further contact between the researcher and the participant.

Observations

Not only do constructivist researchers interview key informants in the research site, they have the opportunity to observe the site. As noted in Part II, such observing, or fieldwork, has stages: preparing for the field, entering the field, routinizing observation, and leaving the field. However, like the critical theorist, the constructivist has certain issues to resolve in relation to observing study participants. In a constructivist study, joint constructions of a research focus are being developed. The only justification for gathering observational data is that it has the potential to add new dimensions to the joint construction. Researchers may gather observational data and so can study participants. Such data is considered to be each person's subjective understanding of what was observed and will be shared with the circle of study participants for review and possible modification.

Preparing for the field includes negotiating and explaining the terms and uses of such observation. The constructivist observer would not disguise his or her role but would openly acknowledge that a research observation is taking place, that the making of the observation is influencing the activities being observed, and that the record of the observation is a subjective account of activities at one time in one particular setting. The site for the observation could be a micro or macro practice setting. Thus it could be the home or other meeting place of families, groups, or individuals, or it could be an agency or community setting. These are not anthropological settings but practice settings where researchers cannot really become insiders and, as outsiders, seriously affect the nature of the activity being observed. In our example HIV-AIDS study, the researcher could have observed the experiences of HIV-AIDS clients seeking services. The presence of the researcher may well have increased the likelihood of the client getting services. The description of these observations would have acknowledged and reviewed the implications of such observer effects. The observer could be behind a one-way mirror, but for a constructivist, this would be an unsatisfactory form of observation since the equal partnership strived for in constructivist research would be lost. It would be possible to make observations with miniature hidden cameras, should the resources be available; however, for the constructivist, data collected in this fashion would be of limited value. The camera does not allow the observer to engage all five senses. There is partial visual and auditory data, but that is all.

Thus the observer role is generally a secondary role to the interviewer role, and any observations are generally made while carrying out an interview and are included in the written account of the interview. However, should the constructivist decide to gather observational data, the structure offered by Bogdewic (1992) will help focus such data collection. He suggests that the observer should ask him- or herself,

1. *Who is present?* What are their roles? How did they enter the setting? Why is each person present? Who seems to be in charge?

2. *What is happening?* Who is involved? What is the tone of the communication? Is it routine or unusual?

3. *When does this happen?* Is this the regular time for this occurrence? How long does it last?

4. *Where is this happening?* Is this the usual place? How is the space used? Who seems to be comfortable here and who is not?

5. *Why is this happening?* What precipitated this occurrence?

6. *How is this activity organized?* What are the rules? How are various events observed connected?

Using this structure to record observations, the constructivist researcher can make observations that contribute to the joint construction being developed. These would be shared with participants for reflection on and development of constructions. Thus there is an interaction between interviews and observations in which observations can suggest questions and informants' constructions can suggest foci for further observation.

Social Artifacts

A third area of data collection is review of documents, reports, and social artifacts in general. Participants might mention influential reports, rulebooks, or legislation. Pictures on the walls or posters may point to significant issues or important shared understandings. Such nonhuman data sources, for the constructivist, would provide context since they are not open to a dialectic that builds and changes the construction, but they can affect the development of individual and joint constructions.

Recording and Reporting Constructions

Methods of data recording range from the absolute fidelity achieved by videotaping each interview or observation to the limited fidelity achieved by making notes after an interview or observation. Videotaping can be an uncomfortable situation for participants, but according to Erlandson et al. (1993), if used, it should be set up and left running for a period of time before data collection begins. At first participants tend to be conscious of the camera and will perform for it rather than continue with their normal behavior, but after a while the camera becomes part of the setting and tends to be ignored. Also, these days, with miniature cameras, videotaping can take place unobtrusively. This may be the case in nonthreatening situations, but in interviews with professionals about, for example, discomfort with providing services to people living with HIV-AIDS, the use of cameras may well inhibit open frank discussion and development of an authentic construction of the research topic.

If videotaping is not feasible, the next most reliable method is tape or digital recording. Again, like the camera, a tape recorder or microphone attached to a computer is something that people tend to be conscious of at first and then ignore. Patton (1990) offers some pragmatic tips for using recording equipment: check equipment; choose a quiet place to record; test voice of respondent before starting; speak clearly; don't make any unnecessary rustling noises; identify the interview on the tape; and if using a transcriber, listen to the tape afterwards and erase any unnecessary conversation; finally, label all tapes.

If video or audio taping the interview is too obtrusive, the researcher must rely on note taking, either during or after the interview. Erlandson et al. (1993) suggest the use of critical incident reporting as a way of recalling the key facets of someone's construction. They suggest that as soon as possible after the interview, the researcher should make a list of critical incidents. A critical incident is something that "either highlights the normal operation of the (setting) or contrasts sharply with it" (p. 103). At first the researcher might not know if the incident is typical or not; however, trying to discover the answer to this question will help the researcher build the joint construction. A description of a critical incident should

1. Contain one event or description. What was the event or main point made by the interviewee? Why was it important to him or her?

2. Identify specific persons, locations, and times. Who were the key players in the incident or point being made? What do they do and when do they do it?

3. Be observed by the researcher or verified by more than one other source. What is the interviewee describing as evidence for the incident or point of view? Is this evidence accurate?

4. Help build the joint construction by identifying typical or atypical features. What has the interviewee said that agrees with other study participants' constructions and what has been said that is unique to this interviewee?

Stages of Data Collection

The process of gathering data to build a joint construction through a hermeneutic dialectic circle is one that starts with an open-ended approach and becomes more structured as the study progresses. At first the researcher is open to all constructions; however, as information starts to be repeated by different participants a focus develops, the joint construction is developed and shared, and action to address the joint construction is developed.

Building the Hermeneutic Dialectic Circle

The initial circle includes the gatekeepers' constructions, the researcher's construction, and the construction identified in the literature. It really doesn't matter which gatekeeper is interviewed first because all members of the circle get the chance to respond to each other's constructions eventually. For the first round of interviews, the researcher starts with an open-ended exploration using the six types of questions noted above. The researcher then asks the respondent to comment on the literature's construction and the researcher's construction. After the interview, all of this is recorded and written up in a narrative form as soon as possible using the critical incident process noted above. This narrative is then sent to the respondent for review and confirmation of the validity of the recorded construction. The respondent may make additions or changes as needed. Once the respondent has agreed that the narrative accurately represents his or her construction at this point in time, the researcher moves on to interview the next member of the circle and follows the same process. However, now the researcher will first gather that respondent's construction, then share the literature construction, then the first respondent's construction, and then his or her own construction. In addition, respondents may suggest artifacts or reports that should be considered or observations that should be made. All of these are added to the initial building of the joint construction by being offered to each participant for consideration. This sounds like a process that makes interviews longer and longer until they reach to infinity. However, redundancies and repetitions will occur in respondents' constructions so that the researcher's representation of other constructions can be structured into a kind of checklist of questions. As it evolves, this checklist can also be shared with the first interviewees via e-mail, phone, or mail so that all participants have the opportunity to respond to all constructions individually.

Thus the productivity stage of the interview builds into the following structure:

1. Participant's construction, using six types of questions;

2. Reflections on literature's construction;

3. Reflections on other participants' constructions;

4. Reflections on social artifacts and/or reports;

5. Reflections on any observational data;

6. Reflections on researcher's construction;

7. Suggestions for other participants for the circle and any other data sources.

When the researcher and participants start to feel that including any more people in the circle would simply be including perspectives already noted and therefore provide redundant data, then the circle is complete and the process moves on to the "membership checking" meeting.

Organizing and Running the Membership-Checking Meeting

Having gathered participants' individual constructions, the constructivist writes the first draft of the group's joint construction and shares it with the circle at a meeting known as a "membership-checking meeting." The function of this meeting is to ensure the "credibility," "dependability," and "confirmability" of the shared construction. The meeting will identify claims, concerns, and issues, that is, areas of agreement, areas of disagreement, and issues to be addressed and acted upon (Guba & Lincoln, 1989). The discussion above described the unique commitments that participants in a constructivist study need to make at the start of the study. As the study moves into this stage, which brings the group together to review and finalize the joint construction, it would be useful to review these commitments with participants. Such reflection will assist both the researcher and participants to truly perceive how constructivist research is both process and product. Data gathering has generated a process that, it is hoped, will have a life of its own beyond the official end of the research project and a product that will be a report on a shared construction at one point in time.

Thus the membership-checking meeting is an important stage of the constructivist project. At this point, the researcher will not only validate the joint construction with the study participants but also motivate circle members to take an active part in continuing the project into its action stages. The researcher has been careful about giving every group member reason to believe that his or her constructions are understood, valued, and included in the final joint construction. When contacting group members to schedule the meeting, this engagement of participants is reinforced by accommodating schedules and setting a meeting place that is familiar and comfortable for as many of the circle as possible. Before the meeting, the researcher shares the joint construction and the meeting agenda with circle members and encourages questions and clarifications. This pre-meeting preparation can be carried out via e-mail, letters, and phone conversations.

At the meeting, the researcher becomes not only the reporter of data but also the group facilitator. At this meeting, the researcher adopts social work group work skills to facilitate understanding of the joint construction and consolidate motivation and commitment to action. Using a generalist approach (Kirst-Ashman & Hull, 2002), engagement, assessment, planning, implementation, evaluation, termination, and follow up are necessary stages for the meeting. Members should be introduced to each other, the purpose of the meeting should be reviewed and clarified, issues to be discussed should be prioritized, action plans should be identified, and the credibility of the group's final construction should be evaluated by group members. Termination of the meeting should be accompanied by a commitment to send the final report to all group members and the allocation of action tasks and roles to group members. This is basic team building where there is a need for organizational support for the project and strong leadership of the team. This group is the entity that is going to carry the project forward. It needs to "form," "storm," and "norm." By the end of the meeting, group members should have understood and taken ownership of the shared construction. They will also have adopted their new roles as leaders of the project.

Example Study of HIV-AIDS

In the HIV-AIDS study (Hogan, 1995), because of concerns regarding confidentiality and stigma, members of the group were reluctant to attend a membership-checking meeting. The researcher was not able to bring together enough of the participants for the meeting to be able to achieve "credibility," "dependability," and "confirmability." The researcher thus confirmed the trustworthiness of individual constructions with individual participants via mail and phone calls (at this time, e-mail was not so prevalent) and then wrote a final report, or case study, which she sent to participants. The study had to end there. It began a process of reviewing services to people living with HIV-AIDS and produced a report but was not able to facilitate continuation of the project at that time. For the constructivist researcher, this was not failed research but a statement of the joint construction in this research context at a certain point in time. As supported by some of the constructions that were developed (reported in the analysis section below), stakeholders in this setting were at a point of acknowledging an issue but not yet able to move forward with joint action to address the issue.

Example Study of Homeless Children

The study of homeless children (Becker, 1994; Kelly, 1995), carried out over two years, was able to complete much more of the constructivist research process. Participants in the original hermeneutic dialectic circle were interviewed in year one. In year two, as a result of these interviews, the circle was expanded and everyone in the final circle was interviewed twice. More was achieved in the second year because interviews became more focused as redundancy and repetition within constructions were identified. At the end of year two, all participants were invited to the membership-checking meeting. This is described by Kelly in her report:

> The networking meeting was held at a city hall, located mid valley, which was easily accessible to all participating agencies. Meeting time and date was scheduled to accommodate the local member of the county board of supervisors, who was interested in the issues addressed in this research report. The meeting agenda was as follows:

Homeless Children Research Networking Meeting

May 24th, 1995

Agenda

Introductions

Agency and Information Sharing
Discussion of Identified Issues
   Families
   Adult Literacy
   Job Skills Training
   Mental Heath Outreach Services
   Additional Health Services
   Transportation
   Affordable Housing
   Shelters
      More Shelters
   Schools
      Identifying and Monitoring Homeless Children
      Funding
   Global Issues
      Agency Restrictions and Policies
      Community Awareness
      Prevention Through Policy Changes
Suggested Solutions
   Networking Regularly
   Sharing Resources
   Liaison, Inter-Agency Representatives
   Expansion of Services
Future Networking Meetings?

Participants from the two separate research inquiries who attended the meeting represented the following agencies: drug-free community based intervention program for the nine valley cities, domestic violence shelter, Western Valley Homeless Shelter, a soup kitchen, a food distribution and transportation resource center, Child Protective Services, The Department of Public Social Services, Riverside County Regional Access Project, Riverside County Office of Education, Riverside County Supervisor, Desert Sands Unified School District, Palm Springs Unified School District, Coachella Valley Unified School District, and the academic tutors for the two participating school districts of the Stewart McKinney Grant Program. Also attending was the professor and research advisor for this project and the former graduate student who was the original researcher for the first round and peer debriefer for this project.

Agency participants who agreed to participate but had to cancel due to last minute emergencies were representatives of law enforcement, the Eastern

Valley Homeless Shelter, representatives of the Public Health Department, representatives of City Government, representatives of the Mental Health Department, and representatives of the regional Child Abuse Council. These participants indicated interest in attending future networking meetings and asked to be kept informed of this meeting outcome.

The first part of this meeting focused on information sharing, with most agencies supplying handouts about their organization and having a question and answer period about various agencies services. (This was a need that had been identified during interviews) . . . .

The discussion phase of the meeting focused on issues of lack of community awareness about homeless children and their families and barriers that school districts have created in the past by "turning children away" because they did not have a permanent address. One tutor participant indicated a concern that many homeless children presently are "out there in a nonexistent" home and are not receiving academic services. School district representatives shared that homeless children is a "new" issue for them and they are still in the process of learning how to deal with this problem. Respondents admitted many school personnel within their school districts do not know how to work with this population and are often insensitive to their needs. As a result of this discussion, the county board of education representative suggested that his office could provide in-service training to all three school districts when requested.

Upon further discussion of identified issues, agency participants focused on possible joint networking meetings with the east and west valley networking groups already in existence. Additionally, shelter and child protective service representatives addressed the need for sharing affordable housing information resources with other agencies . . . . Participants agreed to compile a "housing list" of the entire valley and bring it to the next meeting . . . .

Representatives also agree to participate in future networking meetings and suggested inclusions of G.A.I.N (the local "welfare to work" program) and the Housing Authority in this group . . . . Agency participants agreed to meet in mid-July with this researcher coordinating time, location and date with follow-up communication to all participating agencies.

It is clear here that the project moved a long way toward understanding the issue and taking action to address the issue. The researcher was not able to completely hand over the project to the group, but several participants had taken on responsibilities for additional training, information, and contact to other stakeholders.

Evaluation: Understanding the Meaning of the Data

Data analysis for constructivist researchers will depend on the sources of the constructions included in the hermeneutic dialectic circle. These are mostly qualitative interviews, documents, and readings. However, they could also be quantitative constructions such as data included in reports and documents. Since the goal is not statistical prediction but comprehensive description, this analysis will generally be descriptive rather than inferential. Returning to the qualitative data, like the post-positivist, the constructivist researcher engages in a continual interplay between data collection and analysis. Analysis, therefore, is carried out after each interview, observation, or review of relevant documents. Rather than build a theory, as in the post-positivist approach, this researcher identifies "units" of information. Units are built into categories and then combined into a proposed joint construction that is shared with the whole group at the membership-checking meeting. Eventually the whole group agrees on the joint construction, which includes understanding of the research focus as well as agreed action strategies associated with the construction. The test of whether the analysis is correct is the degree to which the members of the hermeneutic dialectic circle attest to its accuracy. This is not simply collusion between the researcher and a group of study participants but a rigorous process of developing, challenging, and synthesizing subjective data.

Building and Modifying Units

Erlandson et al. (1993) suggest that initial analysis, which is carried out after each interview, should address a set of standard questions that are expanded upon here.

1. What did I learn from this interview, observation, artifact, or data source?

2. How will this shape my next interview, observation, artifact, or data source?

3. What themes or suppositions were identified in this interview, observation, artifact, or data source?

4. Which other data sources were identified in this interview, observation, artifact, or data source?

5. Should I return to gather more information from this interview, observation, artifact, or data source? If so, what am I looking for?

6. What are my emerging working themes and suppositions, and how were they confirmed or challenged by this interview, observation, artifact, or data source?

7. How and where can I gather more information to confirm or challenge these working themes and suppositions?

Table 15.1   Units of Analysis from HIV-AIDS Study

Unit (and category number)	Source	Type of Source	Date and Time Collected	Place Data Collected
1. HIV-AIDS clients invisible	ID number of study participant	Member of client population	February 1, 1995	Restaurant near participant's home
2. Social workers need training in serving this client group	ID number of study participant	Social Worker	February 10, 1995	Agency office
3. Fear of stigma associated with HIV-AIDS	ID number of study participant	In-Home Help Assistant	February 21, 1995	In client home

Having used this analysis to build summary data on the emerging constructions, a more formalized process of analysis that summarizes and interprets data is followed, such as that offered by Lincoln and Guba (1985). The first step is to identify "units" of information within the narrative descriptions. A unit has two characteristics: it must be heuristic (relevant to understanding or action in the research site and focus), and it must be the smallest piece of information that can stand alone (able to be understood without additional explanation). Each unit should be recorded separately in a data processing program that can sort columns and coded with identifying information such as the source, type of source, and time and place the data was collected. For example, units developed in the HIV-AIDS study are shown in Table 15.1.

Having created units, the next step is to group units into categories. The researcher goes back to the first unit and reviews it and, for now, gives it a number, say, number 1. Then he or she reviews the second unit and decides whether it looks like or feels like something similar to the first unit. If so, this unit is given the same number; if not it is given the next number, say, number 2. This process is repeated for all units of information. For any units that do not seem to fit with any other category, a miscellaneous category can be created for now. This is a time-consuming process that combines rather than divides. The "looks like, feels like" process identified above builds categories rather than searches for repetitions of the same category. The core analysis question for the constructivist is, "How does this unit enrich the category?" In contrast, the core question for the post-positivist is, "How often is this unit repeated?" For the constructivist, context is an essential influence that enriches and validates subjectivity. It is as if the constructivist is building up the bones, muscle, blood, and skin of a unique individual while the post-positivist is searching for the common bone structure in each individual. Both are equally valid, but they have very different analysis aims.

A number having been given to each unit, the units can be grouped into their categories. The A-Z function in most spreadsheet programs will create this grouping if the number is in the cell at the beginning of the unit. This will bring all your units together into categories. All the units with the number "1" will be grouped together, all those with the number "2," and so on. Once the units are grouped in this way, the researcher can start to develop criteria for inclusion of a unit in a particular category and give each category a name. This may lead to some re-sorting of units. However, now there are clear criteria that justify the creation of the categories that go beyond intuition.

The next step is to search for relationships between categories. These relationships are not statements that predict repeated relationships between categories but bridges between categories that build a more complete construction. In our example studies, they are the combination of units of information on the HIV-AIDS practice issues that give a complete picture, or the factors that affect practice and the combination of units that identify the package of strategies that address those perceptions and barriers to practice. Or, in the homeless children study, they are the combination of units of information on the characteristic problems of homeless children and the grouping of action strategies set out by the membership-checking meeting. These bridges, according to Guba and Lincoln (1989), are "Extensions" where "The inquirer begins with a known item or items of information and builds on them. He uses these items as bases for other questions or as guides in this examination of documents. Amoeba-like, he inches his way from the known to the unknown" (p. 349).

Example Study of HIV-AIDS

To return to our sample studies, here is a brief overview of the categories that were developed from units.

- Definition: Agreement that HIV-AIDS is a medical condition.
- Role of social work: Confusion among many key players about what social workers are and what they do.
  - People living with HIV-AIDS were confused about what the unique social work contribution to their care could be.

- Social work professionals were clear on their contribution and surprised by the literature findings.
- Volunteer workers with a range of credentials were aware of and critical of social work's reluctance to play a key role in the field. They also suggested that since the gay community was so active and the social work community in the 1980s was focused on licensing, this may be an explanation.

- Image of social work: A consensus that the image of social work has been devalued. Many of the respondents thought of social workers as volunteers who did charitable work, while those with M.S.W. degrees were calling themselves psychotherapists.
- Who is doing social work: A belief that since social workers were actually narrowing their roles to clinician only, nurses and other helping professionals offer the case management and support services and activism that used to be the social work domain.
- Social work leadership: Many noted that there was little social work leadership in the region.
- Influence of medical context: There may be limited opportunities for social workers to get professionally involved, since the medical setting has most of the positions.
- Influence of workplace: Lack of funding for social work positions in HIV-AIDS settings. Mostly grassroots agencies, funded by grants, which cannot hire a social worker.

After these preliminary categories were developed, a membership-checking process via mail was conducted that identified the following constructions:

- Fears and biases: Fear of contagion, stigmatization, discomfort with talking about sexuality, morality, discomfort with death and dying
- Social work education: HIV-AIDS not addressed in many social work programs, lack of faculty expertise, not an institutional priority, political sensitivity
- Ideal social work education: Should include HIV-AIDS information in substance abuse and sexuality courses and at all levels of micro and macro practice; could be issue of diversity or issue of oppression/empowerment
- Factors facilitating HIV-AIDS social work practice: change perception from death sentence to "living with" inspiration coming from working with this group, personal experience

As noted above, this study did not proceed to a membership-checking meeting. The above four joint constructions (summarized) were developed via mail with members of the hermeneutic dialectic circle agreeing individually with their accuracy. They are an initial statement by the hermeneutic dialectic circle of their understanding of social work practice with people living with HIV-AIDS and their suggestions for addressing issues related to social work practice with this client population. Since the group itself was not at a stage that permitted moving forward with building the joint construction and taking action, the case study reported the above constructions. This case study was shared with members of the circle and a general audience of interested readers. Readers of the report were encouraged to decide on the trustworthiness of the constructions and the need for action.

Example Study of Homeless Children

In this study, categories that were identified at the end of the first round of interviews in the first year of the study were

- Homeless characteristics:
  - Families: diverse, economic insecurity, living in a range of settings, affect depressed
  - Children: developmentally and academically delayed, had phobias, shame, anxiety and generally felt unsafe
- Scope of service delivery: shelters, health care services, school district services, social services
- Lack of continuity in children's lives: inadequate network of services with gaps and duplications, needed regular meeting of those providing services to homeless children to better articulate and develop services. Quality of shelters variable, school's response not sensitive to homeless children's struggle to get to school, and lack of continuity in education
- Socialization: kids don't have network of friends
- Health care: can't get records; physicians not willing to treat; no insurance; they don't want to use public health facility; difficult to get indigent status, therefore children tend to be ill
- Mental health services: don't get assessments and interventions, vulnerable to substance abuse and general neglect
- Funding: services not funded, little low-cost housing, slow getting welfare checks, parent education needed, employment needed
- Major recommendation: network of services

In the second year of the study, these categories were revisited with an expanded circle of respondents, as noted above. Two rounds of individual interviews and sharing took place and the following categories were identified.

- Homeless characteristics:
  - Families: low self-esteem of parents, issues of substance abuse and child abuse as well as adult illiteracy
  - Children: need for "safety net" in school system, teenage children embarrassed by clothing, need for outreach coordinator between school districts and service providers, need for a place where they can act normally

- Scope of services
  - Shelters: experiencing increased demand, increased programs addressing substance abuse for children and parents
  - Domestic violence shelter: increased demand, bureaucratic barriers to mainstreaming these families back into community
  - Health care services: hard to keep immunization and children's general medical records as required by service providers
  - School districts: now offering outreach educational services to children at motels, cars, or wherever else children are living, including shelters
  - Social services: maintains food bank and makes referrals

- Lack of continuity in children's lives: agreement with this problem and agreed to participate in networking conference
- Socialization: commitment to outreach, especially mental health services
- Global perspective: need for literacy training, affordable housing, employment opportunities, child care, change of bureaucratic barriers, break cycle of homelessness

This circle revisited and further developed the constructions identified in the first year of the study. As a result of this development, an agenda of action to address the issue of homeless children was developed and a meeting of participants was held. Thus we see that the constructivist implementation and evaluation processes develop from a general focus to a specific construction. Participants are engaged in both a process and a production of a product. Data is gathered and analyzed in partnership with participants and action plans are developed.

To sum up constructivist implementation and evaluation, data collection builds the hermeneutic dialectic and analysis builds individual and joint constructions of the study focus. The circle is constructed using maximum variation and snowball sampling. Data is collected primarily through interviews; however, observational data and data collected from social artifacts may also be used to build constructions. Constructions evolve from individual interviews and the joint membership meeting. The data is analyzed by identifying units and categories of information that describe the construction. A commitment to action associated with the construction is identified and committed to by the study participants who have been engaged in the hermeneutic dialectic process.

Main Points

- Data gathering generally begins with separate interviews with members of the hermeneutic dialectic circle of study participants
- Sampling of participants usually uses maximum variation and snowball procedures

- The constructivist interview is open to exploring tangents, and the interviewer perceives himself or herself as the interview instrument rather than the questions on a questionnaire or interview protocol
- Interviews proceed through stages: preparing for the interview, beginning the interview, maintaining productivity during the interview, and closing the interview
- Observations follow stages: preparing for the field, entering the field, routinizing observation, and leaving the field. There are constraints related to openness and partnership for the constructivist researcher wishing to collect this data.
- Methods for recording data include recording or taking notes during the interview or observation or writing notes immediately after the interview
- The hermeneutic dialectic circle is developed from individual interviews where constructions are shared and a joint membership-checking meeting where agreement is reached on claims, concerns, and issues
- Evaluation, or analysis, of the data requires identifying units and categories of data that should be included in the joint construction

Learning Assignment

Form a small discussion group of about six participants. Assign a community member role to each member of the group. With the study you identified at the end of Chapter 14 in mind, share your constructions of the topic. Identify areas of agreement and areas of disagreement. Identify action that the circle would take about the issue being discussed.

16

Termination and Follow-Up—Reporting on Findings, Exiting the Research Setting, and Communication and Distribution of Findings

A t the end of the research project, the researcher will have completed research journals similar to those described in the post-positivist and critical theory parts of this book. The journal describing the day-to-day processes as the study unfolded will include notes on all stages of the project from assessment and engagement to writing the final case study. It will include rationales for initial constructions, initial data collection procedures, changes in data collection procedures, and the reasoning that went into those changes. In addition, the journal will make reference to the data set showing how units, categories, and constructions were built. This journal will be used as part of the audit check to assess the trustworthiness of the study findings. The second journal will contain narratives of the interview; observational and social artifact data collected during the study; and the units, categories, and the joint construction developed during the study. The final report on the project will be a case study using information from both journals. It is almost as if these documents report on a theatrical production; the journals show what was happening backstage and the report is the performance on stage.

Researcher's Journals

As soon as a constructivist researcher decides to carry out a study, he or she starts a journal. The first entries in this journal are thoughts on why the researcher is interested in the topic and what he or she is trying to learn. It should contain reflections on selection of the research site, possible key players, and the researcher's ideas about what is likely to happen and what the likely findings might be. This helps the researcher develop a constructivist perspective by acknowledging his or her subjective understanding and experience of the topic. It also helps the researcher develop empathy for study participants and how they will experience data collection as they participate in the constructivist process. Entries in the journal should include

> Date
> Focus of entry, e.g.,
> > Development of the research focus
> Thoughts about the site
> Rationales for data gathering processes
> Reflections on data gathering processes
> Explanations for any anticipated changes in data collection strategies
> Reflections on data analysis
> Reasoning behind developing categories and constructions from data
> Thoughts and reasoning for developing the final construction
> Preparation for membership-checking meeting
> Reflections on the meeting
> Final reflections on the study
> Optional Inclusions:
> > Charts and diagrams illustrating thinking
> > Interesting quotes that seem to illustrate an aspect of the study
> > Any emotional reactions to the process and content of the study
> Reference to Coding
> > Section explaining how the final data set is structured so that outside auditor can trace the path of development from narrative, to units, to categories, to constructions

This journal should be organized for easy review. The most useful system would probably be to use headings reflecting the stages of the research project. In a second journal, the researcher simply records the data set. That is, all narratives of interviews, observations, or social artifacts, giving the source and time and date of data collection. Such journals will be kept in electronic form for ease of review, since they are used for the final audit by an outside consultant or a faculty research supervisor. Lincoln and Guba (1985) have given a clear structure for the process of auditing (pp. 385–392). This process is adapted here with student projects in mind.

1. Pre-Entry Phase:
   a. Researcher's subjective understanding of the research focus
   b. Researcher's contact with research site
   c. Auditing Assessment. Was the study clearly conceived? Was the researcher aware of his or her perspective on the study and that this was just one of many possible constructions? Was the initial contact with the research site appropriate given the guidelines for participation in constructivist studies?

2. Auditability Phase
   a. Researcher familiarizes auditor with the study
   b. Researcher familiarizes auditor with auditing trail in journals
   c. Determine "Auditability." Are the journals comprehensive enough to identify and assess a trail from beginning research conceptions to the final joint construction of claims, concerns, and issues?

3. Trustworthiness Phase
   a. Credibility
      i. Review evidence that participants agreed with the researcher's narratives describing their constructions both at the end of individuals' interviews and observations and at the end of the membership-checking meeting. Any social artifacts used can be shown to the auditor with associated interpretations in the data.
      ii. Assess whether the written constructions are indeed accurate descriptions of the study participants' perspectives
   b. Transferability
      i. Review descriptions of settings, participants, and constructions
      ii. Are these descriptions comprehensive enough for readers to be able to assess transferability?
   c. Dependability
      i. Assess appropriateness of methodological decisions and analysis decisions
      ii. Assess whether data collection decisions flowed from evolving constructions or were simply the result of the researcher's biases
      iii. Assess overall dependability
   d. Confirmability
      i. Assess whether findings reported in the final case study are grounded in data

      ii. Assess whether inferences from data are logical
     iii. Assess clarity, explanatory power, and fit with data
     iv. Assess researcher bias
      v. Assess overall confirmability

4. Overall Assessment of Trustworthiness of Study. Is this a "good" study? Give a summary description of the strengths and weaknesses of the study on each of the dimensions of trustworthiness.

The Case Study or Research Report

The structure of this final report has been emerging throughout the study by means of the journal and the ongoing analysis of each interview, observation, or social artifact. Throughout the period of data collection, the researcher has been using the analysis procedures described above to organize and synthesize the data into a shared construction. Individuals' constructions have emerged and been compared and contrasted with other individuals' constructions. Units, categories, and constructions have been built. Claims, concerns, and issues have emerged; that is, areas of agreement have been identified, areas of disagreement have been identified, and issues requiring action have been identified. In our example study of homeless children, there tended to be agreement on the claims and concerns during the meeting, but opinion varied on action issues and strategies. Since this was the first meeting of a network, such disagreements were recorded and identified as possible agenda items for later network meetings. In the HIV-AIDS study, there were claims and concerns, but there was a hesitancy to broach issues and action strategies. Some stakeholders had a vulnerability to a perceived stigma associated with the HIV-AIDS issue. So much so that the membership-checking meeting was not feasible. Thus reflection on how to move forward in the face of this reticence was considered by individual stakeholders but not by the group as a whole.

The final case study, therefore, should include the following:

- The initial research focus
- A detailed description of the research site
- A description of the final membership of the hermeneutic dialectic circle with explanations of how they were identified and why they were selected. If confidentiality is an issue, the roles or agency names can be given rather than names of actual participants.
- A description of data gathering techniques, interviews, and observations. This should include a summary overview of the processes identified in the researcher's journal and changes from the initial focus to the final foci

- A description of the units, categories, and final construction as identified and agreed to at the membership-checking meeting that includes claims, concerns, and issues
- A plan of action addressing the issues that were identified at the membership-checking meeting (Who? What? When? Where?).

The constructivist researcher is committed to creating a dynamic discussion regarding a research focus and its context. The membership-checking meeting and the final report are not seen as the end of the research but the point at which participants take over their own process and continue the ongoing development of the joint construction with all its claims, concerns, and issues. Thus the final case study is simply a report on the joint construction at that point in time. It is assumed that the group will move beyond the findings contained in the case study.

Exiting the Research Setting

When the membership-checking meeting is organized, it should be made clear that this is the time when the researcher will be handing responsibility for the project to the groups and ending his or her involvement in the project. By the end of the membership-checking meeting the researcher should have engaged in a process of terminating with study participants that includes a commitment from the circle of participants to leading and implementing the plan for future action. The hermeneutic dialectic process has engaged the stakeholders in the knowledge generation process to the point where they have taken ownership of the future development of the project. For the social work researcher, this is the same as termination with any other client. The NASW code of ethics tells us that termination should happen when goals are accomplished. In this case, the researcher has facilitated a process and product that now has a life of its own. Again, we can take some advice from the social work practice field. Kirst-Ashman and Hull (2002, pp. 290–291) note that at the end of a project where change has been implemented in systems such as organizations and communities it is important to

- *Routinize procedures and processes.* Encourage the stakeholders to continue the constructivist approach to discussion of claims and concerns and to move forward with action to address issues.
- *Clarify policies and procedures.* Encourage stakeholders to prepare memorandums of understanding with each other regarding future tasks associated with the project (Who? What? When? Where?).

- *Reduce the availability of the researcher to the stakeholder group.* In our example study of homeless children, the researcher agreed to organize the follow-up meeting as her last task. She did not intend to attend the meeting and encouraged the group to select a chair or facilitator at that next meeting.
- *Inform stakeholders of other resources to address the issues that may come up.* Leave stakeholders with resource lists and researcher contact information if they should need consultation as they move forward.

In both of our example studies, the final reports show the flexibility and usefulness of the constructivist approach to research. There was the involvement of key players in gathering data on, and developing a joint understanding of, a local issue and associated actions to address that issue. In both studies, progress was made on this front. The shared power between researcher and participants led to one of the projects ending prematurely because participants were uncomfortable with the growing shared understanding. This in itself, though, gave the local community an understanding of the research issue. In both studies, members of the local community knew more about the issue when the study ended than they did at the beginning of the study. They gained insight into various perspectives on the issue and various possible action strategies. For the constructivist researcher, the product of the research is both the lived experience of the study and the final report. Transfer of findings to other researchers or other settings is a secondary gain.

Main Points

- The final documents are two research journals giving an account of the constructivist process and data collected plus a final report that is written up as a case study
- One journal will describe the study process and the other will contain the data set; they will both be kept in electronic form
- The journals are used for the audit that assesses the study's trustworthiness
- Termination with the hermeneutic dialectic circle happens as the members of the circle take charge of the project and its further development

Learning Assignment

Write a case study of your experiences so far in this research course using the journals you have been keeping and the outline for case studies described above.

Conclusion

This section of the book described an approach to research that seriously challenges most notions of scientific research. It suggests that subjective data is hard data, that the researcher as scientist can be completely involved with participants in a research project, and that data and its analysis should be the result of an evolving discourse between all those involved in the study. It is an approach to research that fits with the social work dictum of "start where the client is." This research starts with study participants' current understanding of an issue and facilitates the development of a more sophisticated understanding and action strategies that emerge from that evolution. It is an approach that can bring us useful micro and macro practice knowledge. One can imagine constructivist studies of, for example, appropriate social work interventions in schools with adolescents exhibiting the potential for violent behavior; appropriate family interventions with child abuse; appropriate group work techniques with gang members; the effectiveness of TANF; and community strategies to address the prevalence of meth labs in a particular neighborhood.

A more traditional scientist may well ask whether this kind of knowledge generation is simply building unsubstantiated hearsay rather than establishing facts. However, the definition of a fact is "a thing certainly known to have occurred or be true." The rigor of the constructivist process, with its commitment to authenticity, makes a strong case for suggesting that facts are being gathered and built into knowledge that is known to be true in this kind of research.

PART V

Cross-Cutting Themes: Ethics, Diversity, and Technology

Introduction to Part V

Having discussed the four paradigms and a generalist approach to research, we can now discuss three cross-cutting themes that apply to all research activities no matter what the approach. These are the ethics and politics of research, the researcher's responsibility to diversity, and the potential uses of technology at each stage of the research process.

Research ethics is an area of social work research that has grown considerably since the 1970s. Frederic Reamer (2001) reminds us that social work and other human service professions' commitment to ethical research grew out of the horrors disclosed at the Nuremburg trials in 1945 that revealed the inhumane experiments carried out by Nazi doctors, and the human rights movements of the 1960s that gave us the consciousness and vocabulary to understand and protect the rights of participants in research projects. More recent specific research practices illustrated the potential for abuse of research participants and the need to establish standardized codes for ethical research and the protection of research participants. The Tuskegee syphilis study (Jones, 1981), begun in the 1930s but only publicized in the 1970s, was a study that allowed poor black men who were diagnosed with syphilis to remain untreated so that the natural progression of the disease could be studied. Also, the Willowbrook (Krugman, Ward, & Giles, 1962) study similarly studied the natural progression of another disease, infectious hepatitis, in a group of children suffering from mental retardation who were intentionally infected with the disease.

The politics of research has always been with us but we rarely make it explicit because . . . it's political. As is clear in the discussion in Part I of this book, traditional positivist research rests on the assumption that the researcher stands outside the research setting as a neutral observer. However, this is not always possible given the demands of those that fund research and powerful gatekeepers of research settings. One of the first things a social work student wanting to carry out a research project in an agency setting learns is that certain questions, especially those regarding the impact or success of the program, are sometimes too sensitive to ask. The first large scale national evaluation of the "Head Start" program, at a time in the late 1960s under President Nixon's new administration when there was a push to cut back many of the programs developed during President Johnson's "Great Society," is a clear example of the influence of politics on research. It is described most clearly by Paul Ballantyne (2002, Ch. 7):

> Reflecting the wider governmental emphasis on scientific accountability in all government departments, an ill-fated attempt at national Head Start evaluation was . . . outsourced to the Westinghouse Learning Corporation in conjunction with Ohio University. This evaluation was outsourced because concerns over the proposed study design were immediately raised within the Department of Education and no internal researchers could be found to carry it out. In the Westinghouse study, Head Start graduates of both summer and full-year programs for years 1965–67 were to be statistically pooled and compared on standardized tests to an ex post facto (after the fact) control group set up three years after the program began (Cicirelli, 1969).
>
> Performance on standardized Psycholinguistic and school readiness tests by 1,980 former Head Start kids (70 percent of whom had attended the initial summer programs) were compared to 1,983 other children (now in grades 1–3). The instruments used to measure cognitive effects included: the Illinois Test of Psycholinguistic Abilities; the Metropolitan Readiness Test; and the Stanford Achievement Test. Westinghouse also developed three ad hoc (and unstandardized) attitudinal measures. The report did not find any positive effect of the summer initiatives but did find some for the full-year programs. These Head Start children, for instance, did better on the Metropolitan Readiness Test (a test used to assess readiness for grade one) than the control group, and their parents were nearly unanimous in voicing strong support for the program. No significant differences were found between groups, however, for the other measures used.
>
> Partisan Republican views against funding the ongoing Johnson era "Great Society" (antipoverty) initiatives were clearly an undercurrent of the design and the conclusions of the Westinghouse report (Hellmuth, 1970). Zigler and other Head Start proponents took issue with the Westinghouse conclusions and so did the main statistician involved in the research (who resigned and refused personal payment for the job in protest). In particular, given that the strongest positive findings turned up for the full-year program group, Zigler was exceedingly surprised when the executive summary of the Westinghouse/Ohio Report concluded that: "Head Start . . . . has not provided widespread cognitive and affective gains" It is exceedingly important to note here that, despite the fact that the initial evaluations of Head Start quickly fell into the "IQ trap" assessment (by utilizing standardized tests as a convenient empirical yardstick), the primary emphasis of the program itself was never to

raise the scores of societally disadvantaged children on such tests. Rather, the founding aims of Head Start were much broader. That is, even in the so-called "naive" era in which Binetesque mental orthopedics was making a resurgence, the central planners of Head Start managed to avoid such naive environmentalism per se. As Zigler would later put it:

"I consider it a real victory that there is no mention in the Planning Committee's recommendations of raising IQs. One of the . . . objectives does specify 'improving the child's mental processes and skills with particular attention to conceptual and verbal skills.' But this language pales by comparison to the fervor of Hunt, Bloom, and other apostles of [naive environmentalism]" (Zigler & Muenchow, 1992, p. 20).

The main problem with evaluation in the early years of Head Start was that the researchers did not know what to measure: "Public health researchers might have assessed the number of measles cases prevented, or the reduction in hearing or speech problems. Sociologist might have looked at the number of low-income parents who obtained jobs through Head Start. But the only people evaluating Head Start were psychologists, and, for a time, that greatly limited the focus of research" (Zigler & Muenchow, p. 51).

Ironically, since the Westinghouse Report on Head Start was the biggest (and most readily accessible) study, it was long assumed to be the best source. The initial findings of fade-out were then enshrined and generalized in general psychology textbooks as evidence of the so-called failure of compensatory educational programs (Cicirelli,1969).

So there we have it. The political intent was to cut back a Johnson-era program; the function of research and evaluation was to serve that agenda. When internal researchers could not be found to implement this agenda, external researchers hired by Westinghouse (yes, that's right, the makers of vacuum cleaners and small kitchen appliances) stepped in. More recent longitudinal evaluations have shown how Head Start children and their families have fared better on quality-of-life indicators such as rates of employment, rates of teenage pregnancy, and rates of substance abuse than children who did not attend Head Start (Love et al., 2002). However, the damage was done and the program was cut back to a much smaller scale as a result of the Westinghouse findings.

When we consider the social work researcher's responsibility to diversity, we are acknowledging the need to be able to carry out research with the diverse communities we work with. Like ethics and politics, consciousness of the need to be sensitive to diversity while implementing a research project has grown in recent decades. Some authors (Rodgers-Farmer & Potocky-Tripodi, 2001) have suggested that simply adopting alternative paradigms to positivism is a step in the right direction. However, even when we adopt worldviews that are focused on understanding empowerment or subjective human experience, we still need to be vigilant about appreciating the impact we have on different people and situations. In our example constructivist study of HIV-AIDS, it was clear that the participants were not ready to move forward with building a joint construction in a membership-checking meeting. The researcher had to step back and reflect on the history and experiences of people living with HIV-AIDS and thus be willing to let the study end when it did.

The uses of technology at each stage of the research process are growing as these words are written. Whatever is included in the following discussion will be embarrassingly out of date almost immediately. However, it is important to acknowledge that there is a technological tool that has the potential to enhance research skills at each step of the way. Only a generation ago, professors talked about taking a month to calculate multiple regressions by hand. Now, with a point and a click of a computer mouse, we can calculate the most complex of multivariate analyses in seconds. The use of technology has gone beyond data analysis. E-mail and Internet communications make it possible to be in contact with anyone anywhere. Cheap miniature cameras and microphones have made it possible to unobtrusively and precisely record data being gathered with individuals, groups, and large community meetings. There is a generation of young people who appear to be more comfortable communicating through text messaging, instant messaging, and cell phones than in a face-to-face conversation with another person in "real time." We may or may not think this is a good thing, but we need to be aware of it.

17

The Ethics and Politics of Research

The National Association of Social Workers (NASW) *Code of Ethics* commits social workers to being knowledgeable about research and carrying out research that respects and protects study participants. It makes the following statements with reference to research in the introduction:

> Social workers promote social justice and social change with and on behalf of clients. "Clients" is used inclusively to refer to individuals, families, groups, organizations, and communities. Social workers are sensitive to cultural and ethnic diversity and strive to end discrimination, oppression, poverty, and other forms of social injustice. These activities may be in the form of direct practice, community organizing, supervision, consultation, administration, advocacy, social and political action, policy development and implementation, education, and research and evaluation. (NASW, 1999)

In the body of the code, the ethics of research are stated as follows:

5.02 Evaluation and Research

(a) Social workers should monitor and evaluate policies, the implementation of programs, and practice interventions.

(b) Social workers should promote and facilitate evaluation and research to contribute to the development of knowledge.

(c) Social workers should critically examine and keep current with emerging knowledge relevant to social work and fully use evaluation and research evidence in their professional practice.

(d) Social workers engaged in evaluation or research should carefully consider possible consequences and should follow guidelines developed for the protection of evaluation and research participants. Appropriate institutional review boards should be consulted.

(e) Social workers engaged in evaluation or research should obtain voluntary and written informed consent from participants, when appropriate, without any implied or actual deprivation or penalty for refusal to participate; without undue inducement to participate; and with due regard for participants' well-being, privacy, and dignity. Informed consent should include information about the nature, extent, and duration of the participation requested and disclosure of the risks and benefits of participation in the research.

(f) When evaluation or research participants are incapable of giving informed consent, social workers should provide an appropriate explanation to the participants, obtain the participants' assent to the extent they are able, and obtain written consent from an appropriate proxy.

(g) Social workers should never design or conduct evaluation or research that does not use consent procedures, such as certain forms of naturalistic observation and archival research, unless rigorous and responsible review of the research has found it to be justified because of its prospective scientific, educational, or applied value and unless equally effective alternative procedures that do not involve waiver of consent are not feasible.

(h) Social workers should inform participants of their right to withdraw from evaluation and research at any time without penalty.

(i) Social workers should take appropriate steps to ensure that participants in evaluation and research have access to appropriate supportive services.

(j) Social workers engaged in evaluation or research should protect participants from unwarranted physical or mental distress, harm, danger, or deprivation.

(k) Social workers engaged in the evaluation of services should discuss collected information only for professional purposes and only with people professionally concerned with this information.

(1) Social workers engaged in evaluation or research should ensure the anonymity or confidentiality of participants and of the data obtained from them. Social workers should inform participants of any limits of confidentiality, the measures that will be taken to ensure confidentiality, and when any records containing research data will be destroyed.

(m) Social workers who report evaluation and research results should protect participants' confidentiality by omitting identifying information unless proper consent has been obtained authorizing disclosure.

(n) Social workers should report evaluation and research findings accurately. They should not fabricate or falsify results and should take steps to correct any errors later found in published data using standard publication methods.

(o) Social workers engaged in evaluation or research should be alert to and avoid conflicts of interest and dual relationships with participants, should inform participants when a real or potential conflict of interest arises, and should take steps to resolve the issue in a manner that makes participants' interests primary.

(p) Social workers should educate themselves, their students, and their colleagues about responsible research practices. (NASW, 1999)

Not only do we have a professional code that requires ethical treatment of people involved in research, but we also have international codes, federal legislation, and national reports that require ethical research practice. The Helsinki agreement drawn up in 1975 to address human rights and fundamental freedoms enjoins us to follow basic humanitarian practices. The Belmont report (National Commission for the Protection of Human Subjects of Biomedical and Behavioral Research, 1979) offers ethical principles to guide research decisions: respect for persons, beneficence, and justice. Such codes and guidelines instruct us to be informed about current thinking and, when carrying out research, to follow guidelines for ethical practice. Other federal mandates include:

- The Code of Federal Regulation–The Common Rule (56FR28003, June 18, 1991)
- The Health Insurance Portability and Accountability Act of 1996 (HIPPAA, Title 11)
- The Family Educational Rights and Privacy Act (FERPA), revised 1997

These mandates instruct us to do the right thing, but our motivation to be ethical is driven by something more than rules and legality. Our morality and values make us search for a just approach to our work. When Greenbank (2003) discussed morality in relation to research, he talked about personal values systems. He cited Rokeach (1973), who developed the concept of instrumental values. There are three kinds of instrumental values: moral, competency, and terminal. Each of these is guided by a different approach to answering the question, "What is the ethical thing to do?"

- *Moral values.* Decisions that are made based on moral values are guided by principles that tell us the "right" thing to do. We may have a value that calls us to respect diversity. Thus we decide that it is wrong to use sexist or racist approaches to carrying out research.
- *Competency values.* Decisions that are based on competency values are guided by principles that tell us the most effective way to do something. By keeping up with current knowledge on best social work practice, we make sure that we intervene in the most effective way possible with our clients. By being knowledgeable about research methods, we make sure that we build authentic knowledge.
- *Terminal values:*
  - *Personal values.* Decisions that are based on personal values are guided by what a person hopes to achieve for himself or herself. If someone strives to be a skilled community worker, then this aspiration will guide approaches to social work practice. Of course, there is a negative aspect to personal values. If a person is, for example, striving for power at any cost, then decisions will be guided by this ambition.
  - *Societal values.* Decisions that are based on societal values are guided by how a person wishes society to operate. A socialist vision calls for sharing and community gain; an entrepreneurial vision calls for individual competitive effort.

When deciding what is ethical, all of these values systems come into play. Sometimes they lead to answers to ethical problems that contradict each other. We have guidelines for basic research practice, but quite often such guidelines are only a starting point and we are left with difficult decisions to make. For example, is it ethical to withhold interventions, which are showing effectiveness during a research project, until the end of the study? Conversely, is it ethical to stop the study and start offering the intervention to all appropriate clients before completing the study? In this dilemma, the moral imperative suggests answering both "yes" and "no" to both questions; the competency principle suggests we follow correct research methodology and finish the study; terminal values lead us to reflect on our personal and societal visions—do we want to be seen as impetuous researchers who ended the study prematurely, or are we sure that the intervention is effective and that society will benefit from premature termination of the study? There are no easy answers to these questions, but it is important that we are mindful of the implications of our ethical reasoning when deciding what to do.

The four approaches to research described in this book raise different ethical and moral questions. Positivist research methodologies raise issues tied to the protection of human subjects where the values that are most pertinent are moral and competency, while terminal values play a less prominent role since they may taint the "scientific" stance of the researcher. For post-positivists, the ethics of intense engagement with study participants for research purposes rather than client intervention, or simply social relationship, need to be addressed. Moral, competency, and terminal values all come into play. For the critical theorist, the potential imposition of an ideological position on individuals or a research setting must be acknowledged and addressed. Thus terminal societal values guide the approach. For the constructivist researcher, moral, competency, and terminal values are acknowledged and interwoven with the dialectic that engages key players.

All studies, no matter what paradigm is being used, must undergo a human subjects review process that is usually carried out by an institutional review board in a university or agency. This process assesses any potential harm to study participants and balances this with the potential benefits of the study's findings. It also evaluates the provisions for protection of a study participant's privacy, confidentiality, and anonymity. Such review processes usually require the following information:

- A summary of the research project
- Evidence of permission to carry out the proposed project at the proposed site
- The written letter of introduction that will be given to gatekeepers of the study site and study participants
- The written informed consent to be signed by study participants before data collection begins. A good template of an informed consent is offered by Reimer (2001, p. 435). His example includes
  - The name of the agency sponsoring the research
  - Brief description of the project
  - Explanation of who the researcher is
  - Explanation of how the project relates to your academic program
  - Description of procedures that will be followed during data collection, including rationale for data collection procedure, timetable, risks, inconveniences, benefits, any withholding of services, and the participant's choices regarding participation
  - Explanation of confidentiality, legal constraints on revealing information, and how the data will be used
  - Contact information
  - Space for signatures and dates
- The data collection instrument(s)
- The written debriefing statement, which will be similar to the informed consent with the addition of suggestions for services should the topic of the study have made the participant aware of a need for services

Turning to the politics of research, we know that powerful groups and gatekeepers who control funding and dissemination of findings can dictate a discipline's research agenda. Indeed, the first experience of research politics most social work students will have will be when they approach a site and ask for permission to carry out a project. If such a student wishes to study the effectiveness of a program, the gatekeepers for that program will immediately be concerned about the impact of negative findings on funding sources and the general viability of the program. The student may well need to negotiate a formative (process) evaluation rather than a summative (outcome) evaluation so that such concerns can be assuaged. Another aspect of politics is the power differential between the researcher and the population that is being researched, as discussed by Martin and Knox (2000). These authors suggest a brokering model where both the researcher and the study participants give and receive something they need. A variety of political issues come into play when we consider our four paradigms: positivists struggle with the need for scientific freedom in a context where the research sponsor is the source of funding; post-positivists confront the politics of observing and interviewing people when the focus of the study may change, since it raises questions about who has power and control over the project and the extent of informed consent; critical theorists must think through the political implications of direct action to address oppression that can both harm as well as help a community; and for constructivists, sharing power with study participants can threaten the completion of a study. In the discussion below, both the ethics and politics of each of the four paradigms are reviewed.

Ethics

Positivism

Since the plan for the implementation of positivist research is prepared before data collection begins, with minimal input from participants besides the instructions from the sponsors, a number of ethical issues arise concerning the assumptions the researcher is making about study participants. The positivist researcher, in the past, had the potential to ignore the rights of study participants in the name of science. Now such a researcher, in the planning stage, must anticipate harm that might be done by the study, review the impact of any deception of participants, guarantee anonymity and confidentiality, and acknowledge the possible distorting influence of the researcher's commitment to the study sponsor.

Even with these protections, this approach to research requires a power differential between researcher and study participant that can lead to unintended unethical treatment of study participants. This precipitates a conscious formal consideration of whether a study is moral and legal. If a positivist researcher believes that study participants' knowledge about the study will threaten the scientific approach to the proof of causality, then the necessity for deceptions and the potential for harm must be reviewed and assessed (terminal value). For example, if a social work researcher wishes to prove that parent education training is more effective in reducing families' incidents of child abuse than an alternative intervention such as family therapy, it will be important for the families in the study to be unaware of the researcher's hypothesis regarding the enhanced efficacy of the parenting program. The question for the human subjects committee would be whether the harm and deception resulting from withholding a program that the researcher believes is more effective in protecting children is balanced by the families' access to the family therapy and the need to know which of these interventions protects children most effectively.

All research projects sponsored by universities must undergo a human subjects review process managed by an institutional review board. A university committee assesses the research project's potential for harm using federal guidelines. Practice agencies also tend to have research review committees. Such institutional review procedures were put in place after a number of now famous abuses of the research process (the Milgram study of obedience, Milgram, 1963, 1965, 1974; the Humphreys study of male homosexuals, Humphreys, 1975; and the Zimbardo et al. study of prison behavior, Zimbardo et al., 1974), and they review research projects for possible physical, psychological, and legal harm to participants. The social work researcher must also consider the potential harm arising from coercion of special populations such as mandated clients or clients who may well feel that their services will be threatened if they do not agree to be in the study. One strategy for reducing harm is offered by Elaine Wethington (2003), who gives examples of two studies where she spent a year pretesting telephone interview protocols specifically to discover whether they caused harm to participants. She asked a small sample of study participants to engage in the process and then give specific feedback on the experience of being interviewed about sensitive topics on the phone. She then adjusted the training of interviewers, so that when the large-scale study was carried out, harm was minimized.

In addition to doing no harm and not coercing study participants, researchers also need to address study participants' privacy, anonymity, and confidentiality. Is the researcher intruding into the study participants' privacy by observing their behaviors in a parenting class? Is the study important enough to warrant this? Anonymity is the protection of a person's identity while confidentiality is the protection of that person's information. Again, the researcher must develop procedures for such protections before data collection begins. The solution to many of these ethical concerns, for positivists, is to obtain a signed informed consent form from study participants at the beginning of the study and offer a debriefing at the end of the study. The informed consent will describe the study, how it will be carried out, any potential risks, any guarantees as outlined above, who the researcher is, and the auspices of the project. However, this is not always as straightforward as it appears. Many researchers will admit that the more information you put into an informed consent, the less likely it is that a participant will sign it. Participants have no say in the design of the project and can either trust that the researcher will treat them ethically or refuse to participate in the study. Many disenfranchised groups have reacted to this situation and now demand more collaborative approaches to research; thus the exploration of alternative approaches to research illustrated in this book.

A further ethical issue for positivist researchers is their relationship with the research sponsor. Should the researcher reveal the funding source? What pressure is there to look for certain positive findings and suppress unpalatable findings? The only real answer to these questions for a social work researcher is to look to his or her own personal ethical standards and to the NASW code of ethics for his or her professional ethical standards. Continued discussion of these issues with peers can only increase awareness of potential ethical pitfalls and help to avoid the mistreatment of study participants or collusion with study sponsors.

Post-Positivism

Post-positivists face many of the ethical issues addressed above with reference to positivism. Like any other researcher, the post-positivist must undergo a human subjects review and develop procedures for informed consent, debriefing, and any ethical issues associated with his or her projects. However, since there is an engagement with study participants when the initial research focus is developed, there is more opportunity for consideration of and response to any ethical concerns that participants may mention during the initial stages of the project. Post-positivist research entails an intense social involvement for both the participants and the researchers. The informed consent procedures need to be thoroughly thought through. If the mode of data collection is the interview, the interviewee needs to be informed at the beginning about the subject of the interview and the length of time the interview is likely to take. Researchers and respondents always meet each other in this form of research, and thus there is a potential to betray anonymity and confidentiality. Researchers need to take extra care to make sure that respondents' names are not made public and that either the data they give is separated from their name or, if data needs to be linked to its source, that the list of names connected to data is kept in a secure place. If the research is a formative or summative program evaluation, then the interviewee, whether staff member or client, needs to be made aware of the potential uses of the evaluation data, with particular reference to the politics of the agency.

If the mode of data collection is observation, those being observed need to be given the opportunity to think through the implications of close watching for them. In a formal work setting, what risks are those being observed taking regarding supervisory reaction to observations made by researchers? If the researcher/observer masks his or her role in some way, how is voluntary informed consent gained, how is the right to voluntary withdrawal from the study protected, and what are the procedures for debriefing participants? Many of these ethical issues make observation, especially if it involves deception, an undesirable data collection mode. Indeed, Adler and Adler (1994) suggest that its future as a sole method of data collection looks bleak. They suggest that its most fruitful use is as an integrated technique combined with interviewing. In this context, it can enrich researchers' understandings of participants' statements during interviews. However it is used, the ethical treatment of study participants must be addressed.

Critical Theory

The ethical issues for critical theory research relate to the impact of education about oppressions and action for empowerment. The harm that might be done by taking an ideological position and acting on it should be thoroughly reviewed in relation to the vulnerability of the oppressed group that is the focus of the study. For example, our example study of eating disorders in adolescent female high school students took a feminist position on the causes of those eating disorders and intervened in the school to educate a group of adolescent girls about the feminist position on eating disorders and body image. The researcher needed to first make it clear that the girls had permission to challenge and debate these positions. The researcher also needed to make it clear that success in high school was not influenced by their acceptance, or non-acceptance, of these ideas. Regarding the action that critical theorists take to challenge power over an oppressed group, there needs to be an acknowledgment of the potential for harm. For example, a study that confronts differential services to racial groups has the potential to antagonize service providers so that they withdraw from an underserved neighborhood, and the unintended impact of the action is that the services, although inadequate, completely disappear.

The critical theory researcher is clearly bound by the traditional human subjects mandates of doing no harm, avoiding deception, assuring privacy and confidentiality, and formally gaining informed consent. However, an additional constraint for these researchers is the importance of informing participants about the ideological orientation of the study and the intent to empower. Since the study has a political agenda that may be contradictory to participants' own ideologies or experiences, the critical theory researcher must engage opposing opinions and clearly explain the rationale for the ideological orientation and intent of the study. Study participants must be informed about the activity that they are getting involved in, including the potential for coercion by others who disagree. The teaching-learning dialogue is seen as the key to keeping all participants informed and negotiating conflict.

An additional ethical issue for some critical theorists is the commitment that many make to a lifelong relationship with participants in the research project (Brown & Strega, 2005). Those that take this position are implying that the boundary between social work practitioner and client should be erased if genuine empowerment is to take place. This contradicts much of the practice wisdom about such relationships, not to mention parts of the NASW code of ethics, specifically Conflict of Interest §1.06(b), which states that "social workers should not take unfair advantage of any professional relationship or exploit others to further their personal, religious, political, or business interests"; and (c), which states that "social workers should not engage in dual or multiple relationships with clients or former clients in which there is a risk of exploitation or potential harm to the client. In instances when dual or multiple relationships are unavoidable, social workers should take steps to protect clients and are responsible for setting clear, appropriate, and culturally sensitive boundaries." The potential exists for the social work researcher using the more "committed" critical theory approach to become unclear about the personal boundary between a social work practitioner who is carrying out research as part of practice and the participants in the study who are looking to the researcher for professional services. As stated above, clear boundaries must be identified and maintained throughout the period of the study.

Constructivism

As with all the other approaches to research, constructivist research is subject to human subjects review processes assuring that participants are not harmed and that privacy, confidentiality, and anonymity are protected. This is a challenge, given the open nature of the data collection process. The ever-changing focus of the study, the desire to build accurate constructions for each respondent, the goal of sharing those constructions, and the openness of the membership-checking meeting intensifies and broadens informed consent. Protection of privacy and confidentiality becomes an intensive process of constant renegotiation throughout the study as the focus emerges and evolves. Anonymity is difficult to guarantee in constructivist research. Even if a name is removed from the construction, the point of view may be a known one and easily identified by other key players in the research project. The only solution to this is to make sure that study participants are aware of the risk. Remember, the goal of the constructivist researcher is to empower, educate, and connect participants (Erlandson et al., 1993), and a failure to openly confront the issues would weaken the methodology of the study and threaten the validity of the data collected for the constructions. Thus the dilemma should be openly shared with participants so that they can make a decision about the terms of their participation.

If a stakeholder decides not to participate and another person cannot be found who plays a similar stakeholder role, then that construction is missing from the final joint construction. This would be noted when reporting the final construction. A stakeholder group can be informed that a particular perspective has not yet been included in the process of building the joint construction. That is useful data for the constructivist and the members of the hermeneutic dialectic circle. A participant who is comfortable sharing data at the beginning of a study may be put in a politically or professionally embarrassing situation by some of the issues that surface during data collection as the focus of the study emerges and changes. Thus it is difficult to anticipate exactly what the ethical issues will be as the study continues, but adjustments and accommodations will need to be made throughout the process. This was particularly evident in our HIV-AIDS study example. Many participants asked for anonymity, and most participants were not comfortable with a joint meeting of the circle of informants. This was a sad but valid comment on the HIV-AIDS situation in that region at that time. Anonymity was perceived as necessary, and this need limited the progress of the study. However, reporting of the separate constructions of the key stakeholder groups and acknowledgment that a joint meeting was not possible at that point in time was useful information for the stakeholders and gave a direction for further action.

The principles of sensitivity and integrity that guide constructivist research are required for collection of valid and reliable data that guarantee trustworthy constructions. These principles determine appropriate solutions to ethical dilemmas regarding harm to participants. With such a fluid process, unanticipated situations that may harm the participant or researcher may surface. Acknowledging these and changing the study so that protection from harm is achieved will not weaken or even threaten a constructivist study. Such accommodations are all part of the process of building the joint construction and accurately reporting subjective under-standings. Deceiving participants would not be a strategy that constructivist researchers would use, since such deception would threaten the process and product of constructivist research. If participants should find out, for exam-ple, that the researcher was really studying HIV-AIDS but was pretending to study substance abuse or sexually transmitted diseases in general, the process by which participants were engaged in the project would be com-promised. Indeed, the accuracy of the subjective data and the likelihood that the action stage will be implemented would be compromised if partic-ipants were not clear on the focus and intent of the study. By sharing, con-fronting, reflecting, and changing perspectives, the constructivist process is believed to offer a comprehensive approach to protecting those who engage in these studies.

Politics

Positivism

The politics of positivist research are revealed when a series of macro issues and questions listed below are posed.

1. Who decides appropriate arenas and topics for research? In the research world, some topics become the "hot" topics while others go away. In the 1960s, poverty was a hot topic. Now we may see a study of income mainte-nance or the effectiveness of TANF, but we rarely see studies on the causes of poverty and its amelioration. HIV-AIDS is a hot topic, but it tends to be studied in the USA rather than Africa where per capita incidents are higher. Since child welfare is a major employer of social workers, in the social work arena we tend to see a lot of research on child abuse and neglect but not so much on aging, even with the infusion of Hartford Foundation funding for the integration of aging content into social work curricula.

2. How are such choices made? Well, as Deep Throat said in the movie *All the President's Men*, "Follow the money." If there is money, either government or private, for a research topic, then it will be studied. Private funding usu-ally comes from foundations with a particular mission, while public funding is linked to political decisions about important topics. As I write this, Ronald Reagan's funeral is on the television and members of his family are making a plea for the funding of stem cell research to find a cure for Alzheimer's. When

the O.J. Simpson case was on the television, research into spouse abuse was advocated. After any high school shooting, studies of adolescent violence are called for. Government decisions about research are influenced by public opinion that favors certain topics and public criticism of other topics. In the early 1980s when HIV-AIDS was seen as a "gay" disease, limited funding was made available for research, but once it was seen as a threat to us all it became an expanded, acceptable, and fundable research arena.

3. Who defines social constructs? Employment is a good example of the issues related to this question. In the 1960s the unemployment rate was calculated by simply adding up the number of people who did not have a job. It was the total workforce minus those who had a job. However, when these numbers crept up, definitions of both the workforce and unemployment began to be massaged so that numbers of unemployed decreased. The workforce was redefined as those employed in non-military positions. The unemployed were redefined as "those actively seeking employment." The requirements for being officially unemployed were, therefore, tightened and rates declined. The example of child abuse raises a different political problem with definitions. The only data we have enumerating rates of child abuse is numbers of reports of child abuse. However, some reports are substantiated and others are not. If we use substantiated reports of child abuse, we notice a correlation with poverty. In fact, checking the correlation of child abuse rates with rates of poverty is often the method researchers use to determine the validity of the data on substantiated rates of child abuse. However, the poor are more likely to be reported for child abuse since they tend to experience more public scrutiny from social workers and other health and human service officials than other classes of society. The poor are labeled as child abusers while middle and upper class families, not subject to the same scrutiny, are not.

4. What data is available and how was it collected and organized? The census bureau has collected demographic data on the US for about 200 years. However, collecting valid and reliable data on ethnicity has only been addressed in the last 10 to 15 years. Until quite recently, data on the Latino ethnic group was collected by noting those with a Spanish last name. These could have been members of any ethnic group who had married someone with a Spanish last name. Also, the need for a category of identification for those of mixed ethnicity or race has been responded to only recently. Another issue arises when the source of data for a project is social service case records. Often, these data have been collected for the purposes of auditing rather than research. Thus a client service might have been checked off in the file, but the length of service and its content may well not be there. The auditor wants to know whether the service was delivered; the researcher wants to know how much of the service was delivered and what kind of service was delivered. It is the auditor to whom social services agencies must pay much more attention.

Ethics, Diversity, and Technology

5. Who sponsors and funds the research and for what reasons? This is a major issue with program evaluation. Generally the agency funds its own evaluation. Outcome evaluations address program effectiveness. However, an agency may well have difficulty paying to be told that it is ineffective. The pressure on the positivist researchers is, therefore, to cushion the blow or perhaps modify the findings.

6. Who will know about the research findings? What will be done with the research findings? This brings us to the question of exploitation of research participants and research sites. Most positivists report research findings to the academic community in academic journals. They may write a report for the funder and they may promise access to findings to respondents, but the reality is that study participants have to take the initiative to find out about the study; positivists do not, generally, see a return to the research site to give feedback as a stage of the research process. Researchers will make a name for themselves by being an expert on a certain area as a result of the study, but the same is not true for participants in the study. This is sometimes addressed by payment to participants, but generally, it is not addressed at all.

Post-Positivism

Since the purpose of post-positivist research is to develop theory, it does not have the same political issues as positivism. The notion of politically sensitive or "hot topic" research foci does not tend to apply to this kind of research. The political issues here relate more to the combination of a positivist worldview that allows the researcher to be more powerful than the respondent and an intense social engagement between researchers and study participants that implies a partnership. The post-positivist can consult with participants, but he or she keeps the power to decide which data shall be collected and how data will be used. Post-positivists attempt to curb the influence of their values on the research project and maintain the positivist stance that the researcher, if careful, will not affect the research setting. Thus, for the post-positivist, study participants are a source of data, not collaborators in the project. For example, in the study of homeless children described in Part IV, it needed to be made clear that the artwork and poems that were being produced in sessions on building children's self-esteem were being used as data to discuss the hopes and aspirations of the children and would be reported in a research report to an academic setting.

Critical Theory

Of course, everything about critical theory research is political: the choice of ideology, the teaching-learning process, and the action to promote empowerment. In fact, the explicit political agenda of critical theory research is one of its strengths. It openly defines power relationships in the research setting, takes action to address them, and then reports back to the community on the impact of the action. Meanwhile the relationship between the researcher and the researched is an action partnership. Thus the political issues that are associated with this approach are not the differential power relationship between researcher and study participant but more the potential for conflict and emotional responses to the actual study. The political issues highlighted by this approach are likely to generate emotional responses to injustice and the success or failure of action for empowerment. The researcher will need to think through a responsible plan for these experiences in partnership with study participants. For example, in our example study of eating disorders in teenage girls, the high school students in the study needed to be aware of, and ready to discuss, the impact on both their friends and teachers of adopting feminist interpretations of issues.

Constructivism

The politics of a constructivist study are negotiated before the study starts. Study sponsors commit to the constructivist process that requires sharing of power, honesty, and an intense commitment. If these conditions cannot be agreed to then the study cannot commence. The constructivist commitment to developing partnerships with study participants and explaining the process and product of the research during initial negotiations with the site is a powerful strategy. It practically eliminates the possibility of colluding with study sponsors to produce favorable findings since the concept of favorable or unfavorable findings does not make sense. In the constructivist context, there is an assumption that the shared constructions will identify both areas of agreement and areas of disagreement between stakeholders and a plan for action to improve the situation. The judgment, and the need to "get it right" associated with impact studies, is not a part of the constructivist approach. Even if stakeholders tend to agree that a particular program or issue is being handled badly, the commitment of the stakeholders is to building a joint construction of solutions and action strategies for progress rather than an assessment of failure or success. At the end of the study there is an agenda for action that addresses collaboratively the areas of agreement and disagreement.

Conclusion

This chapter has reviewed the ethics and politics of research for each of our paradigms. We can see that the issues change as our worldview changes. We are never free of these concerns, and the solutions to the problems they raise are not always obvious. However, as social workers we have a commitment to ethical practice and awareness of political contexts. Through continual dialogue with our colleagues and research partners we will meet the evolving demands that are generated by our professional commitment to building new knowledge.

Main Points

- The NASW code of ethics charges social workers with a responsibility to be knowledgeable about research and integrate research into social work practice
- Researchers must consider the morality and legality of their research projects
- Each paradigm has its own ethical issues to be addressed
  - For positivists it is the potential harm when a study is designed in isolation from participants
  - For post-positivists it is the impact of intense engagement of study participants by researchers
  - For critical theorists it is the potential harm done by the powerful to those seeking empowerment
  - For constructivists it is the threats to anonymity and confidentiality created by such an open data sharing process

- Each paradigm has its own political issues to be addressed
  - For positivists they are associated with outside influences on "science"
  - For post-positivists it is the confusion that might arise when activities taking place in natural informal settings are used as a source for research data
  - For critical theorists they are associated with the impact of the chosen ideology on various interest groups
  - For constructivists it is a consciousness that power must be shared if the approach is to work

Learning Assignments

1. Read the brief description of the Humphreys tearoom study below. In groups, imagine that you are the university institutional review board reading the proposal for this study. Should it be approved? What are the pros and what are the cons? Do the potential benefits outweigh the potential harm? What is your decision?

   In the 1970s, homosexuality was widely assumed to be an illness or a psychiatric disorder. Since most gay men did not reveal their sexual orientation it was also assumed to be a rarity. Sociologist Laud Humphreys

(1970) studied homosexual behavior in a way that was widely criticized. There are two parts to his study that present ethical dilemmas.
First, he observed homosexual behavior using participant observation
and deception. He knew that some male homosexuals meet for impersonal sex in public restrooms, which they call "tearooms." Homosexuals
who engage in sex in tearooms like to have a third person present,
someone they call a "watch queen." This person warns them if he sees
a stranger approaching. Humphreys volunteered to take on this role so
that he could carry out participant observation of sexual behaviors in
"tearooms." In this way he developed detailed descriptions of homosexual sexual behavior. The second part of the study involved finding
out more about the men who were using these tearooms. When they
left, he followed them to their cars and took down their license plate
numbers. He got their addresses from the department of motor vehicles
and sent university staff to their homes, in the guise of pollsters, to find
out more about them. Humphreys found that 38% of the men who
were having tearoom sex were married and identified themselves as heterosexual. Homosexuality was not, perhaps, the rarity that it was
thought to be and appeared not to be an illness.

2. Imagine you are a critical theory researcher preparing to carry out a feminist
   study of homeless women. Form pairs. One person takes on the role of the
   researcher and the other takes on the role of the homeless women living in a
   temporary shelter. Engage in the teaching-learning process with each other.
   Which of the political and ethical issues discussed above did you become
   aware of?

18

The Researcher's
Responsibility to Diversity

Like any other social work practitioner, the social work researcher must deliver services that acknowledge and engage the diverse characteristics and contexts of study participants, who are his or her clients, at both the micro and macro levels of human organization. During the engagement and assessment phases of the project, the researcher identifies the unit of analysis, the unit of observation, the people who will participate in the study, and the research setting. These can be individuals, families, groups, organizations, or communities. The unique characteristics of these human beings in various settings who are "sources of data" should be immediately considered. What is their history? What are their demographic characteristics? What are their cultural norms? What is their history with being involved in research projects? How will their unique identities be acknowledged, honored, and respected during the research project? What is their history with members of the researcher's socioeconomic group? One way to think about these questions is to reflect on and understand the following differences between the researcher and the researched:

- Differences in appearance: not only dress but the more significant differences of gender, ethnicity, age, and so on. What are the differences between researchers and researched and how will they be recognized, discussed, understood, and addressed so that the research project can be effectively carried out from the beginning conceptualization stages to the final reporting stage, from engagement to termination and follow up?

- Differences in perceived power over the situation: male versus female, minority versus majority ethnic identity, and vulnerable client versus researcher with status. Can a partnership be formed between the researcher and the researched by acknowledging and reflecting on these differences? What arrangements of mutual benefit can be brokered?

- Differences in assumptions and norms about the topic being researched and the actual implementation of research: for example, there will be differences in assumptions about what a happy child looks like, or what a healthy functioning family looks like, or the extent of involvement in groups and communities, or organizational norms and cultures. How are these being identified and integrated into the study processes?

- Differences in norms about appropriate behavior: how will researcher and researched recognize and honor each other's code of behavior, both formal and informal? What strategies will be used to explore and understand these assumptions? For some, the formal and transitory engagement of filling out a survey to give personal information will be offensive and ineffective in the end. Feminist researchers have repeatedly stressed women's reticence to give any meaningful data in such situations. On the other hand, for some, the intense engagement of observation and in-depth interviews is intrusive. How will the researcher become knowledgeable about these assumptions and accommodate them?

- Differences in perspective: the anthropologists refer to this as the emic/etic distinction. Is the researcher looking at things as an outsider looking inward or an insider looking outward? How will this affect the exchanges between the researcher and the researched, and what can be done about these effects?

- Differences in language, or vocabulary within a language: if language is the difference, how will interpreters be used? If vocabulary (research terms versus informal language, or informal street talk versus formal language) is the issue, whose language will be used and who will be accommodated?

- Differences in history: what is the immigration experience of the researcher's ethnic group compared to that of the study participants? What is each group's historical experience in the country they now live in? Will this history have an impact on data gathering?

If we focus on the social engagement between the researcher and participants in a research project, a number of quite specific questions surface. Can a man carry out feminist research? Can a white person, male or female, research the oppression of minority ethnic groups? Can a heterosexual person gather valid data on the gay and lesbian community? Can a young person gather valid data on the old? These are just a few of the questions, and, of course, opinions vary on the answers to them. Those who doubt peoples' ability to learn cultural competency would answer "no" to all of the above questions. However, a more optimistic outlook suggests that anybody could gather data about anything or anyone with the appropriate effective training. In reality it is not that simple or stereotypical. We all have individual reactions to others that depend on our ancestry, life experiences, and current consciousness of diversity. Thus, for all of us, it is important to be aware of differences between others and us as we engage in our work.

At the micro level of human interaction, Evans et al. (2004) give some useful advice about differences when they summarized their experience with "the micro-counseling approach," which has been used throughout the world with over 500,000 professionals. They note that "through wide use and cultural feedback" they have learned that attending and listening skills have the following cultural differences:

Eye Contact. The direct European North American pattern of eye contact is considered intrusive and rude in some cultures. Many Native Americans, Latinos/Latinas, and people from other countries prefer less eye contact. For some cultures a reverse pattern is considered appropriate. You should gaze at the person while talking and avoid eye contact when listening.

Body Language and Space. The shaking of the head for "yes" or "no" varies across different cultures. For many, an arm's length is a comfortable distance between people. However, some, such as those of recent Arab descent, may be comfortable with a closer 6 to 12 inches separating people engaged in conversation, and others (such as Australian aborigines) may need a distance.

Verbal Following. Being direct about listening and reflecting back what you hear may not be appropriate for Chinese Canadian or Japanese American participants in a study.

Listening First, then Acting. For some groups, action is needed early to develop trust. For example, in a critical theory study it may be necessary to take some action during the ideological analysis stage. This could be as simple as contacting key informants suggested by the group. The point is to show that the researchers are capable of doing more than just gathering data. (p. 19)

At the macro level of human organization, Chavez, Duran, Baker, Avila, and Wallerstein (2003) discuss race in relation to community-based research (CBR). They note three kinds of racism:

- institutionalized racism, which is exhibited through differential access to services such as quality education and health care as well as to information and power;
- personally mediated racism, which is exhibited through discrimination and prejudice; and
- internalized racism, which is exhibited through peoples' belief in negative messages about their own race or ethnicity.

CBR, reliant as it is on community collaboration, addresses these forms of racism by (1) being aware of the class and ethnic makeup of the research team; (2) being aware of the potential to stereotype community members as "insiders" with deficits that need to be addressed by the researcher as an "outsider" who has privilege and knowledge; and (3) making it possible for researchers of color to acknowledge their own experiences with racism and being in the role of outsider or insider. When discussing "white privilege," Chavez et al. (2003) quote Omni (2000) who states,

> Whites tend to locate racism in color consciousness and find its absence in color blindness. In so doing, they see the affirmation of difference and racial identity among racially defined minority students as racist. Black students, by contrast, see racism as a system of power, and correspondingly argue that they cannot be racist because they lack power. (p. 90)

With this perspective in mind, these authors' recommendations regarding carrying out CBR include the following:

- Acknowledge the diversity within racial and ethnic groups. Expand data collection to include questions on ancestry, migration history, and language. Be attentive to the increasing heterogeneity of racial/ethnic groups, and rethink the nature and types of research questions asked.
- Acknowledge that race is a social construct, not a biological determinant, and model race as a contextual variable in multivariate analysis.
- Address the present-day existence and impacts of racism not only as variables to measure but also as lived experiences within the research process as the study is carried out.
- Emphasize the "intersectionality" (e.g., black women versus black men or poor Latino women versus wealthy Latino women) of race, gender, age, and class to examine how the resultant different categories engage with racism and with each other.
- Use the research process and findings to mobilize and advocate for change to reduce disparities and enhance race relations.
- Listen, listen, listen. Pay close attention and try to recognize both hidden (discourse by those without power when they are not in the presence of those with power) and public transcripts (the official discourse that happens in the presence of those with power); speak out about white privilege and racism.
- Accept that outsiders cannot fully understand community and interpersonal dynamics. Do not, however, let this stop you from taking part.
- Recognize that privilege, especially white privilege, is continually operating to some degree and creating situations of power imbalance. Such an understanding is crucial in honest, ongoing communication that builds trust and respect. Build true multicultural working relationships; in partnership mode, develop guidelines for research data collection, analysis, publication, and dissemination of research findings. (pp. 92–93)

Examining the research process as a whole, Rodgers-Farmer and Potocky-Tripodi (2001) have considered the stages of the research process and addressed traps that may lead to insensitivity to diversity. In the problem definition stage, relying on past literature and hypothesis testing models may lead us to focus on the "'problems' of minority groups (often in relation to the dominant group) rather than focusing on strengths and resiliencies" (p. 447). In the design stage, both between- and within-group comparisons raise questions about stereotyping of ethnic groups. In the past, between-group comparisons have stressed deficits in various ethnic groups, while within-group comparisons have not been generalizable because of differences in conceptual and measurement equivalence between various ethnic groups. For example, comparisons of indicators such as poverty and child abuse stress the overrepresentation of certain minority groups in poor and abusing populations. However, comparisons of community commitment or ability to collaborate to solve a problem would show strengths. Or, in another example, comparisons between middle class Latinos and working class Latinos in California are not generalizable to similar groups in, say, Mexico. In the data collection stage, Rodgers-Farmer and Potocky-Tripodi (2001) suggest the need for training of data gatherers and note that researchers should be sensitive to the processes used to gain access to the population of interest, the selection of data gatherers, and the selection of data gathering methods. To address these, they suggest "gaining the sponsorship of a well known ethnic community service agency, explaining the purpose of the research to a variety of appropriate community groups, and training indigenous personnel to participate as interviewers or in some other staff capacity" (p. 449). With the above general pointers in mind, we can proceed to our discussion of diversity and difference at each stage of the research process.

Engagement—Gaining Entrée to the Research Setting

On a continuum of intensity, a researcher's engagement with the targets of research can range from formal contracting with study sponsors and the signing of informed consents to an intense long-term social involvement with the study sponsors and participants. Whatever the degree of intensity of involvement, researchers need to take a close look at diversity as it affects the initial human engagement. When developing the study, researchers should consider at least the gender, ethnic, and age makeup of potential participants and educate themselves in the ethics and politics of working with such subpopulations. For the positivist, this may simply be awareness and sensitivity, rather than a need to demonstrate culturally competent engagement skills, since the positivist (as defined in this book) tends to have a more formal, limited engagement with study sponsors and study participants so that the "science" of the approach is not compromised. However, explicit training in the history and current manifestations of differences for specific subpopulations are essential elements of the post-positivist, critical theorist, and constructivist researcher's preparation if they are to engage study participants to the extent that is required by these approaches to research. Post-positivists need an intense engagement in interviews. Critical theorists need the partnership of the teaching-learning process to promote empowerment. And constructivists need the dialogue of the hermeneutic dialectic to gather valid subjective data. All the differences noted above (appearance, power, assumptions, norms of appropriate behavior, perspective, and language) need to be acknowledged and addressed. For example, if the constructivist researcher needs to work with an interpreter, how will this affect data gathering? The presence of the interpreter is assumed to affect the construction being offered. The constructivist researcher, when contracting with an interpreter, would need to know something of that interpreter's experience and perspective regarding the research focus. Monolingual Spanish-speaking participants were not included in our example HIV-AIDS study. However, the region in which that study was carried out is at least 30% Hispanic. The student researcher did not have the resources to hire a Spanish/English interpreter. If she had, then she would have assumed that interpreter had feelings and partial knowledge about the topic. She would have documented the interpreter's construction and included it in the circle of individual constructions as well as the joint construction.

Assessment—Developing an Understanding of the Research Focus

When talking about research with lesbians and gay men, Martin and Knox (2000) discuss problem development and the role of established theories in promoting misinformation. They note that until recently, theories of sexuality had an implicit assumption that heterosexuality was normal while homosexuality was either abnormal or just did not exist. For the positivist researcher in particular, such assumptions in theory are problematic, since their question(s) and hypotheses are built on current knowledge. It is important that positivists screen the assumptions of the theories they are adopting for erroneous assumptions about diversity. Asking the following questions, adapted from questions on the elements of thought from the Foundation for

Critical Thinking (Paul & Elder, 2004), about each reading that is used to develop the research focus facilitates this review.

1. What was the purpose of the reading? Does this purpose include a discussion of diversity (gender, ethnicity, age, sexual orientation, income levels, education levels, etc.)?

2. What evidence was used to develop the reading's purpose? Did that evidence include acknowledgment of diverse groups, and did it make implicit assumptions about diverse groups?

3. What inferences were made using that evidence? Were these inferences appropriately or inappropriately extended to diverse groups?

4. What are the concepts and variables in the reading and how are they defined? Was the data collection instrument used to operationalize these variables tested on diverse groups?

5. What assumptions are being made in those definitions and what do those assumptions say about diverse groups?

6. If this reading is accepted as valid knowledge, what are the implications for members of diverse groups?

7. What point of view has been taken in this reading? Are there other possible points of view on this topic that tend to be held by members of diverse groups?

8. Overall, what does this reading assume or demonstrate regarding diversity?

For post-positivists, the current literature is considered at the beginning of the study but does not direct the study. Such researchers can carry out the diversity assessment suggested above, but they are not as dependent as positivists on the literature as the foundation of the study. If study participants challenge assumptions based in theory, post-positivists will explore those challenges and look for patterns in those challenges that can lead to development of new theory. For critical theorists, assessment of diversity in the literature is the key to finding the research focus. The ideological analysis carried out during the assessment phase identifies societal assumptions regarding power and difference and is used to develop the focus of a research project aimed at empowerment. Finally, the constructivist explicitly identifies any readings used at the beginning of the study as subjective constructions of the research focus. Such constructions are presented to study participants for consideration and comment. Thus for the positivist, the pitfalls of misunderstanding diversity during the assessment phase rest in the researcher's preparation while for the other three paradigms such pitfalls can be avoided by involvement of study participants in considering the implications of previous theory.

Planning—Rationales and Plans for Carrying Out the Research Project

In her book on feminist research methods, Reinharz (1992) reviews various approaches to research and suggests modifications that are sensitive to the needs of women. Her discussion suggests that feminist research, rather than being critical theory research only, is any research project carried out by those who identify themselves as feminists or those who are focused on an aspect of a feminist agenda. The methodologies she reviews are traditional positivist designs. When discussing survey research and experimental designs, she suggests that although such approaches may not be sensitive to women in their conceptualization and data collection modes, they provide quantitative data that can be used to document the oppression and empowerment of women. She makes the same argument for experimental designs when she references Lenore Walker's (1979) use of animal experiments to illustrate learned helplessness and develop behavioral theories of how women become helpless in battering relationships. She also notes that many feminist researchers believe that experiments can be used to address feminist topics if a contextual explanation of the observed behaviors is added to the study (Vaughter, 1976). The concerns with positivist research designs that Reinharz raises, however, can be allayed by adopting the alternative approaches to research planning described in this book, which, to various extents, include study participants in planning. Involving participants in planning, of course, means a commitment to partnership and negotiation. True partnership does not mean that the researcher approaches study participants with a plan and, in essence, says, "This is what I plan to do. Do you agree?" Partnership requires a two-way negotiation of the plan in which modifications are made as the result of input from all key players. The researcher using the postpositivist, critical theory, or constructivist paradigms needs to make a commitment to listening, hearing, and being responsive. When developing partnerships with study participants, the key is to listen for the issues that are unique to each participant and reflect consideration of these issues in the plan for data collection. There is *not* one set of issues that will be the same for all women, or all ethnic groups, or all disenfranchised groups;

people's concerns will vary both intergroup and intragroup. Knowing this and responding appropriately is the key to developing a plan that is sensitive to diversity.

Implementation—Gathering the Data

Data collection takes the form of surveys; interviews; observations; and reviews of social artifacts, documents, and secondary data. Surveys are used to gather data that is translated into numbers. When developing items for a survey instrument, the researcher generally reviews validity and reliability. When assessing validity, the researcher considers face, content, criterion, and construct validity. When making such assessments, it is important to (a) ask a diverse group to assess face validity; (b) consider whether the content includes items that address diversity when considering content validity; (c) review whether the comparison criteria being used in tests of criterion validity acknowledge diversity; and (d) consider whether all the indicators measure the same way for various diverse groups when assessing construct validity. For example, a survey instrument measuring social work knowledge of micro practice, when being assessed for face and content validity, should be reviewed by a diverse group of experts to see that interventions unique to certain cultures are at least considered for inclusion. If being assessed for criterion and construct validity, the instrument should be evaluated on whether it includes interventions that have been found to be effective with diverse groups.

The conceptualization and measurement techniques that are adopted for surveys can frequently be of concern to certain groups of participants. Martin and Knox (2000) discuss the measurement tools for sexual orientation that assume mutually exclusive categories of sexual orientation. They suggest that this may not be true since a person may fall into several categories of sexual orientation. Feminist researchers such as Dee Graham and Edna Rawlings (1980) have gone so far as to insist that quantitative research cannot address feminist research issues because the use of quantitative data reflects a patriarchal definition of science that categorizes numbers rather than words as "hard" facts.

Turning to interviews, the impact of differences between the interviewer and interviewee, as listed above, needs to be reviewed and included in any interviewer training. Generally, according to Neuman and Kreuger (2003), interviewees are more truthful with interviewers who look and sound similar to them. However, if such matching is not possible, training in effective interviewing is crucial to gather authentic data. On the one hand, the intense involvement with participants that is required by the forms of qualitative research described here acknowledges the unique contribution each participant will make to the data set; on the other hand, this involvement can be a major intrusion into someone's private opinions and feelings. When Armitage (in Anderson et al., 1990) talked about a methodology for taking women's oral histories, they noted that researchers and academics tend to focus on activity and generalizations. Thus when someone reveals feelings about a topic, researchers tend to disregard such an expression as irrelevant to the research topic or assume that it is not a "fact" and thus ignore or dismiss such data during the interview. These authors, therefore, noted that research interviewers should learn how to listen actively. Dana Jack (in Anderson et al., 1990) talked about interviewing depressed women and realizing that she needed to acknowledge that definitions of maturity and health imply self-reliance and autonomy and exclude some female notions of maturity such as connection and relationship to others. She worked to avoid interpreting women's stories for them and encouraged the female interviewees to be the experts on their own experience and its meaning. Reinharz (1992) discusses feminist interviewing and concluded that a feminist approach to interviewing assumes that interviewees are human beings to be engaged rather than subjects with identification numbers who are a source of predetermined data. She also notes that the interviewer needs to reflect on the implications of his or her relationship with the interviewee. Is the interviewee perceived to be a friend or a stranger? One suggested answer to this question was to call the interviewee the "knowledgeable stranger," someone who is between a friend and a stranger. With this notion of a relationship between the interviewer and interviewee, some feminists have made commitments to interviewing practices that would not be accepted by traditional positivists. For example, some believe that during an interview the interviewer should intervene with the interviewee if he or she has a problem or a need for information (Webb, 1984). Many believe that the interviewer should self-disclose during the interview (Melamed, 1983; Bristow & Esper, 1988; Bombyck, Bricker Jenkins, & Wedenoja, 1985), although Bombyck et al. felt that such disclosures should be paced and timed appropriately. Thus the consideration of diversity when interviewing challenges positivist notions of scientific data gathering when carrying out interviews and indeed rejects such notions as insensitive and unresponsive to the diverse groups who are invited to participate in research.

Observation, as a data gathering method, has been criticized for its subjective quality and expression of a power relationship between the observer and the observed. As stated in the discussions of this approach in Parts II, III, and IV of this book, the implementation of observation and the use of the resultant data need to be discussed with those who are being observed if it is to be an ethical and sensitive process. The diversity issues for this mode of data collection, namely the impact of the differences between observer and observed and how this impact can be understood and addressed, return us to the emic and etic concepts derived from anthropology. As a reminder, the emic perspective is the perspective of the insider on a particular social setting, while the etic perspective is that of the outsider. Do we have the right to say that we have gathered data on the insider's (the person being observed) reality just because we have observed him or her? Or do we only have an "etic" understanding of what has been observed—a setting viewed and interpreted using an outsider's orientation? The implications of these questions are illustrated in the famous controversy about Margaret Mead's work in Samoa. The Australian Derek Freeman (1983) challenged the validity of Mead's work and her findings regarding adolescent promiscuity as described in her book *Coming of Age in Samoa: A Psychological Study of Primitive Youth for Western Civilization*. His account of why he believed her to be wrong about her accounts of promiscuity in adolescents in Samoa makes the following points.

- First, she brought with her to Samoa a belief in ideology, impressed upon her by her mentors Franz Boas and Ruth Benedict, that human behavior is determined by cultural patterns.
- Second, her involvement with ethnology studies for the renowned Bishop Museum created a crisis regarding her original research of adolescence and she turned to informants in Samoa such as Fa'apua'a and Fofoa in hopes of finding a cultural pattern that would allow her to solve the problem that Boas had sent her to Samoa to investigate.
- Third, she arrived in Samoa with a false preconception from Edward Handy, director of the Bishop Museum, that she would find premarital promiscuity as the cultural pattern in Samoa.
- Fourth, she idolized Franz Boas and wanted to reach a conclusion that he would find acceptable.
- Fifth, Mead had inaccurate knowledge of the responses she received from Fofoa and Fa'apua'a when she asked them about their sexual behavior. (pp. 12–15)

Freeman himself has been criticized for the methodology he used to conclude that Mead had gathered inaccurate data. However, the rights and wrongs of this debate need not concern us here. It is the above list of potential mistakes that gives us pointers to the personal reflection we need to make when we gather observational data. He is giving several good reasons to wonder whether Margaret Mead, wedded to an "etic" perspective, could have misinterpreted what she saw and heard. He notes her biases, her need to please her mentors, and the potential for her to misinterpret humorous responses to her questions from two study participants. If Margaret Mead can be accused of making such mistakes, then we mere social work researchers need to beware.

Review of artifacts, documents, and secondary data, of course, needs to include an acknowledgment of the context of such sources, their history, and their authors' perspectives so that the reader can assess the import of that data. Howard Zinn's (1980) approach to writing history in his *A People's History of the United States* clearly reminds us that when looking at any document, we need to reflect on whose perspective is being portrayed and who sponsored the document before we assess the authenticity of the data in the document. His history gives us perspectives of the recent history of the United States from the point of view of Native Americans, various ethnic groups, women, and the poor.

Evaluation—Developing an Understanding and Interpretation of the Data

Debates about interpreting the meaning of data have taken some interesting twists and turns. Not only has there been the criticism of quantitative statistics as representing a patriarchal definition of "hard" facts, but there has also been criticism of qualitative analysis of language as being too linear and still tied to patriarchal definitions of rational thought and synthesis. Alternatives, such as the use of poetry and drama to explain the meaning of qualitative data, have challenged usual definitions of analysis.

Feminist criticisms of quantitative statistics range from Betty Gray's (1971) writing in the *Nation* magazine in the 1970s about a "statistical industrial complex" that undercounts women's participation in the labor force and overstates women's progress in employment to Margaret Anderson (1983) writing in the 1980s about underreporting of crimes against women and the Oakleys' (1981) accusation of sexism in the ways data are collected, processed, and presented, referring to examples of how we understand terms such as "heads of households," "work," and "crime." The essential message of these critiques is that a statistic, once written on a piece of paper, becomes a "hard" fact even though there are questions about the biases that influenced the label given to a phenomenon. The desire to create order out of the complexity of human experience, as well as the acceptance of probability theory, has led us to use rules of mathematics to manipulate numbers derived from a data collection instrument that measures constructs said to represent human experience. We use bivariate and multivariate analysis procedures to create statistical findings that dictate conclusions about the relationships between these constructs. However, any reservations about these conclusions, on the basis of questioning the relationship between statistical manipulation of numbers and authentic human experience, are rarely expressed since this would suggest that one of the primary approaches to "science" in social science research rests on a shaky foundation. The pressure to be scientific and "get it right" embedded in the positivist approach to research discourages an open discussion of the limitations of quantitative measurement of human behavior. Numbers are quickly understood summaries of a phenomenon; words take longer to describe that phenomenon but may well offer a more complete representation of the complexity of a phenomenon. This is not to say that we should stop counting and measuring human behavior. However, we need to be open to admitting that the diversity of human experience cannot be fully understood with the production of a statistic.

Ironically, qualitative analysis of words that represent human experience has also been criticized as representing a linear, patriarchal thinking process. The top-down and bottom-up qualitative analysis procedures described in this book are said to be approaches to understanding data that fragment human experience and force its meaning into categories and theories of explanation that ignore the diversity of human experience. The more radical thinkers who have taken this position suggest that turning qualitative data into poetry, scripts for dialogues between key players, and the representation of people's ideas through art rather than words are analysis and synthesis procedures that are more true to the human experience. Coffey and Atkinson (1996) discuss the presentation of results through conversations between key players or the development of plays and sketches that outline and develop the alternative points of view that emerged from the data. This form of representative data analysis has developed to a point where it has been termed "ethnographic theatre" (Mienczakowski, 1994, 1995), and has been used as a vehicle for presenting data in a way that expresses diverse perspectives and experiences.

Termination and Follow-Up

While for constructivists and critical theorists termination and follow-up are critical stages of the research project, positivists and post-positivists are often left scratching their heads when asked about their procedures for this phase of the project. For them, termination and follow-up may be as simple as leaving a business card and identifying a place where a copy of the report can be found. The debriefing statement may mention places to go if the study participant is troubled by the data collection process, but the notion that there should be an identifiable process of termination and follow up with study participants is overlooked. At the other extreme are community-based researchers such as Minkler and Wallerstein (2003), who see the commitment to research as a permanent commitment to a partnership with members of a research setting. When describing a protocol for community-based research, with reference to this stage of the project, they note that the following questions must be asked by *both* community members participating in the study and researchers:

- What perceptions about the community are likely to be created or persist as a result of analysis and publication of the results? Will the spirit of confidentiality be violated as a result of making public the research findings?
- How, when, and by whom should findings be released?
- What is the focus of research vis-à-vis addressing long-term community needs? (p. 408)

It is clear that they see this stage as crucial to the success of the study and the community research partnership.

Main Points

- Researchers need to reflect on and understand all dimensions of difference between researcher and study participants
- At the micro and macro levels of human organization and social work practice, there are principles and characteristics of diversity that can guide researchers' methodologies
- For all stages of the generalist model of intervention, a consciousness of diversity is required if the research project is to gather valid social work knowledge

Learning Assignments

1. With your partner, discuss and share what you know about your ethnic ancestry including the history of your family in this country. As one partner talks, the other should take notes. Then, together, discuss the analysis of the data you have collected and decide on the most appropriate way to present that data.

2. Take the "Type A" personality test at http://www.2h.com/personality-tests.html. Do you think this test is sensitive to gender and ethnic diversity? Why?

19

The Function of Technology at Each Step of the Way

Technology, as discussed here, is any mechanical enhancements that support the research process. These include phones, computers, video, cameras, microphones, software, the Internet, computer Webcams and two-way compressed video. This discussion is not a detailed review of how to use technology but rather a review of some current potential uses of technology and resources offering more guidance. The role of technology in research has evolved to the point where there is a mechanical enhancement available to assist each stage of the research process. It can range from something as low tech as a telephone and as high tech as computer software that supports analysis of both quantitative and qualitative data or the use of the Internet for community development. Use of these enhancements will depend on the researcher's judgment, resources, and expertise, as well as the research participants' willingness to embrace technology. Their benefits are their time-saving contributions to routine tasks and enhanced access to knowledge, while their drawbacks include a loss of control of certain decision processes, for example, when the computer programmer decides on the conceptual assumptions behind the software for qualitative analysis or when there is a lack of quality control of Web sites. This discussion of technology takes us through the stages of the generalist model for researchers and discusses some possible functions of technology at each of these stages.

Engagement—Gaining Entrée to the Research Setting

Apart from using phones for initial contact arrangements, the Engagement stage is the stage in which human contact is crucial. The researcher needs to build a foundation of trust and commitment to the project with research site gatekeepers and study participants. Gatekeepers and participants, though, are busy people and will not have time for protracted meetings. Thus once initial personal comfort has been established, phone and e-mail contact can assist development of the relationship. A further possibility for ongoing efficient communication is the use of computer "cams" and software allowing two people to converse and see each other while sitting at their computers at a distance from each other. As engagement proceeds, such mechanical mediations of human contact can be integrated with face-to-face meetings with individuals and groups. Also, listservs can be set up for ongoing communication between researchers and participants in the study. Fawcett, Schultz, Carson, Renault, and Francisco (2003) note that the U.S. Department of Health and Human Services supports ongoing listservs for those working on disability, aging, and long-term care. Also, the U.S. Administration on Aging has an online guide with guidelines for engaging underserved or underrepresented groups at http://www.aoa.gov/prof/adddiv/cultural/addiv_cult.asp.

After initial engagement, both critical theorists and constructivists need to develop a more intense engagement that includes a commitment to a partnership based on a set of values and commitment to action. Fawcett et al. (2003) discuss the use of Internet tools when developing this intense relationship with community groups. These authors have an online resource for community change (Fawcett et al., 2000) that can be found at http://ctb .ku.edu. With reference to understanding community context and collaborative planning, these authors offer six core competencies. These are creating and maintaining coalitions, assessing community needs and resources, analyzing community-identified problems and goals, developing a framework or model for change, developing strategic action plans, and building leadership. Creating and maintaining coalitions parallels the Engagement phase of research discussed in this book. Such coalitions are built at both the micro and macro levels of human interaction. These authors cite Web sites containing resource information that can be downloaded by researchers or community members looking for help with group discussions of community problems (such as http://www.communityhlth.org/community hlth/index.jsp and http://www.ncl.org). These resources are not a substitute for engagement skills, but they can enhance and inform the engagement process.

Assessment—Developing an Understanding of the Research Focus

During the phase in which the research focus is developed, literature is reviewed and, for some paradigms, study participants are consulted. The literature review has been made immensely more convenient by the availability of electronic journals and books via the Internet. Most university libraries can offer this service through their library Web sites, and full-text articles can be downloaded to the personal computer at home or at the office. The reading, of course, still has to be done. There is no mechanical enhancement that will do that for you, but word processing programs and spreadsheets have made indexing the literature quick and easy, as explained in discussions of the literature review in other parts of this book. A recent development related to the demand for research to support evidence-based practice is the establishment of Web sites such as The Campbell Collaboration (www.campbellcollaboration.org). This is a repository for reviews of the research and has sophisticated guidelines for synthesizing literature on a particular topic.

Regarding additional sources of information and involvement of research participants in development of the research focus, again, major federal departments such as the Department of Health and Human Services, the U.S. Centers for Diseases Control, and the Department of Aging offer statistics and listservs that assist this process.

Planning—Rationales and Plans for Carrying Out the Research Project

For planning, again the telephone, e-mail, and computer cameras can increase efficiency. Fawcett et al. (2000) again offer some useful Web-based resources such as the Network for Good (http://www.networkforgood.org), which offers information and strategies for advocating for community change. These authors' own Web-based Community Tool Box (http://ctb.ku.edu) offers assistance with building capacity for community change, learning and adjustments to be made during the process of community change, and evaluation and analysis of the contribution made by the intervention to community change.

Implementation—Gathering the Data

Tape recorders, digital recording, and cameras can assist the researcher immensely with data gathering. The participatory, partnership-oriented approaches to research, however, have chosen to put the tape recorders and cameras in the hands of study participants. Caroline Wang (2003) defines "photovoice" as a "process by which people can identify, represent, and enhance their community through a specific photographic technique" (p. 179). It has three goals:

> (1) to enable people to record and reflect their community's strengths and concerns, (2) to promote critical dialogue and knowledge about important community issues through large and small group discussion of photographs, and (3) to reach policy makers and others who can be mobilized for change. (p. 179)

In the case study described by this author, homeless people are given cameras, trained, and then sent out to take pictures of homeless issues in their community that they consider to be important. These researcher/photographers are asked to explain each photo, describe what is happening in the photo and how it affects the lives of local homeless people, and suggest any action that should be taken in relation to the issue being illustrated in the photo. After discussion with the research partners, the information from the photos is shared with policy makers, journalists, and the wider community so that action can be advocated and later assessed.

Another technology that has begun to assist data collection is the Web-based survey instrument (Soloman, 2001; Eiler & Fetterman, 2000). While this has the limitation of only being accessible to those who can log onto the Internet, response rates to such surveys have been increased by e-mail cover letters, follow-up reminders, and the use of simple research designs. A number of software programs have been developed to promote such methods of data collection, and Web sites such as http://lap.umd.edu/survey_design/tools.html provide design guidelines and principles for Web-based survey instruments. This particular Web site designs survey instruments based on the principles of cognitive psychology, heuristics, and design theory. However, many other for-profit and nonprofit sites can be found that provide a range of resources and software.

Evaluation—Developing an Understanding and Interpretation of the Data

When understanding and interpreting the data, we can use computer software programs to do either quantitative or qualitative analysis. Quantitative analysis software packages can perform any kind of statistical analysis in seconds. Qualitative software programs can organize reams of narrative and assist in conceptualizing units of data and the connections between those units so that theory can be developed or the general meaning of data can be described.

Quantitative Analysis

Most students are familiar with computer programs that carry out quantitative data analysis. At the simplest level, we have spreadsheet programs such as Windows Excel that permit us to lay out scores on items on a questionnaire for each member of our sample. In these programs we can create totals and mean scores and, in fact, any manipulation of numbers if we can create the correct formula. Beyond spreadsheet programs, statistical packages such as SPSS (Statistical Package for the Social Sciences) and SAS (The Statistical Analysis System) have developed to such a user-friendly point that we can not only generate descriptive statistics (frequencies, means, medians, and modes) and bivariate analyses, but we can also carry out the most complex of multivariate analyses with just a point and click of a mouse. It is not the province of this book to explain how to do this but merely to acknowledge that such packages are available and that we still have to understand the principles of statistics to use them correctly.

Qualitative Analysis

Coffey and Atkinson (1996) have provided a helpful review of the use of computers for various stages of managing qualitative data: creating and managing data, coding and retrieving data, language meaning and narrative, and theory building and hypothesis testing. Before discussing these topics, it might be obvious but useful to remind ourselves that computers are very useful tools for the general organizational tasks associated with qualitative research, such as keeping lists of contacts; communicating via e-mail and the Internet with experts, study participants, and colleagues; managing bibliographies and reference lists; and preparing reports, papers, and presentations. These authors concluded that a word processing package can perform the functions needed for creating and managing data, such as initial write-up of notes; numbering of lines, paragraphs, and pages; cross-referencing and indexing, including creating contextual and other headings; and summarizing longer data documents.

However, when it comes to coding and retrieving data, programs such as Ethnograph, NUD.IST, and ATLAS/ti are more useful since they have routines for attaching codes to chunks of data identified by the researcher and then searching for the repeated occurrence of the code to identify the underlying regulatory mechanism that is emerging from the data. They also allow the researcher to write memos during this process, linked to the codes, that explain the reasoning behind the codes. This facilitates production of both the record of data collection and analysis and the journal of reasoning behind coding and analysis decisions required in post-positivist, critical theory, and constructivist research. Once data is entered and coded, a program such as ATLAS/ti allows the researcher to draw diagrams identifying the links between the codes (axial coding) and develop evidence for identifying the core theme (selective coding). All of this is done more quickly and efficiently than is possible by using index cards and paper notes. It is a very useful way of combating the data overload that often overwhelms the qualitative researcher facing pages and pages of narrative. Drisko (1998) gives an overview of the various qualitative data software programs. He concludes that if the researcher is careful to use a program that can fulfill the purpose of the chosen approach to research, such software is a great asset to managing and interpreting qualitative data. It is important, however, to remember that the researcher, not the computer, is in charge here. Programs such as ATLAS/ti encourage the researcher to use his or her own insight in building codes and their connections and dimensions. This can be a most productive partnership between technology and humanity.

A final suggestion offered by Coffey and Atkinson (1996) is the use of hyperlinks to make connections in the data. The researcher identifies the patterns of links between parts of the narratives by creating hyperlinks in the narrative that allow the reader to "click" on a word or phrase and be sent to its category, or core theme, or other related category. This truly is the most flexible approach to synthesis of narrative and rescues us from the linear thinking represented in many discussions of qualitative analysis.

Termination and Follow-Up

As with engagement, human contact is an important piece of the termination process since its main purpose is to wind down or redefine the human contact between researcher and study. The researcher personally thanks the study gatekeepers and participants and, at least, presents the results of the study to the group. Such presentations can be in the form of PowerPoint presentations. For research approaches where further follow-up is required, though, such contact can be enhanced by the use of a Web site to post the study report and to host a discussion board for further comment on the study, or a listserv for ongoing discussion and contact.

Main Point

- There are technological tools that can assist the researcher with each stage of the research process

Learning Assignment

With your partner, discuss the usefulness of technology for each stage of the research process. Which stages are considerably enriched by technology and which stages cannot be distinctly enhanced by technology? Why?

Glossary

Action Analysis: The review of change strategies that emerge from ideological analysis, using a conceptual matrix to categorize each strategy and therefore understand the significance of the activity.

ANOVA: A statistical measure that tests the difference between the means of two or more groups.

Anti-Oppressive Research: An approach to research that fosters social justice.

Applied Research: An approach to research that takes the findings of basic research and applies them to real-world problems.

Auditing Trail: The record kept in a diary of the processes of data collection and data analysis in a constructivist study.

Axial Coding: The second stage of qualitative analysis for grounded theory in which relationships between themes or categories are proposed; these relationships are tested in further rounds of data gathering.

Basic Research: In this book it is defined as grounded theory development, as described by Strauss and Corbin (1990), that requires lengthy intensive fieldwork.

Bivariate Analysis: Analysis of the relationship between two variables.

Bottom-Up Qualitative Evaluation of Data: An approach to evaluating qualitative data where the meaning of the data emerges from the narrative through development of codes and categories of data.

Categories: The groupings that units of data are put into during analysis of data in a constructivist study.

Conceptual Ideological Analysis: An approach to analyzing an ideology that gives a rationale for the ideological development that has been described by diachronic and discursive analyses and synthesizes the progression of thought over time, giving a historical and social context for the changes.

Conditional Matrix: The last stage of qualitative analysis for grounded theory in which the statements emerging from axial coding are placed into current knowledge about the human environment in terms of the individual, family, group, organization, and community.

Confidence Level and Confidence Interval: The limits within which we can assume estimates of sampling error, and therefore of the parameter, are correct.

Confirmability: In constructivist research, the reliability of the interpretations of the data.

Constructivism: A paradigm that assumes a subjective reality, that the observer discovers this reality in partnership with participants in that reality, and that data is gathered by means of a hermeneutic dialectic from which a joint construction of a reality unique to time and place evolves.

Credibility: In constructivist research, the degree to which written constructions are accurate descriptions of study participants' perspectives.

Credible Intervals: The percentage likelihoods that something is true.

Critical Theory: A paradigm that assumes an objective reality governed by laws and mechanisms, that the observer distorts this reality using the ideologies of his or her social group, and that true research uncovers the impact of such ideologies and takes action to address oppression.

Dependability: In constructivist research, the validity of the data.

Dependent Variable: The variable that is changed by the independent variable.

Descriptive Statistics: Statistics that summarize and describe data.

Diachronic Ideological Analysis: An approach to analyzing an ideology that traces the thematic transformation as the ideology develops over time.

Discourse Analysis: An approach to analyzing language that is a compromise between a need for, on the one hand, form and regularity when analyzing narrative and, on the other hand, a need to include general principles of interpretation by which we all understand each other.

Discursive Ideological Analysis: An approach to analyzing an ideology that tracks the evolving ideology that is identified when the themes of the diachronic analysis are integrated.

Element: The unit about which the information is collected (individuals, families, groups, organizations, or communities).

Emergent Analysis: An approach to qualitative analysis that has six characteristics: social science framing, socializing anxiety, coding, memoing, diagramming, thinking flexibility.

Emic: A perspective on a social setting that is taken by a member of that setting.

Ethics of Research: Specific research practices that reduce the potential for abuse of research participants and adhere to established codes for ethical research and the protection of research participants.

Ethnography: A method of studying people that involves the study of a small group in their own environment. Ethnographic accounts include detailed descriptions and interpretations of the significance of what is observed.

Ethnography and Ethnoscience: Methods for researching culture as a whole and as a cognitive map of social organizations, shared meanings, and semantic rules.

Ethnomethodology: An approach to qualitative research that is an offshoot of symbolic interactionism and studies how people who are interacting with each other create the illusion of a shared social order when they don't really understand each other and have different points of view.

Ethology: An approach to qualitative research that has emerged in psychology that studies behavior and events over time and in context.

Etic: A perspective on a social setting that is taken by an outsider.

Evaluation Research: An approach to research that assesses both the operations and the impact of the solutions to problems that have been implemented through policies and programs based on the results of basic and applied research.

Experimental Design: A positivist research design that, if followed, facilitates proof of causality.

External Validity: The strength of the proof that findings from a sample can be generalized to the population from which the sample was drawn.

Feminism: The theory that men and women should be equal politically, economically, and socially.

Generalist Social Work Practice: The knowledge, values, and skills needed to intervene at the micro (individuals, families, and groups) and macro (local, national, and international organizations and communities) levels while acknowledging the interlocking influences of all those levels of human organization on the target of the social work intervention.

Grounded Theory: An approach to developing theory using qualitative data so that the theory is grounded in data, as opposed to being the result of only hypothetical reasoning.

Hermeneutic Dialectic: The process of gathering data in constructivist research where there is a dialogue between study participants and researchers from which the study's constructions emerge.

Ideological Analysis: An approach to analyzing, gathering, and interpreting qualitative data in critical theory research that offers a synthesis that describes the oppression and empowerment experienced by study participants.

Independent Variable: The variable that causes the change in the dependent variable.

Inferential Statistics: Statistics that permit a statement to be made about a population based on findings in a sample drawn from that population.

Internal Validity: The strength of the proof of causality that is constructed by the research design.

Linguistics: The study of language.

Macro Social Work Practice: An approach to social work practice with organizations and communities (local, national, and international) that assesses and intervenes with these levels of human organization in combination, rather than as separate entities.

Marxism: A societal analysis carried out by Karl Marx that states that the most important features of a *society* are its economic *classes* and their relations to each other in the modes of production of each historical epoch.

Membership Checking: The process of checking back with study participants to ask whether the narratives of their contribution to the study are accurate. This is done both individually and at a membership checking meeting.

Micro Social Work Practice: An approach to social work practice with individuals, families, and groups that assesses and intervenes with these levels of human organization in combination, rather than as separate entities.

Multivariate Analysis: Analysis of the relationships between more than two variables.

Neo-Marxist: Term for a group of French anthropologists who, during the 1970s, applied Marxist theory on the study of non-Western societies, often under the influence of French structuralism. In time, important adjustments were made in the theory: in particular, the understanding of the concept of *production* changed. From assuming (as in many earlier readings of Marx) that "productive work" was just another way of saying "the economy," one now started to speak of a more general "production" of the overall preconditions of the existence of society as such (also, meaning is thus "produced").[1]

Non-Parametric Statistics: Statistical procedures that are not based on assumptions drawn from probability and sampling theory.

Open Coding: The first stage of qualitative analysis for grounded theory in which narratives are grouped into categories of information.

Operationalization: The process by which a concept is redefined in terms of measurable variables that can be observed.

Paradigm: A worldview or overriding viewpoint that shapes ideas and actions within a particular field.[2] In this book a paradigm is defined as an overriding viewpoint that defines the nature of knowledge, the relationship between the researcher and his or her source of data, and the methodologies to be used to carry out the research.

Parameter: A summary description (e.g., mean) of a variable in the population of interest.

Parametric Statistics: Statistical procedures based on assumptions drawn from probability and sampling theory.

Phenomenology: An approach to understanding the world that uses reflection, evidence (i.e., awareness of something), and description.

Politics of Research: The effect that those who have power will have on the research process.

Positivism: A paradigm that assumes an objective reality governed by laws and mechanisms that can be identified, that reality is separate from the observer, and that scientific observation requires objective methodologies that manipulate reality.

Post-Positivism: A paradigm that assumes an objective reality governed by laws and mechanisms that can never be truly understood; that although the observer can never be truly separate from reality, researchers should work to control the influence they might have on reality; and that data gathered in naturalistic settings gives us an accurate understanding of reality.

Power Analysis: An approach to data gathering in critical theory research that identifies arenas in which study participants have influence.

Probability Theory: A mathematical theory that underpins statistical inferences and estimates of the likelihood that something will happen.

Purposive Sampling: A sampling procedure in which the researcher selects study participants who will give the most complete data about the study focus.

Reliability: The degree to which a survey instrument measures the same thing the same way each time it is used.

Sampling Error: The degree of error between a statistic and a parameter.

Sampling Frame: The list of sampling elements or units from which a sample is selected.

Sampling Theory: A theory that guides selection of samples and estimates the amount of error that will be made when a finding from a sample is generalized to the population from which that sample was drawn.

Sampling Unit: The same as an element in simple designs. In a complex design the unit could vary from the element.

Selective Coding: The third stage of qualitative analysis for grounded theory, in which a theoretical statement is developed.

Statistic: A summary description (e.g., mean) of a variable in the sample.

Study Population: The total of elements from which the sample is selected.

Symbolic Interactionism: A term invented by Herbert Blumer to describe a sociological perspective that sees humans as pragmatic actors who must continually adjust their behaviors to those of others by interpreting other people's behaviors symbolically.

Teaching-Learning Process: An approach to gathering data in critical theory research in which the researcher and the study participants teach each other and learn from each other regarding the research focus.

Top-Down Qualitative Evaluation of Data: An approach to evaluating qualitative data in which the same analysis framework is applied to all data.

Transferability: In constructivist research, the accuracy with which the findings from one study can be applied to another setting.

Trustworthiness: In constructivist research, the assessment of the validity of a piece of research using the criteria of credibility, transferability, dependability, and confirmability.

Type I Error: The decision to reject the null hypothesis when, in the population of interest, the null hypothesis is indeed true.

Type II Error: The decision to accept the null hypothesis when, in the population of interest, the rejected null is not true.

Unit of Observation: In positivist research, the source of numerical data.

Units: The groupings that the qualitative data is put into during analysis of data in a constructivist study.

Units of Analysis in Positivism: The category of people about whom assertions rising from the findings of the study will be made.

Units of Analysis in Post-Positivism: The whole entity being researched. However, while the study is being carried out, various units of analysis are identified.

Univariate Analysis: Analysis of the distribution of one variable at a time.

Validity: The degree to which a survey instrument actually measures the concept or construct it is intended to measure.

Variables: A measurable characteristic whose value can change.

Notes

1. From the Dictionary of Anthropology at http://www.anthrobase.com/Dic/eng/def/neo-marxism.htm
2. McArthur, 1992, p. 747.

Bibliography

Adler, P. A., & Adler, P. (1994). Observational techniques. In N. K. Denzin & Y. S. Lincoln (Eds.), *Handbook of qualitative research* (pp. 377–392). Thousand Oaks, CA: Sage.

Alasuutari, P. (1995). *Researching culture: Qualitative method and cultural studies.* Thousand Oaks, CA: Sage.

Anderson, K., Armiage, S., Jack, D., & Wittner, J. (1990). Beginning where we are: Feminist methodology in oral history. In J. M. Nielsen (Ed.), *Feminist research methods* (pp. 69–93). Boulder, CO: Westview.

Anderson, M. (1983). *Thinking about women: Sociological and feminist perspectives.* New York: Macmillan.

Austin, J. L. (1962). *How to do things with words.* Oxford: Clarendon Press.

Ballantyne, P. F. (2002). Questioning the ideology of testing: The modernist search for an appropriate mental yardstick (1964–1981). In *Psychology, society, and ability testing (1859–2002): Transformative alternatives to mental Darwinism and interactionism.* Retrieved November 29, 2004, from http://www.comnet.ca/~pballan/C7P1.htm

Ballantyne, P. F. (2003). *Psychology, society and the rise of ability testing (1947–2002).* Unpublished doctoral dissertation, York University, Toronto, Canada.

Becker, J. E. (1994). *A constructivist study of the social and educational needs of homeless children.* Unpublished manuscript.

Bell, S. (1998). Self-reflection and vulnerability in action research: Bringing forth new worlds in our learning. *Systemic Practice and Action Research, 11*(2), 179–191.

Berg, B. L. (1995). *Qualitative research methods for the social sciences.* Boston: Allyn & Bacon.

Bernstein, R. J. (1988). *Beyond objectivism and relativism: Science, hermeneutics, and praxis.* Philadelphia: University of Pennsylvania Press.

Bloomfield, L. (1933 & 1935). *Language.* New York: Holt, Reinhart and Winston and London: Allen and Unwin.

Bogdewic, S. P. (1992). Participant observation. In B. F. Crabtree & W. L. Miller (Eds.), *Doing qualitative research* (pp. 45–69). Thousand Oaks, CA: Sage.

Bombyck, M., Bricker Jenkins, M., & Wedenoja, M. (1985). *Reclaiming our profession through feminist research: Some methodological issues in the feminist practice project*. Paper presented at the Annual Program Meeting of the Council of Social Work Education.

Brewer, J., & Hunter, A. (1989). *Multimethod research: A synthesis of styles*. Newbury Park, CA: Sage.

Brislin, R. W., Lonner, W. J., & Thorndike, R. M. (1973). *Cross-cultural research methods*. New York: John Wiley.

Bristow, A. R., & Esper, J. A. (1988). A feminist research ethos. In The Nebraska Sociological Feminist Collective (Eds.), *A feminist ethic for social science research*. Lewiston, NY: The Edwin Mellen Press.

Brown, G., & Yule, G. (1991). *Discourse analysis*. New York: Cambridge University Press.

Brown, L. B., & Strega, S. (2005). *Research as resistance*. Toronto, ON: Canadian Scholars' Press.

Campbell, D. T., & Stanley, J. C. (1963). *Experimental and quasi-experimental designs for research*. Boston: Houghton Mifflin Company.

Charles, N., & Kerr, M. (1986). Food for feminist thought. *Sociological Review*, 34(3), 537–572.

Charlesworth, M. (1982). *Science, non-science, & pseudo-science*. Victoria, Australia: Deakin University Press.

Chavez. V., Duran, B., Baker, Q. E., Avila, M., & Wallerstein, N. (2003). The dance of race and privilege in community based participatory research. In M. Minkler & N.Wallerstein (Eds.), *Community based participatory research* (pp. 81–97). San Francisco: Jossey-Bass.

Cheatham, A., & Shen, E. (2003). Community based participatory research with Cambodian girls in Long Beach, California. In M. Minkler & N. Wallerstein (Eds.), *Community based participatory research for health* (pp. 316–331). San Francisco: Jossey-Bass.

Chernin, K. (1981). *The obsession*. New York: Harper & Row.

Chernin, K. (1986). *The hungry self*. New York: Harper & Row.

Chomsky, A. N. (1957). *Syntactic structures*. The Hague: Mouton.

Chomsky, A. N. (1968). *Language and mind*. New York: Harcourt, Brace, and World.

Christopulos, J. (1995). *Oppression through obsession: A feminist theoretical critique of eating disorders*. Unpublished manuscript.

Clough, P. T. (1992). *The end(s) of ethnography: From realism to social criticism*. Newbury Park, CA: Sage.

Cochran, W. G. (1954). Some methods for strengthening the common X2 tests. *Biometrics, 6*, 426–443.

Coffey, A., & Atkinson, P. (1996). *Making sense of qualitative data*. Thousand Oaks, CA: Sage.

Cohen, J. (1988). *Statistical power analysis for the behavioral sciences*. New York: Lawrence Erlbaum Associates.

Cohen, J. (1994). The earth is round (p<.05). *American Psychologist, 49*(12), 997–1003.

Corbin, J., & Stauss, A. (1990). Grounded theory research: Procedures, canons, and evaluative criteria. *Qualitative Sociology, 13*(1), 3–21.

Coulthard, M. (1985). *An introduction to discourse analysis.* New York: Longman.

Crabtree, B. F., & Miller, W. L. (1992). *Doing qualitative research.* Newbury Park, CA: Sage.

Davis, L. V. (1986, Spring). A feminist approach to social work research. *Affilia,* 32–47.

Delphy, C. (1981). Women in stratification studies. In A. Roberts (Ed.), *Doing feminist research* (pp. 114–128). London: Routledge.

Denzin, N. K., & Lincoln, Y. S. (1994). *Handbook of qualitative research.* Thousand Oaks, CA: Sage.

Dillman, D. A. (1983). Mail and other self-administered questionnaires. In P. H. Rossi, J. D. Wright, & A. B. Anderson (Eds.), *Handbook of survey research* (pp. 359–378). Orlando, FL: Academic Press.

Dilts, R., Grinder, L., Bandler, R., Bandler, L. C., & DeLozier, J. (1980). *Neurolinguistic programming: The study of the structure of subjective experience.* Cupertino: Meta Publications.

Drisko, J. (1997, Winter). Strengthening qualitative studies and reports: Standards to promote academic integrity. *Journal of Social Work Education, 33*(1), 185–197.

Drisko, J. (1998). Using qualitative data analysis software. *Computers in Human Services, 15*(1), 1–18.

Durkheim, E. (1895/1938). *The rules of sociological method.* New York: Free Press.

Eiler, M. & Fetterman, D. (2000, November). *Empowerment and web-based evaluation.* Paper presented at American Evaluation Association, Honolulu, Hawaii.

Epstein, N. B, & Bishop, D. S. (1981). Problem centered system therapy of the family. In A. S. Gurman & D. P. Kniskern (Eds.), *Handbook of family therapy* (pp. 444–482). New York: Brunner/Mazel.

Erlandson, D. A., Harris, E. L., Skipper, B. L., & Allen, S. D. (1993). *Doing naturalistic inquiry.* Thousand Oaks, CA: Sage.

Evans, D. R., Hearn, M. T., Uhlemann, M. R., & Ivey, A. E. (2004). *Essential interviewing: A programmed approach to effective communication.* Belmont, CA: Brooks Cole-Thomson Learning.

Farquhar, S., & Wing, S. (2003). Methodological and ethical considerations in community-driven environmental justice research. In M. Minkler & M. Wallerstein (Eds.), *Community-based participatory research for health* (pp. 221–241). San Francisco: Jossey-Bass.

Fawcett, S. B., Francisco, V. T., Schultz, J. A., Berkowitz, B., Wolff, T. J., & Nagy, G. (2000). The community tool box: A web-based resource for building healthier communities. *Public Health Reports, 115,* 274–278.

Fawcett, S. B., Schultz, J. A., Carson, V. L., Renault, V. A., & Francisco, B. T. (2003). Using internet tools to build capacity for community based participatory research and other efforts to promote community health and development. In M. Minkler & M. Wallerstein (Eds.), *Community-based participatory research for health* (pp. 155–178). San Francisco: Jossey-Bass.

Feyerabend, P. (1988). *Against method*. London: Verso.

Finn, J. L., & Jacobson, M. (2003). *Just practice: A social justice approach to social work*. Peosta, IA: Eddie Bowers.

Fontana, A., & Frey, J. K. (1994). Interviewing: The art of science. In N. K. Denzin & Y. S. Lincoln (Eds.), *Handbook of qualitative research* (pp. 361–376). Thousand Oaks, CA: Sage.

Frankel, M. (1983). Sampling Theory. In P. H. Rossi, J. D. Wright, & A. B. Anderson (Eds.), *Handbook of survey research* (pp. 21–67). Orlando, FL: Academic Press.

Freeman, D. (1983). *Margaret Mead and Samoa: The making and unmaking of an anthropological myth*. Cambridge, MA: Harvard University Press.

Freeman, D. (1999). *The fateful hoaxing of Margaret Mead: A historical analysis of her Samoan researches*. Boulder, CO: Westview Press.

Gergen, K. J. (1985). The social constructionist movement in modern psychology. *American Psychologist, 40*, 266–275.

Gergen, K. J., & Gergen, M. M. (1991). Toward reflexive methodologies. In F. Steier (Ed.), *Research and reflexivity* (pp. 76–95). Newbury Park, CA: Sage.

Gibbs, J. A. (2001). Maintaining front line workers in child protection: A case for refocusing supervision. *Child Abuse Review, 10*, 323–335.

Gibson, R. (1986). *Critical theory and education*. London: Hodder & Stoughton.

Glaser, B. (1978). *Theoretical sensitivity*. Mill Valley, CA: Sociology Press.

Glaser, B. G., & Strauss, A. L. (1967). *The discovery of grounded theory: Strategies for qualitative research*. New York: Aldine De Gruyter.

Gleick, J. (1988). *Chaos*. London: Heinemann.

Goffman, E. (1964). *Stigma*. Englewood Cliffs, NJ: Prentice Hall.

Goffman, E. (1971). *The presentation of self in every-day life*. Harmondsworth: Penguin.

Goodman, N. (1978). *Ways of worldmaking*. Indianapolis, IN: Hacket.

Goodman, N. (1984). *Of mind and other matters*. Cambridge, MA: Harvard University Press.

Graham, D., & Rawlings, E. (1980). *Feminist research methodology: Comparisons, guidelines and ethics*. Paper presented at the Annual Meeting of the American Psychological Association.

Gray, B. M. (1971, June 14). Economics of sex bias: The 'disuse' of women. *The Nation*, pp. 742–747.

Greenbank, P. (2003). The role of values in educational research: The case for reflexivity. *British Educational Research Journal, 29*(6), 791–801.

Greenwood, D. J., & Levin, M. (1998). *Introduction to action research*. Thousand Oaks, CA: Sage.

Grinnell, R. M., Jr. (1997). *Social work research and evaluation: Quantitative and qualitative approaches*. Itasca, IL: Peacock.

Grossman Dean, R., & Fleck-Henderson, A. (1991, March). *Teaching clinical theory and practice through a constructivist lens*. Paper presented at CSWE-APM, New Orleans, LA.

Guba, E. G. (1981). Criteria for assessing the trustworthiness of naturalistic inquiries. *Educational Communication and Technology Journal, 29*, 75–92.

Guba, E. G. (1990). *The paradigm dialog.* Newbury Park, CA: Sage.

Guba, E. G., & Lincoln, Y. S. (1989). *Fourth generation evaluation.* Newbury Park, CA: Sage.

Hanson, N. (1958). *Patterns of discovery.* Cambridge: Cambridge University Press.

Harvey, D. L., & Reed, M. H. (1996). The culture of poverty: An ideological analysis. *Sociological Perspectives, 39*(4), 1–20.

Hesse, M. (1980). *Revolutions and reconstructions in the philosophy of science.* Brighton, UK: Harvester Press.

Hogan, P. (1995). *A constructivist study of social work's involvement with HIV-AIDS.* Unpublished manuscript.

Hope, A., & Timmel, S. (1999). *Training for transformation: A handbook for community workers.* London, UK: Intermediate Technology (ITDG Publishing).

Horkheimer, M. (1972). *Critical theory.* New York: Seabury.

Hudson, W., & Nurius, P. S. (1994). *Controversial issues in social work research.* Boston: Allyn & Bacon.

Hull, C. (1914). The service of statistics to history. *Publications of the American Statistical Association, 14*(105), 30–39.

Humphreys, L. (1975). *Tearoom trade: Impersonal sex in public places.* Chicago: Aldine.

Jaynes, E. T. (2003). *Probability theory: The logic of science* (G. L. Bretthorst, Ed.). Cambridge: Cambridge University Press.

Johnsen, H. C. G., & Norman, R. (2004, June). When research and practice collide: The role of action research when there is a conflict of interest with stakeholders. *Systemic Practice and Action Research, 17*(3), 207–235.

Jones, J. H. (1981). *Bad blood: The Tuskegee syphilis experiment.* New York: Free Press.

Kelly, G. (1995). *A constructivist second year study of the social and educational needs of homeless children.* Unpublished manuscript.

Kincheloe, J. L., & McLaren, P. L. (1994). Rethinking critical theory and qualitative research. In N. K. Denzin, & Y. S. Lincoln (Eds.), *Handbook of qualitative research.* Thousand Oaks, CA: Sage.

Kirst-Ashman, K. K., & Hull, G. H., Jr. (2002). *Understanding generalist practice.* Pacific Grove, CA: Brooks Cole.

Krieger, S. (1984). Fiction and social science. In N. K. Denzin (Ed.), *Studies in symbolic interaction 5* (pp. 269–286). Greenwhich, CT: JAI.

Krugman, S., Ward, R., & Giles, J. P. (1962). The natural history of infectious hepatitis. *American Journal of Medicine 32*, 717–728.

Kuhn, T. S. (1970). *The structure of scientific revolutions.* Chicago: The University of Chicago Press.

Lakatos, I., & Musgrave, A. E. (Eds.). (1970). *Criticism and the growth of knowledge.* Cambridge: Cambridge University Press.

Lincoln, Y. S., & Guba, E. G. (1985). *Naturalistic inquiry*. Beverly Hills, CA: Sage.

Lofland, J., & Lofland, L. H. (1995). *Analyzing social settings: A guide to qualitative observation and analysis*. Belmont, CA: Wadsworth.

Lonner, W. J., & Berry, J. W. (1986). *Field methods in cross-cultural research*. Beverly Hills, CA: Sage.

Love, J. M., Brooks-Gun, J., Paulsell, D., & Fuligni, A. S. (2002). *Making a difference in the lives of infants and toddlers and their families: The impacts of early Head Start*. Washington, DC: Department of Health and Human Services. Retrieved May 18, 2004, from http://www.mathematica-mpr.com/publications/pdfs/ehsfinalsumm.pdf

Lyons, J. (1970). *Chomsky*. London: Fontana/Collins.

Mach, E. (1883/1959). *The analysis of sensations*. New York: Dover.

Mahowald, M. B. (1992). To be or not to be a woman: Anorexia nervosa, normative gender roles, and feminism. *The Journal of Medicine and Philosophy, 17*, 233–251.

Manicas, P. T. (1988). *A history and philosophy of the social sciences*. Oxford, U.K.: Blackwell.

Marcuse, H. (1964). *One dimensional man*. Boston: South End.

Martin, I. M., & Knox, J. (2000). Methodological and ethical issues in research on lesbians and gay men. *Social Work Research, 24*(1), 51–59.

Mascia-Lees, F. E., Sharpe, P., & Cohen, C. B. (1989). The postmodern turn in anthropology: Cautions from a feminist perspective. *Signs, 15*, 7–33.

Matsumoto, D. (1994). *Cultural influences on research methods and statistics*. Pacific Grove, CA: Brooks Cole.

McArthur, T. (Ed.). (1992). *The Oxford companion to the English language*. London: Oxford University Press.

McCarl-Neilson, J. (1990). *Feminist research methods*. Boulder, CO: Westview.

Mead, M. (1973). *Coming of age in Samoa: A psychological study of primitive youth for western civilization*. New York: Modern Library.

Melamed, E. (1983). *Mirror mirror: The terror of not being young*. New York: Simon & Schuster.

Mienczakowski, J. E. (1994). Reading and writing research: Ethnographic theatre. *National Association for Drama in Education (Australia), 18*, 45–54.

Mienczakowski, J. E. (1995). The theatre of ethnography: The reconstruction of ethnography into theatre with emancipatory potential. *Qualitative Inquiry, 1*, 360–375.

Milgram, S. (1963). Behavioral study of obedience. *Journal of Abnormal and Social Psychology, 6*, 371–378.

Milgram, S. (1965). Some conditions of obedience and disobedience to authority. *Human Relations, 18*, 57–76.

Milgram, S. (1974). *Obedience to authority*. New York: Harper & Row.

Minkler, M., & Wallerstein, N. (2003). *Community-based participatory research for health*. San Francisco: Jossey-Bass.

Morgan, G. (1983). *Beyond method*. Beverly Hills, CA: Sage.

Morris, T. (1990, March). Culturally sensitive family assessment: An evaluation of the family assessment device used with Hawaiian-American and Japanese American families. *Family Process, 29,* 105–116.

Morris, T. (1992). Teaching social workers research methods: Orthodox doctrine, heresy, or an atheistic compromise. *Journal of Teaching in Social Work,* 6(1), 41–62.

Moustakas, C. (1990). *Heuristic research: Design, methodology, and applications.* Newbury Park, CA: Sage.

Mulkay, M. J. (1979). *Science and the sociology of knowledge.* London: George Allen & Unwin.

Mulkay, M. J. (1985). *The word and the world: Explorations in the forms of sociological analysis.* London: George Allen and Unwin.

National Association of Social Workers. (1999). *Code of Ethics.* Retrieved September 18, 2005, from http://www.naswdc.org/pubs/code/code.asp

National Commission for the Protection of Human Subjects of Biomedical and Behavioral Research. (1979). *The Belmont report: Ethical principles and guidelines for the protection of human subjects of research.* Retrieved September 18, 2005, from http://poynter.indiana.edu/sas/res/ belmont.html

Neuman, W. L., & Kreuger, L. W. (2003). *Social work research methods: Qualitative and quantitative applications.* Boston: Allyn & Bacon.

Oakley, A. (1990). Interviewing women: A contradiction in terms. In A. Roberts (Ed.), *Doing feminist research* (pp. 30–61). London: Routledge.

Oakley, A., & Oakley, R. (1979/1981). Sexism in official statistics. In J. Irvine, I. Miles, & J. Evans (Eds.), *Demystifying social statistics* (pp. 172–189). London: Pluto.

Oldroyd, D. (1986). *The arch of knowledge.* Kensington, Australia: New South Wales University Press.

Omni, M. A. (2000). The changing meaning of race. In N. J. Smelser, W. J. Wilson, & F. Mitchell (Eds.), *America becoming: Racial trends and their consequences*(Vol. 1, pp. 243–263). Washington, DC: National Academy Press.

Parsons, T. (1951). *The social system.* London: Routledge & Kegan Paul.

Patton, M. Q. (1990). *Qualitative evaluation and research methods.* Newbury Park, CA: Sage.

Paul, R., & Elder, L. (2004). *The miniature guide to critical thinking: Concepts and tools.* Dillon Beach, CA: Foundation for Critical Thinking.

Pellecchia, G. L. (1999). Dissemination of research findings: Conference presentations and journal publications. *Topics in Geriatric Rehabilitation,* 14(3), 67–69.

Phillips, D. C. (1990). Postpositivistic science: Myths and realities. In E. Guba (Ed.), *The paradigm dialog* (pp. 31–45). Thousand Oaks, CA: Sage.

Popkewitz, T. S. (1990). Whose future? Whose past? Notes on critical theory and methodology. In E. Guba (Ed.), *The paradigm dialog* (pp. 46–66). Thousand Oaks, CA: Sage.

Popper, K. (1959). *The logic of scientific discovery.* London: Hutchinson. (Original work published 1934)

Popper, K. (1972). *Objective knowledge: An evolutionary approach*. Oxford: Clarendon Press.

Potts, K., & Brown, L. (2005). Becoming an anti-oppressive researcher. In L. Brown and S. Strega (Eds.), *Research as resistance* (pp. 255–286). Toronto, ON: Canadian Scholars' Press.

Rapoport, R. N. (Ed.). (1985). *Children, youth, and families: The action-research relationship*. Cambridge, UK: Cambridge University Press.

Reimer, F. G. (2001). *The social work ethics audit: A risk management tool*. Washington, DC: N.A.S.W. Press.

Reinharz, S. (1992). *Feminist methods in social research*. New York: Oxford University Press.

Richardson, L. (1992). The consequences of poetic representation: Writing the other, writing the self. In C. Ellis & M. G. Flaherty (Eds.), *Investigating subjectivity: Research on lived experience* (pp. 125–137). Newbury Park, CA: Sage.

Riech, J. R. (1994). *Psychotherapy encounters curanderismo: Implications for clients treated in the United States by culturally insensitive social workers*. Unpublished manuscript.

Roberts, A. (1990). *Doing feminist research*. London: Routledge.

Rodgers-Farmer, A.Y., & Potocky-Tripodi, M. (2001). Gender, ethnicity and race matters. In B. A. Thyer (Ed.), *The handbook of social work research methods* (pp. 446–453). Thousand Oaks, CA: Sage.

Rodwell, M. K. (1998). *Social work constructivist research*. New York: Garland Publishers.

Rokeach, M. (1973). *The nature of human values*. New York: The Free Press.

Rossi, P. H., Wright, J. D., & Anderson, A. B. (1983). *Handbook of survey research*. Orlando, FL: Academic Press.

Rubin, A., & Babbie, E. (2001). *Research methods for social work*. Belmont, CA: Wadsworth.

Russell, B. (1903). *Principles of mathematics*. Cambridge: Cambridge University Press.

Ruttman, D., Hubberstey, C., Barlow, A., & Brown, E. (2005). Supporting young peoples' transitions from care: Reflections on doing participatory action research with youth from care. In L. Brown & S. Strega (Eds.), *Research as resistance* (pp. 153–180). Toronto, ON: Canadian Scholars' Press.

Sachs, H., Schegloff, E. A., & Jefferson, G. (1974). A simplest systematics for the organization of turn-taking for conversation. *Language, 50*, 696–735.

Sapir, E. (1921). *Language*. New York: Harcourt, Brace, and World.

Schriver, J. M. (2001). *Human behavior and the social environment: Shifting paradigms in essential knowledge for social work practice*. Boston: Allyn & Bacon.

Schulz, A., Israel, B. A., Parker, E., Lockett, M., Hill, Y., & Wills, R. (2003). Engaging women in community based participatory research for health. In M. Minkler & N. Wallerstein (Eds.), *Community based participatory research for health* (pp. 293–315). San Francisco: Jossey-Bass.

Schwandt, T. A. (1994). *Handbook of qualitative research.* Thousand Oaks, CA: Sage.

Seid, R. P. (1989). *Never too thin.* New York: Prentice Hall.

Sheatsley, P. B. (1983). Questionnaire construction and item writing. In P. H. Rossi, J. D. Wright, & A. B. Anderson (Eds.), *Handbook of survey research* (pp. 195–230). Orlando, FL: Academic Press.

Sinclair, J. McH., & Coulthard, R. M. (1975). *Towards an analysis of discourse.* Oxford: Oxford University Press.

Skinner, B. F. (1953). *Science and human behavior.* New York: Macmillan.

Soloman, D. J. (2001). Conducting web-based surveys. *Practical Assessment, Research & Evaluation, 7*(19). Retrieved April 15, 2004, from http://pareonline.net

Special Issue on the Scientist Practitioner. (1996, June). *Social Work Research, 20*(2), 65–128.

Spencer, H. (1902). *Principles of psychology* (3rd Ed.). New York: Appleton.

Stack, C. B. (1974). *All out kin: Strategies for survival in a black community.* New York: Harper & Row.

Stanfield, J. H., II. (1994). Ethnic modeling in qualitative research. In N. K. Denzin & Y. S. Lincoln (Eds.), *Handbook of qualitative research* (pp. 175–188). Thousand Oaks, CA: Sage.

Stephan, F. (1948). History of the uses of modern sampling procedures. In *Journal of the American Statistical Association, 43*(241), 12–39.

Stouffer, S. A., & Associates. (1947–1950). *Studies in social psychology in World War II.* (4 vols.). Princeton: Princeton University Press.

Strauss, A. (1987). *Qualitative analysis for social scientists.* New York: Cambridge University Press.

Strauss, A., & Corbin, J. (1990). *Basics of qualitative research.* Newbury Park, CA: Sage.

Strauss, A., & Corbin, J. (1998). *Basics of qualitative research* (2nd Ed.). Thousand Oaks, CA: Sage.

Stringer, E. T. (1996). *Action research: A handbook for practitioners.* Thousand Oaks, CA: Sage.

Sudman, S. (1983). Applied Sampling. In P. H. Rossi, J. D. Wright, & A. B. Anderson (Eds.), *Handbook of survey research* (pp. 145–194). Orlando, FL: Academic Press.

Susman, G. I. (1983). Action research: A sociotechnical systems perspective. In G. Morgan (Ed.), *Beyond Method* (pp. 95–113). Beverly Hills, CA: Sage.

Talshir, G. (2003). A threefold ideological analysis of Die Grunen: From ecologized socialism to political liberalism? *Journal of Political ideologies, 8*(2), 157–184.

Telles, C., & Karno, M. (1994). *Latino mental health: Current research and policy perspectives.* Los Angeles: U.C.L.A., Neuropsychiatric Institute.

Thyer, B. A. (Ed.). (2001). *The handbook of social work research methods.* Thousand Oaks, CA: Sage.

Tripodi, T. (1994). *A primer on single-subject design for clinical social workers.* Washington, DC: NAWS Press.

302 Social Work Research Methods

Tudor, A. (1982). *Beyond empiricism: Philosophy of science in sociology.* London: Routledge & Kegan Paul.

Tully, C. T. (1995). *Lesbian social services: Research issues.* New York: Harrington Park Press.

Turbayne, C. M. (1962). *The myth of metaphor.* New Haven: Yale University Press.

Tutty, L. M., Rothery, M. A., & Grinnell, R.M., Jr. (1996). *Qualitative research for social workers.* Boston: Allyn & Bacon.

Tyson, K. (1995). *New foundations for scientific social and behavioral research.* Boston: Allyn & Bacon.

Van Olpen, J., Freudenberg, N., Galea, S., Palermo, A. S., & Ritas, C. (2003). Advocating policies to promote community reintegration of drug users leaving jail: A case study of first steps in a policy change campaign guided by community based participatory research. In M. Minlker & N. Wallerstein (Eds.), *Community-based participatory research for health* (pp. 371–389). San Francisco: Jossey-Bass.

Vaughter, R. M. (1976). Psychology. *Signs: Journal of Women in Culture and Society, 2,* 120–146.

Von Glasersfeld, E. (1989). Cognition, construction of knowledge, and teaching. *Synthese, 80,* 121–140.

Von Glasersfeld, E. (1991) Knowing without metaphysics: Aspects of the radical constructivist position. In F. Steier (Ed.), *Research and reflexivity* (pp. 12–29). Newbury Park, CA: Sage.

Walker, L. (1979). *The battered woman.* New York: Harper & Row.

Walters, R. M. (1995). *Treating the abusive male: A constructivist study.* Unpublished manuscript.

Wang, C. C., & Pies, C. A. (2004, June). Family, maternal, and child health through photovoice. *Maternal and Child Health Journal, 8*(2), 95–102.

Wang, C. W. (2003). Using photovoice as a participatory assessment and issue selection tool: A case study with the homeless in Ann Arbor. In M. Minkler & M. Wallerstein (Eds.), *Community-based participatory research for health* (pp. 179–196). San Francisco: Jossey-Bass.

Watson, J. B. (1948). Psychology as the behaviorist sees it. In W. Dennis (Ed.), *Readings in the history of psychology.* New York: Appleton-Century-Crofts.

Webb, C. (1984). Feminist methodology in nursing research. *Journal of Advanced Nursing, 9,* 249–256.

Weinbach, R. W., & Grinnell, R. M., Jr. (2004). *Statistics for social workers.* Boston: Pearson, Allyn & Bacon.

Weinberg, E. (1983). Data collection: Planning and management. In P. H. Rossi, J. D. Wright, & A. B. Anderson (Eds.), *Handbook of survey research* (pp. 329–358). Orlando, FL: Academic Press.

Weiss, H. B., & Jacobs, F. H. (1988). *Evaluating family programs.* New York: Aldine de Gruyter.

Wethington, E. (2003, December 1). Research protocols grounded in ethics. *Human Ecology, 1.*

Wexler, P. (Ed.). (1991). *Critical theory now*. New York: Falmer.

Willer, D., & Willer J. (1973). *Systematic empiricism: Critique of a pseudo-science*. Englewood Cliffs, NJ: Prentice-Hall.

Wolcott, H. F. (1973). *The man in the principal's office: An ethnography*. Prospect Heights, IL: Waveland Press.

Wolcott, H. F. (1990). *Writing up qualitative research*. Newbury Park, CA: Sage

Wolf, M. (1992). *A thrice told tale: Feminism, postmodernism, and ethnographic responsibility*. Stanford, CA: Stanford University Press.

Young, M. L., & Creacy, M. (1995). *Perceptions of homeless children*. Unpublished manuscript.

Zimbardo, P. G., et al. (1974). The psychology of imprisonment: Privation, power, and pathology. In Z. Rubin (Ed.), *Doing unto others* (pp. 61–73). Englewood Cliffs, NJ: Prentice Hall.

Zinn, H. (1980). *A people's history of the United States*. New York: Harper Collins.

Index

About the Author

Teresa Morris is professor and chair of the Department of Social Work at California State University, San Bernardino (CSUSB). Her undergraduate education was at the University of Loughborough in England. She received her M.S.W. from the University of Hawaii and her Doctorate from the University of California, Berkeley. She is from England via Australia and now lives in California. In England she worked as a secondary school teacher and a youth and community worker. In Australia she was a community worker in rural Western Australia and later an academic at the University of Melbourne. In 1989 she went to California to help start a new M.S.W. program in San Bernardino in a new Department of Social Work at CSUSB. She now heads that department. She has published in the areas of refugee resettlement, philosophy of science, and alternative paradigm research methods. She teaches research methods.